How critical is education in the development struggle of a Third World country? Responding to popular demands for more accessible education, the Guyanese government instituted numerous educational reforms, hoping to promote economic growth in both the modern and the traditional sectors of the economy. Many in the traditional sector, however, saw education as a means of economic advancement, and sought increasingly to move into higher social strata through employment in the modern sector. Consequently, the civil service and private firms gained an oversupply of personnel, while agriculture and small business suffered, and unemployment increased. The author examines Guyana's educational system from historical, political, social, and economic perspectives, and draws implications for other developing countries.

M. K. Bacchus is Professor of Sociology of Education at the University of Alberta, specializing in education and Third World development. He has held important teaching and administrative positions in England, Guyana, the West Indies, and the United States. His numerous publications on education and the Third World include Education and Socio-cultural Integration, *published by the Centre for Developing-Area Studies, McGill University. He holds the Ph.D. degree from the University of London.*

Development Perspectives

EDUCATION FOR DEVELOPMENT OR UNDERDEVELOPMENT?

Development Perspectives is edited from the Centre for Developing-Area Studies, McGill University, Montreal, Canada and sponsored by the Canadian Interuniversity Consortium for Publication on International Development (Association Interuniversitaire Canadienne: Publication sur le Développement Internationale). The purpose of the series is to publish without regard for disciplinary boundaries research work, conducted in Canadian universities or by Canadians in other organizations, on the problems of development in third world countries. The primary focus will be on works that contribute to our general understanding of the process of development. Books in the series will be published in either French or English.

Consortium Members

Institut de la Coopération Internationale, Université d'Ottawa

Third World Studies Co-Ordinating Committee, International Studies Programme, University of Toronto

Centre for Developing-Area Studies, McGill University

University of Western Ontario

Co-ordinating Editor: Rosalind E. Boyd

EDUCATION FOR DEVELOPMENT OR UNDERDEVELOPMENT?

Guyana's Educational System
and its Implications for the Third World

M. K. Bacchus

DEVELOPMENT PERSPECTIVES 2

Wilfrid Laurier University Press

Canadian Cataloguing in Publication Data

Bacchus, M. K.
  Education for development or underdevelopment?

(Development perspectives ; 2)
Bibliography: p.
Includes index.
ISBN 0-88920-084-X bd.   ISBN 0-88920-085-8 pa.

1. Education − Guyana.   2. Underdeveloped areas −
Education − Case studies.   3. Guyana − Economic
conditions.   4. Guyana − Social conditions.   I. Title.
II. Series.

LA576.B32   370'.9881   C80-094733-9

Wilfrid Laurier University Press
Waterloo, Ontario, Canada
N2L 3C5

80 81 82 83 4 3 2 1

Cover Design: Michael Baldwin MSIAD

To my wife Shamie
and my children Narry, Zeeda and Fahiem
who had to put up with my constant absence from home
during the collection of the data for this book—a period
which lasted far too many years

Contents

List of Tables and Charts

Tables

Charts

Preface

The objectives of this study are threefold: (1) to describe and analyze recent changes and developments which took place in the educational system of a third world country—Guyana—and to identify the major factors which were responsible for them; (2) to examine how effective these educational efforts were in helping the nation meet some of its development needs; (3) to discuss the applicability of these findings to other third world developing countries.

There is at present a dearth of studies of individual third world countries which focus on the contribution that their education programmes have made or are making to their socio-economic development. Such work is necessary in order to document the role that education has been playing in the development process. In addition, the findings can provide valuable insights for educators in other third world countries seeking to increase the efficiency of their educational systems.

The country selected for this study was Guyana which, though situated on the mainland of South America, is more akin to the former British West Indies in its history, economy, and social structure. The results indicate that while there were many developments and some changes in the Guyanese educational system between 1945 and 1974, these failed to increase substantially the contribution which education was making to overall national development. This was, to a large extent, due to the fact that while education reforms were being attempted, the basic colonial economic and social structure of Guyanese society had remained relatively intact and was frustrating the success of most of these educational changes.

Foremost among the structural features of this ex-colonial society was the dualistic nature of its economy. This was characterized on the one hand by a relatively small modern sector comprising the sugar plantations and the bauxite mining enclaves, the large civil service and the armed forces, and the more progressive commercial and small-scale manufacturing firms and, on the other, by a large traditional sector comprising mainly subsistence farmers. Another marked feature of this dualism was the great difference in incomes between workers in these two sectors.

An examination of the effect of this economic dualism led to the conclusion that unless there was a radical reduction in the income differences in Guyana and, in fact, in other third world countries, efforts at trying to encourage individuals to be trained for and enter the low-income occupations which are considered essential for national development are not likely to be successful. The considerable inequalities in the wages received by those in various occupations will continue to distort, as they did in the colonial days, the supply of trained and educated personnel towards these high-income jobs, ir-respective of the objective development needs of the nation. Further, simple quantitative increases in the supply of educated personnel would not necessarily help in the development and transformation of these societies and in fact might even be anti-developmental.

During the period of colonial rule there was a substantial congru-ence between the economic sub-structure of colonial societies and their education super-structure which was developed essentially to support, reinforce, and reproduce the existing economic and social order. Therefore, educational changes in these societies are not likely to be effective if there are not corresponding basic changes in the economic and social structure that these societies inherited under colonialism. What has been happening is that while these societies have attempted to modify the nature and type of educational programmes being of-fered in their schools, the substance of the programmes and the func-tions of the educational institutions have to a large extent remained unchanged. These are still seen mainly as instruments to help indi-viduals escape the realities of life as it has to be lived by the great majority of the population and move into the white-collar or other highly paid jobs in the small, modern sector.

The data for this study were collected over a period of ten years. During part of that time I was employed as a senior edu-cational administrator in the Ministry of Education in Guyana; later I worked at the University of the West Indies and the University of Alberta where I continued my research. I must express my thanks to these latter two institutions which, in one way or another, gave me assistance with the collection of my data. This book has been pub-lished with the help of a grant from the Social Science Federation of Canada, using funds provided by the Social Sciences and Humanities Research Council of Canada. The University of Chicago afforded me a "home" when I was doing the first draft of the study in 1973-74, and the Institute of Development Studies in Sussex, England, granted me a visiting fellowship which allowed me to use its library and other facilities.

Other assistance through comments and discussions was obtained from Dr. Philip Foster and Dr. Jean Bowman, former faculty mem-bers of the Comparative Education Centre, University of Chicago, and from Dr. George Psacharopolous of the London School of Economics and Mr. Herman McKenzie of the University of the West Indies, who were at the University of Chicago during the year I spent there as visiting professor. In addition I benefited greatly from the many comments and observations on the manuscript made by Professor Ron Dore, Senior Fellow of the Institute of Development Studies, Sussex. Thanks are also due to M. T. Lowe, Chief Education Officer, Guyana, who kindly reviewed Chapter 5 on secondary education.

Lastly, my thanks to those who assisted with the preliminary editing and typing of the various drafts of the book, and especially to Mrs. Doris Dobson and Mrs. Susan El-Nahhas of the University of Alberta, Miss Ann Genett and Mrs. Sharon Gibson of the College of the Bahamas, and Mrs. Joan Theander.

M. K. Bacchus
University of Alberta
February 1979

1. Historical Introduction to Guyanese Society

Guyana, the former colony of British Guiana, experienced the most rapid expansion in its educational system during the three decades following the 1940s, despite the fact that the country had a Compulsory Education Act since 1876. This increase in educational services for the general population occurred especially at the secondary and tertiary levels.

For about a century following the emancipation of its slaves, the country had experienced little basic change in its economic and social structure and in its distribution of political power. True, there were some limited economic developments such as the emergence of the rice and later the bauxite mining industries. But the transition from slave to creole society was on the whole distinguished more by marginal modifications than by major structural changes in the economy. This was largely due to the dominance of the "plantation" system, which was characterized by a concentration of political power in the hands of the white planters or their agents who were not primarily interested in and were often opposed to the emergence of major alternative economic opportunities outside the plantations. They were usually afraid that such developments might reduce the dependency of the labour force on the plantations.

However, where new jobs did emerge, as in the bauxite industry, the basis on which they were allocated reflected and reinforced the existing stratificatory system in a society where colour was an important criterion of social differentiation. So the jobs on the lowest rungs of the occupational ladder went to the Africans and occasionally to the East Indians, and the junior white-collar positions to the children of the coloured middle class, while Europeans from the metropole were recruited to fill the senior and sometimes not-so-senior administrative, professional, and technical posts.

The number of Afro- and Indo-Guyanese who were able to rise higher on the local occupational and social ladder by virtue of their education was, therefore, very limited. In fact, education was then essentially an instrument of status reconfirmation, helping to reinforce the legitimacy of ascribed status based on colour, which itself was a heritage of slave society. For example, children from the lower-status groups received only an elementary education, since school attendance at this level was compulsory though not rigidly enforced, and, like their parents, ended up in the lowest-paid jobs in the society. The children of the coloured middle class had more opportunities to attend secondary schools, after which they, like their fathers, moved towards filling positions in the intermediate status categories. Personnel for politically sensitive positions, or for positions requiring professional or technical training, were recruited from Britain and, in some cases, from the "white" dominions, especially Canada. The relatively few East Indians and Africans who were able to rise higher on the social and occupational ladder through their educational achievement were those who qualified for one of the independent professions—law, medicine, and later, dentistry.

However, with the gradual redistribution of political power, which began more noticeably after the 1940s, some changes began to occur in the basis on which status was distributed in the society. The previous caste-like features gradually began to give way to a more open class-structured society in which status became increasingly distributed on the basis of achievement criteria such as education, rather than on ascription based mainly on colour.

This opening up of opportunities for low-status, dark-skinned ethnic groups, mainly Africans and East Indians, to rise on the occupational ladder, resulted in a marked increase in their educational aspirations; as a consequence, they began to exert more pressure on the Government to provide the necessary educational facilities. Political developments occurring after the mid-1940s, such as the extension of the franchise and the increasing substitution of popularly elected representatives for nominated members in the Legislative assembly, also made the political system more responsive to these popular demands. The combination of these forces, increasing popular demand for education, and an elected Government more responsive to such demands resulted in a rapid increase by the Government in the number of its educational institutions located throughout the country and at all levels of the system.

But in addition to the growing popular demand and the rapid increase in the school-age population which occurred after the 1940s, there were other factors responsible for the educational expansion. Among them were the desire of the political leaders themselves to increase the opportunities for children from the lower socio-economic groups to move into the middle- and higher-level jobs in the society and to enlarge the supply of trained local manpower for the emergent nation. The achievement of both these objectives rested heavily on the provision of more educational services. As a result, educational planners, administrators, advisers, and even Ministers of Education were involved in developing new programmes aimed at diversifying, expanding, and making more "relevant" the educational system of the country with the hope that these new and additional facilities would be effective in helping the nation achieve its new social and economic goals. In short, pressures for educational expansion and changes came jointly from the general population and from the Government and its officials.

But quite often there was conflict between these two sources as to the kind of education which should be provided. The type which the masses wanted for their children was not usually the type which the Government and the educational planners thought best for the society. However, the educational changes which were more successfully implemented were those which resulted from popular demand. The masses were very perceptive about the realities of the existing reward structure and tended to seek the kind of education which would best prepare their children for the jobs offering the greatest rewards.

Those educational changes sponsored by the Government to meet certain national objectives, which were in conflict with those popularly demanded, had more difficulty taking root. This was mainly because the basic economic and social changes which were necessary to make such educational programmes economically and socially rewarding to the individual did not take place or were slow to emerge. The various Governments were somewhat naively hoping that their proposed educational changes would be a major factor in spearheading social and economic reforms—a very difficult task for education alone. Rewards remained wedded to the occupational structure which emerged during the colonial era and these, rather than the objective needs of the economy, were largely responsible for the type of education that was demanded by the public. For example, most of the Government-sponsored educational changes were aimed at getting the population better equipped to work in the low-income sectors of the economy, in areas such as agriculture, which the Government wanted to develop. But since incomes from this sector remained low, parents continued to be interested in securing for their children the type of education which was likely to lead them out of agriculture and into the more prestigious and financially rewarding white-collar jobs.

This does not mean that planned educational changes which at first do not stem from popular demand cannot be successfully introduced into a society. All it points to is the difficulty of initiating educational changes aimed at de-emphasizing the more prestigious type of education traditionally offered in a society unless there are corresponding changes in the reward structure which would make the educational innovations economically and socially more attractive.

Another important feature of these developments was that "educational inflation" was beginning to occur, i.e., there were already too many "educated" individuals on the job market chasing too few jobs. This was reflected both in the increase in unemployment among the young and in the rising educational levels of the unemployed population.

Early History of Guyanese Society

To understand the reasons for the very rapid expansion of Guyanese education after 1945 and why the content of education offered in the schools proved so resistant to change it is necessary to look, from a historical perspective, at the developments in the society since its early days of colonization and slavery.

The early years of the seventeenth century marked the beginning of intense rivalries among such European nations as Spain, Holland, England, and France for control of lands in the circum-Caribbean area including Guyana. The ultimate result of their scramble was the "political balkanization" of the region and the conflicts among these nations were reflected in the early history of Guyana.

This competition for new lands was a natural extension of the mercantilist philosophy of these nations which was "characterized by an aggressive desire among rulers to exert maximum extension of territory under their sovereignty or of resources under their absolute control."[1] The then prevailing belief was that power bred wealth and command of the seas and key possessions overseas was necessary to protect the power and hence the wealth of the mother country.

Martin, writing in 1835, attempted a classification of colonies according to their importance to the mother country using the criteria of territorial expansion, commercial value, and maritime position, and placed Guyana and some of the West Indian islands as territories which combined all three.[2]

According to the Papal Bull of 1494, Guiana, a name which technically referred to all the lands between the Orinoco and the Amazon rivers, fell within the sphere of influence of Spain. But the Spaniards, with their many problems and their efforts concentrated on the colonization of other territories in the region, had little time left to defend the Guianese coast against "intruders."

The region first came to the attention of the Western world through the efforts of the Englishman Sir Walter Raleigh, whose published account of the country, *The Discovery of the Large, Rich and Beautiful Empire of Guiana*, was an attempt to gain the support of his countrymen for building a grand empire in the Caribbean. As a result of Raleigh's lead, successive groups of Englishmen tried to establish colonies on the coast of Guiana, but most of these early efforts were short-lived.

[1] K. E. Knorr, *British Colonial Theories 1570-1850* (Toronto: University of Toronto Press, 1944), p. 5.

[2] R. M. Martin, *The British Colonies, their History, Extent, Condition and Resources*, Vol. 1 (8 vols.; London and New York: J. & F. Tallis, n.d.).

The first successful settlement was established up the Essequibo River in 1616 by the Dutch; it was followed by one in Demerara and another in Berbice. The last named remained a separate administrative unit until 1834, while the other two were merged into one colony. In 1620, when the Pilgrim Fathers thought of settling in Guiana, the Dutch had already been there for about four years.

The Dutch were at first mainly interested in trade, and to this end formed the Dutch West India Company in 1621. Dutch traders penetrated the interior of Guiana and established an extensive trading network spreading as far south as the Rupununi and as far west as the Orinoco. The main products obtained from the local Amerindian population with whom they traded were cotton, dyes, and letter wood.

From Trading to Cultivation

However, the Dutch settlers soon began to cultivate cotton, tobacco, and coffee. As agriculture expanded they began the search for a supply of unskilled labourers and after unsuccessfully attempting to enslave the Amerindians turned their attention to importing African slaves.

The relationship between the Dutch and the Amerindians eventually became fairly cordial and the former even passed legislation forbidding the enslavement of the latter. In fact, those planters who owned Amerindian slaves had to surrender them in exchange for African ones.

A rapid expansion of sugar production occurred in the early eighteenth century, and this increased the demand for Negro slaves. Tobacco and cotton cultivation had begun to decline with a fall in price for these commodities due to the competition from the North American colonies and, as a result, many plantations switched over to sugar cane cultivation. The largest expansion of the colony at this time occurred about 1746, when the Dutch Commander Laurens Storm Van Gravesande declared Demerara open to settlement and offered new settlers a ten-year exemption from poll tax as well as 250 acres of land. This open invitation attracted the English and their slaves from the nearby colony of Barbados, and by 1760 they were reported to be in the majority in Demerara. By this time the colonies of Demerara and Essequibo had 4,000 slaves and 161 plantations, while Berbice in 1762 possessed 3,833 Negro slaves. The ratio of whites to Negro slaves in Berbice was about 1:12. The shift to sugar cultivation further increased the demand for slaves and since the Dutch West India Company, which had the monopoly on supplying slaves to the planters, was unable to meet this demand, slave smuggling began.

The changeover to sugar production also affected the relationship between planters and their slaves. Both the size of the plantations and the number of slaves employed per acre increased, and this transformed the planter from a co-worker to a supervisor and helped to create a rigid hierarchical structure of authority and a more impersonal and autocratic relationship between the white planters and their black slaves.

British Takeover

In 1781, during the War of American Independence, Admiral Rodney captured the Dutch colonies in the West Indies and Guiana. But they were soon recaptured in 1782 by the French and returned to the Dutch at the Treaty of Versailles in 1783.

In 1796, following the defeat of Holland during the French Revolution, a British expeditionary force from Barbados captured Guiana; this British occupation saw another influx of English settlers. But after eight years of British rule the colony was again restored to the Dutch in 1802 at the Treaty of Amiens. With the renewal of war, the colonies were recaptured by the British in 1803, and in 1814 were finally ceded to Great Britain. They were amalgamated into the colony of British Guiana in 1831, and, after about one and a half centuries of British rule, the country was formally granted political independence in 1966.

The Changing Social Structure

During the early years of British occupation there was no great or immediate change in the colony. Chattel slavery, which was "the cornerstone of the whole edifice of colonial society,"[3] continued and the status boundaries between black and white became more sharply defined with the shift to sugar cane cultivation, the increase in the number of slaves, and the greater influx of white women in the society.

For a short period towards the end of the eighteenth century the colony was the greatest cotton producer in the world and the largest coffee grower in the British Empire. But the production of sugar began to increase rapidly, while the output of coffee and cotton was drastically reduced (Table 1). "The initial impact of British sovereignty," as one historian noted, "can be best summarized as the elevation of sugar to a position of unchallenged pre-eminence in the economic life of British Guiana."[4]

The slave population grew substantially—from about 8,000 in the 1780s to over 100,000 by 1826—and the ratio of slaves to whites had

[3] Raymond T. Smith, *British Guiana* (London: Oxford University Press, 1962), p. 26.

[4] W. B. Mitchell *et al.*, *Area Handbook for Guyana* (Washington, D.C.: The American University, 1969), p. 34.

Table 1 *Production of Sugar, Coffee, and Cotton in Guyana, 1814-1833*

Period	Sugar (hogsheads)	Coffee (000s lbs.)	Cotton (000s lbs.)
1814-18	21,770	10,817	8,422
1829-33	71,496	5,165	1,741
Percentage increase or decline	+228	−52	−79

Source: Alan H. Adamson, *Sugar without Slaves* (New Haven and London: Yale University Press, 1972), p. 25.

reached about 26:1 by the latter year. Out of an estimated total population of 100,836 in the three colonies, only about 3.5% (3,529) were whites, about 7.5% (7,521) were free coloureds and blacks, and the remainder were slaves.

The relationship which developed between the black slave workers and the whites, as a result of the shift to sugar cane cultivation, eventually acquired caste-like features based on race and colour and came to characterize relationships in all other institutions in the society. This was as one student observed, because the plantation "not only produces its own class structure but has an inhibiting effect on the formation of any alternative class structures within its own area of control."[5]

The third factor contributing to the emerging rigid status distinctions between whites and non-whites was the increasing number of white women who came to reside in the colony. Kirke, who lived in Guiana during the last quarter of the nineteenth century, observed that with the arrival of white women "a regular English society was forming itself."[6] Miscegenation was increasingly frowned upon by the women and the relationship between whites and non-whites became even more polarized.

Social Stratification and Education

Education of the White Population

The earlier Dutch settlers did attempt to provide some education for their children and in 1685 established a school in Essequibo. But

[5] Eric R. Wolf, "Specific Aspects of Plantation Systems in the New World," in *Plantation Systems of the New World*, ed. by Vera Rubin, Pan American Union and Research Institute for the Study of Man, Social Science Monographs No. 7 (Washington, D.C., 1959), p. 17.

[6] H. Kirke, *Twenty-Five Years in British Guiana* (London: Sampson, Low, Marston and Co., 1898), p. 45.

since there was at the time no economic need for manpower with any level of formal education, the main objective of these settlers was to provide a religious education for their children.

However, with the introduction of sugar cane cultivation the situation changed somewhat; there developed a demand for attorneys, doctors, bookkeepers, clerks, and others with various levels of formal education. In addition, the major objective of the whites, especially those of higher status, was to make their fortunes as quickly as possible and return to England permanently or at least for long periods of time. Because of this, and the fact that primogeniture ensured that only the eldest sons inherited their property, the planters were anxious to provide their children with the educational opportunity which would later facilitate their absorption into the upper echelons of British society.

These "primary" whites—planters, professional men, and merchants—therefore provided their children with an elementary education locally through specially employed private tutors, and later sent them off either to the famous public schools or to finishing schools in Britain. The sons, after completing their education at Eton or Harrow and other such prestigious schools, proceeded to the older British universities, mainly Oxford or Cambridge. Some eventually entered the Inns of Court to obtain professional training in law. Incidentally, the majority of these never returned to Guiana or to the West Indies.

Below this elite group were the "secondary whites" or "*petits blancs*"—the overseers, shopkeepers, clerks, and artisans who did not need, for their economic and social advancement, an education beyond that which provided them with basic literacy and numeracy skills. For example, with the increase in the slave population, whites were relieved of the lowest-status jobs in the society. These were taken over by the slaves, allowing the whites to move into the somewhat higher-level occupations. Also, as the primary whites returned to England, the "secondary" whites, by a hydraulic process of mobility, were moved up to fill the vacancies thus created. With such opportunities for social and economic advancement open to the whites because of their skin colour, they did not see the need for much formal education and considered education beyond the very rudimentary level as unnecessary. This attitude was shared throughout the West Indies and, as one observer noted, "learning is at its lowest ebb [in these colonies]; they don't seem to be fond of the thing [education]."[7]

The result of this situation—the "primary" whites sending their children to Britain for their secondary education and the "secondary" whites having no use for this level of schooling—was that secondary

[7] Quoted in Frank W. Pitman, *The Development of the British West Indies 1700-1763* (Hamden, Conn.: Archon Books, 1917), pp. 24-25.

schools were not established in Guiana until after the abolition of slavery. By this time the lower-level whites and even the coloured population began to fear that the children of the masses, large numbers of whom were receiving an education under the Negro Education Act of 1834, would advance educationally too near their own children. This was likely to reduce the existing social distance between these groups and even put the children of the ex-slaves in a competitive position for some jobs, which were traditionally the preserve of the coloured population and the lower-level whites. These higher status groups, therefore, became increasingly interested in giving their children a secondary education of the classical type which would help to maintain the social and economic distance between themselves and the lower social orders. This demand for classical secondary education led to the establishment of the Queens College Grammar School by the Anglican Church in 1844—just six years after emancipation; this was followed by the opening up of St. Stanislaus College for boys by the Catholics in 1866.

Education of the Free Coloureds and Free Blacks

Because of the limited number of white women in Guiana, especially during the early years of settlement, there developed regular mating relationships between white males and female Negro slaves. If the fathers of the offspring resulting from such relationships were economically well off, they tended to provide for the educational welfare of their illegitimate coloured children almost in the same way as they did for their legitimate white children—arranging for them to have private tuition and then sending them off to Britain to receive further education. Kirke noted that in the nineteenth century lawyers in Guiana were a mixed lot—white, black, and coloured—and he further commented on the many coloured doctors and barristers who, as offspring of white fathers, were sent to Britain for their education. However, these free coloureds continued to be accorded inferior status to the whites even when they were more educated and wealthier. Dalton noted that many young coloured persons were sent to Europe and brought back with an excellent education and polished manners, only to find that "in spite of high connections and the refinements they had acquired they were still excluded from what was considered the *first society.*"[8]

Also, a number of black slaves were able to secure their freedom either through the generosity and affection of their masters or more commonly through their own efforts. Limited opportunities did exist for slaves to earn money and some of those who saved enough

[8] Henry G. Dalton, *A History of British Guiana*, Vol. 1 (London: Longmans, 1855), p. 313.

bought their own freedom. Although their numbers were few, some of the early black professionals in Guyanese society came from fathers who were in this group.

Education Among the Slaves

While a few of the more liberal planters encouraged and made provision for the religious education of their slaves, the planters as a group were opposed to the provision of formal education for the children of the slave population. While such opposition was found throughout the West Indies, it was most marked in Guiana.

Obviously the major concern of the planters was the maintenance of order and stability in the society, and they felt that once a slave received an education he could no longer be kept in his "proper place." They shared the belief that "reading provokes thinking and this is dangerous" among slaves.[9] Even a liberal plantation owner like Hermanus Post, who brought the Reverend John Wray to Guiana to minister to the spiritual needs of his slaves, made it quite clear that he did not want the missionary to teach them to read. Similarly, when Wray's successor, the Reverend John Smith, arrived in the country in 1817, the Governor warned him that if he taught a slave to read he would be banished from the Colony.[10]

The editor of the *Colonist*, a local mouthpiece of the planters, put the views of the white group on this matter of the education of slaves very clearly. Following the death of the Reverend John Smith, one of the most controversial missionaries ever to work in Guiana, he wrote an article castigating planters for not speaking out in time against the first advocates of missions and education for the slaves. He pointed out that these advocates should have been told that "the missionary system is in fact undermining the institutions and endangering the political existence of the colonies." Continuing, the editor noted:

> While we have no desire to treat Africans with undue rigour . . . we cannot be ignorant [of the fact] that our power over them can exist only so long as we are more highly *educated* and *enlightened*. We are few, they are many, and if their moral qualities or *education* be allowed to be made equal to ours, it follows that the power of government or the right of government which is the same thing, will be determined by the amount of physical force.[11] (Emphasis added.)

The Governor of Martinique made a similar point in objecting to the education of slaves on that island where, he argued, "the safety of the whites, fewer in number, demands . . . that the Negroes should be

[9] See Vere T. Daly, *A Short History of the Guyanese People* (Georgetown, Guyana: Daily Chronicle, 1966), p. 135.

[10] Shirley Gordon, *A Century of West Indian Education—A Source Book* (London: Longmans, 1963), p. 9.

[11] Quoted in Daly, p. 254.

kept in the most profound ignorance."[12] As Coleridge saw it, the education of the slaves would place the planters in a dilemma because they would then jeopardize their own safety if they continued to withhold from the educated slaves those privileges to which the slaves would soon feel that they had "acquired an equitable right. It would be impossible," he continued, "to march Negroes on the road to knowledge and compel them to stand at ease within the old entrenchments of ignorance."[13]

Incidentally, there were also economic reasons why the planters did not want to allow slave children to attend school. At the age of six, they were already working in the grass gangs, making an economic contribution which was enough to cover the expenses involved in their upkeep.

Guyanese Society After the Abolition of Slavery

One of the greatest fears expressed by the planters was that emancipation would totally ruin the economy of the colony, since they expected that the free slaves would no longer want to work on the plantations. So they initially took every step possible to maintain the dependence of the ex-slaves on the plantations. For example, the Imperial Government provided in the Abolition Act of 1834 for the ex-slaves to serve their masters for up to four years before they were finally freed. This was to give the planters a chance to cope with the emerging new status of their workers, thereby helping to ensure that the ex-slaves did not leave the estate as soon as they finally obtained their freedom. In addition, the planters took their own steps to get the slaves to remain on the plantation and accept low wages. On many estates it was reported that

> the provision grounds, plantation walks and fruit trees cultivated and reared by the peasantry while in bondage were destroyed . . . in order to control their dependence on plantation work; and but few planters were willing to sell or lease small portions of land large enough to provide a living for families.[14]

Further, some planters began to import small numbers of indentured labourers even before the apprenticeship period was over in order to influence the ex-slaves to make "moderate" wage demands when they finally obtained their freedom.

But despite these steps, the ex-slaves in Guiana began to withdraw from the plantations as soon as their legal obligations were ful-

[12] Quoted in F. R. Augier and S. G. Gordon, *Sources of West Indian History* (London: Longmans, 1962), pp. 145-46.

[13] H. N. Coleridge, *Six Months in the West Indies in 1825* (London: John Murray, 1832), p. 321.

[14] Martin, Vol. 8, p. 175.

filled, producing a sharp decline in agricultural production after 1838. Sugar output in Guiana fell about 62% between the period 1831-34 and 1838-42 and the number of sugar plantations declined from 230 to 180 within a decade. The number of active coffee and cotton estates fell from 174 to 16 during the same period.

The ex-slaves who left the sugar estates attempted to establish an independent peasantry; groups of them, using money they had saved up—some of it during their apprenticeship—bought out abandoned sugar estates and set themselves up as independent farmers. By 1848 they had acquired about 446 estates on which were settled 44,443 persons, as compared with the 20,000 who still remained on the sugar estates.

But the freed slaves faced many problems in establishing themselves as farmers. After making their initial capital investment in land—usually under very harsh terms—they did not have enough working capital to allow them to become independent sugar producers. The purchase price for their estates was also exceedingly high, especially in comparison with land values a few years later; e.g., between 1847 and 1850 estates were being sold at auction at $9.70 per acre, including building and machinery, while the ex-slaves had purchased their land in the early 1840s at $242.50 per acre.[15] In fact, many planters exacted these exorbitant prices because so few wanted to sell out their estates to ex-slaves.

Attempts to equalize the distribution of fertile and less fertile lands among the many purchasers led to fragmentation of the estates and militated against large-scale production. In addition, many legal restrictions about the size of land that could be sold or leased to the ex-slaves, and the lack of drainage and irrigation facilities in some of the new areas, made it difficult for them to establish an economically vibrant peasantry. Most of them were, therefore, condemned to eke out a meagre existence on subsistence farming for "ground provisions"—cassava, yams, eddoes, and plantains.

Some Africans did remain on the sugar estates where they sought employment as skilled workmen in the factories—positions which in the past had had considerable prestige among the slaves. This tendency has continued to the present and Africans working on the sugar estates today are largely employed in the factories as skilled workmen.

Arrival of New Migrants

The exodus of the ex-slaves from the sugar plantations created a shortage of cheap labour and led the planters to search for new

[15] Alan H. Adamson, *Sugar without Slaves: The Political Economy of British Guiana, 1838-1904* (New Haven and London: Yale University Press, 1972), p. 164.

sources of "unfree labour" through a system of indentureship. Between 1839 and 1928 (Table 2) a total of 340,792 immigrants from different parts of the world arrived in Guiana. Those from the West Indies and Africa were Negroes, who in time followed the patterns of life of the local Negro population, even though efforts were at first made to isolate them from this latter group since it was believed that such association would adversely affect their attitude to work.

Table 2 *Number of Contract Immigrants Arriving in British Guiana after 1834*

Country of origin	Number	Dates of main immigration
India	238,960	1838-1917
Madeira, Azores, and Cape Verde Islands	31,628	1835-1882
West Indies	42,562	1835-1928
Africa	13,355	1838-1865
China*	14,189	1853-1912
U.S.A.	70	1840
Total	340,792	

* The bulk of the Chinese (12,631) arrived before 1866.
Source: Quoted in R. T. Smith, *British Guiana* (London: Oxford University Press, 1962), p. 44. Originally appeared in Dwarka Nath, *A History of Indians in British Guiana* (London: Nelson, 1950).

The Portuguese from Madeira, Azores, and Cape Verde Islands were the first groups of indentured labourers to arrive in large numbers, but, as Rodway[16] noted, they were never regarded by the African population as "buccra" or "gentlemen" or as "ideal white men." They did not prove to be good labourers on the sugar estates and on completion of their indentureship turned to commercial activities. Because of their skin colour, they found it relatively easy to obtain credit and other favours from the existing white-dominated institutions. They were, therefore, soon able to oust the African traders from commerce. This became an early source of conflict between the two groups, resulting eventually in the Angel Gabriel Riots of 1856.

Further, with the establishment of a Catholic secondary school in 1866 some Portuguese were able to obtain a secondary education locally and, with their financial success in commerce, were able to send their sons abroad to obtain a university education and profes-

[16] J. Rodway, *History of British Guiana from 1668* (3 vols.; Georgetown: n.p., 1891-1894).

sional training. Their skin colour plus their education not only ensured their entry into the civil service at levels commensurate with their qualifications, but enabled them to rise to fairly senior positions even prior to the 1940s.

The Chinese, who began arriving in 1953 as indentured labourers, also proved unsuccessful as field-hands on the sugar plantations. They, too, entered the field of commerce but did not have the same facilities open to them as the Portuguese. Hence, most of their operations were on a much smaller scale. Some of them did obtain the necessary funds to give their children secondary education; this ensured their acceptance into the lower levels of the civil service.

The East Indians proved more successful as field labourers than either the Portuguese or the Chinese, and as a result, India continued to be the major source of indentured workers for the next seventy-five years. By 1917, when Indian immigration was finally abolished, about 240,000 East Indians had migrated to Guiana. The conditions under which they lived and worked at first were not much better than those of the liberated slaves, although these conditions gradually improved over time. After their indentureship expired many moved away from the sugar estates and a large percentage of them returned to India, some with relatively substantial savings. But as other economic opportunities opened to them locally, an increasing number settled in Guyana.

Understanding Guyanese Society Prior to the 1940s

Guyanese society prior to the 1940s continued to be stratified mainly on the basis of colour and ethnicity. This perpetuated the position of the two major ethnic groups in the country—the Africans and the East Indians—on the lowest rungs of the social and occupational ladder. There was also little diversification in the economy and the sugar industry remained the largest employer of wage labour. The close relationship between ethnicity, educational opportunity, and social and occupational status meant that the role of education in upward social mobility was still very limited. The independent professions continued to provide the only means whereby Africans and East Indians who had the necessary ability and funds to pay for their education overseas could move up the status hierarchy.

To understand why this relative lack of openness in the social structure persisted for so long after slavery was abolished, why social stratification continued to be based on ethnicity and colour, why the economy remained so dependent on sugar, and why so few alternative economic opportunities emerged, one has to examine the nature of the plantation system which dominated the society throughout the period. An understanding of these issues should lead to an appreciation of why, despite the relative economic prosperity of the country during the late eighteenth and early nineteenth centuries and the introduction of a Compulsory Education Ordinance in 1876, education did not become more important at least prior to the 1940s, as a vehicle for the economic and social advancement of the children of Africans and East Indians. It should also help to indicate why the role of education remained relatively unchanged in the society up to that period of the country's history.

The Plantation System in Guyanese Society

The basic social, economic, and political fabric of Guyanese and most West Indian societies was woven out of the "plantation system" which evolved from slave society. The following vivid description by Dr. C. B. Jagan of plantation life in Guyana in the 1920s drew attention to the fact that plantations influenced all institutions within their boundaries. Writing about his boyhood on a sugar estate Jagan observed:

> The plantation appeared to me as representing the hub of life. Everything revolved around sugar and sugar planters seemed to own the world. They owned the canefields and the factories. Even the small parcels of land rented to some of the workers for rice farming and ground provision cultivation belonged to them. They owned the mansions occupied by the senior staff and the cottages occupied by the lesser beings like dispensers, chemists, engineers, book-keepers and drivers. They owned the logies where the labourers lived, the hospitals and every other important structure. At one time they also owned and operated a rice mill. Even the churches and schools came within their patronage and control.
> The plantation was indeed a world in itself. Or rather it was two worlds: the world of the exploiters and the world of the exploited; the world of the whites and the world of the non-whites. One was the world of the managers and the European staff in their splendid mansions; the other the world of the labourers in their logies in the "niggeryard" and the "bound-coolie-yard." The mansions were electrically lit; the logies had kerosene lamps . . . electricity like so many other things was a status symbol.
> Sitting at the apex of this world was the plantation manager. At Port Mourant . . . the manager was J. G. Gibson. His reputation extended far and wide; he was czar, king, prosecutor, judge, all in one. Almost everyone looked upon him with awe and fear. . . . Between these white and non-white worlds there were distances—social [occupants of these two worlds did not associate] and physical [the mansions were out of bounds]. There was also a psychological distance. I recall vividly my great curiosity about the manager's mansion. I wanted to know how it felt to be inside the gate.
> The plantation hierarchy had an unwritten but nevertheless rigid code. Managers and overseers could have sex relations with non-white women but inter-marriage was forbidden.

> Between the world of the bosses and the bossed was the middle strata of shopkeepers, pandits, parsons, teachers, dispensers, book-keepers and drivers. They depended for their status and social position on the patrónage of the manager. They could be penalized at any time if they lost grace with him.[17]

Major Structural Features of the Plantation Economy of Guyana

There is much literature pertaining to the general characteristics of plantations but here some observations will be made on the Guyanese situation. Plantations in Guyana were engaged in the production of sugar for export and in the days of slavery and for many years after, the whole country was virtually a series of sugar plantations. This export orientation led to major links between the colony and the metropole, links which were strengthened as the planters attempted to increase their profits by widening their commercial interests. For example, Bookers—the largest company in Guyana—was in 1968, as Beckford[18] observed, engaged in the following business activities: shopkeeping at both the wholesale and retail levels; distilling; manufacturing and marketing of rum, liquors, and other spirits; ocean and coastal shipping; trawling in the Caribbean waters; warehousing and stevedoring; the manufacturing of sugar machinery, mining equipment, and hydraulic press and pumps; drug manufacturing and sugar refining.

Some of these activities were undertaken in the metropole where the company headquarters and the major focus of its operations lay. The local plantations became branch plants, vertically integrated into the company's metropolitan economic enterprises and horizontally tied into the overall strategies and policies of all its operations overseas. The result of this centralization of activities in the United Kingdom was the development of a "segmental economy consisting of a number of firms, each of which is a self-sufficient unit almost independent of the rest of the economy."[19] R. T. Smith in commenting on Guyanese and West Indian societies in general, also noted that they were in fact segmentary societies, "with the plantations constituting a simple linear series of segments having little or no organic interrelation."[20]

The economic repercussions of this structure were indicated by Beckford, who observed, "So far as the colony is concerned, then, very little money income is available to the residents from plantation production and the plantation does not provide the impetus for de-

[17] C. B. Jagan, *The West on Trial* (London: Michael Joseph, 1966), pp. 17-18.
[18] George L. Beckford, *Persistent Poverty* (London: Oxford University Press, 1972), p. 144.
[19] *Ibid.*, p. 46.
[20] Quoted in *ibid.*, p. 62.

velopment."[21] This was responsible for one of the major structural defects of plantation economies observed by economists—the lack of "intermediate and final demand linkages" between the plantations and the rest of the rural and urban sectors of the economy—a factor that has been seen as an important one contributing to the economic under-development of all plantation societies.

A second important feature was the power the owners on the plantations had in ensuring the continued dependence of a large enough number of workers on the sugar estates. Guyana was, as far as land was concerned, an "open resource situation." This meant that most of the land was not previously taken up in permanent settlement or, where necessary, was made free by the enslavement and sometimes genocide of the local Amerindian population. The best of these lands were commandeered for plantation use at little or no initial cost to the planters. Even those lands which they did not cultivate were brought under their control and were used as an instrument to control labour. The objective was to block the development of an economically viable peasantry which would reduce the source of cheap labour for the plantations. Also, continued control of land, which was a major basis of the original stratification system, to a large extent meant the persistence of this system—with the high-status white groups owning the land and the low-status black slaves and later indentured East Indians working for them.

Further, since the commercial banks were heavily dependent on and sometimes controlled by the plantocracy their credit facilities were opened up mainly to the planters and not to peasant farmers. Even small entrepreneurs and commercial traders who did not have the necessary contacts found it almost impossible to obtain a loan from the banks. This made it very difficult for many individuals to acquire a decent livelihood outside the plantations except in the few low-status positions in the public service. Later, as other business ventures were launched, most notably in bauxite mining, Africans and eventually also East Indians were able to secure employment primarily as manual labourers in the operations.

In addition, when research relating to agricultural production was launched even by the Government, it was the type which was of direct benefit to the plantations. There was no attention paid to the increased production and processing of crops cultivated in the peasant sector though later when rice became an important export commodity some research work was carried out on it.

A third feature of the plantation system is the "totality of the institutional arrangements surrounding the production and marketing of plantation crops."[22] Some social scientists have noted strong

[21] *Ibid.*, p. 46.
[22] *Ibid.*, p. 8.

parallels between plantations and total institutions partly because the former were fairly autonomous sub-systems meeting nearly every need of their members. The plantations were not just the focus of one's work activities but represented a whole way of life, providing for most if not all of one's economic, social, health, education, and recreational needs. They had their own hospitals, stores, schools, places of worship and often their own institutions for the settlement of disputes among their sub-population. All these facilities were under the ownership, control, or patronage of the plantation authorities.

It was virtually impossible to escape from the system, partly because of the dominant influence of the plantation over the rest of the economy and partly because the monoculture of sugar meant that few opportunities were open outside the plantations. Beckford made the same observation when he noted that "to rebel against it [i.e., the plantation] is to threaten one's own survival, for alternative opportunities are hard to find."[23] This considerably enhanced the ability of the planters or their agents to control every aspect of life on the plantation and also resulted in the development of autocratic relationships between management and labour. On the estates the managers, as Jagan pointed out, exerted almost total control over the lives of the workers both within and outside the work situation. This was made easier because of the dominant position which they held, not only on the plantations but in the political, economic, and social structure of the country.

Finally, since the plantations provided little opportunity for upward social or economic mobility for these non-white workers, their social structure developed caste-like features. The difference in colour and ethnicity between the owners and the workers made it even easier to perpetuate this fairly rigid system of stratification. The maintenance of such a system, which had no religious or other ideological underpinning to support it, was best ensured by unfree labour and so, the importation of indentured labourers from India for the plantations continued until 1917.

Persistence of Plantation Systems

The fact that the system of social stratification on the sugar estate, as described by Jagan for the 1930s, strongly resembled that of the plantations during and just after slavery, gives an idea of the rather slow-changing nature of plantation society. Its tendency for persistence was remarkable; we find that a century after the abolition of slavery, the "bosses" were still white, holding all managerial and supervisory posts, living in geographically separate areas which were "out of bounds" to the rest of the population, mixing socially only with

[23] *Ibid.*, p. 54.

each other, and having sexual relationships but not inter-marrying with the non-whites. The "bossed," on the other hand, who were mainly East Indians and some Africans, lived in the "bound coolie" and "nigger yard" and were allowed to hold only the lowest jobs on the plantations. They were mainly agricultural labourers and never rose above the position of "driver."

The persistence of the plantations with little modification of their basic social structure was largely due to their major features identified above. These all stemmed from the amount of political power and influence which the planters enjoyed locally and in the metropole. For example, their continued control of the most valuable land resources in the country, even when these were not cultivated, was due to their power in the local legislature and their influence on the colonial administration, making it possible for them to use the state apparatus in their favour.

Another source of influence and mutual support were the churches and later the schools which helped in the "proper" socialization of the population, directly and indirectly developing in them an acceptance of and even support for the plantation system. In 1865, the Government, comprised mainly of the planters, found it useful or necessary to pass an ordinance "to provide for the maintenance of Ministers of the Christian Religion in the Colony of British Guiana" from public funds. But even before then the state contributed towards the financial support of various Christian churches and between 1841 and 1844 nearly 25% of all expenditure from the civil list was towards the upkeep of the ministers of these churches.[24] In 1876, when a Compulsory Education Act was passed, the aim was not only to have all children attend school, but also to ensure that they were brought up in the Christian faith. The hope was that the churches would help to socialize children to accept their lowly position in the society, the dominant position of the plantocracy, and the superiority of European culture. As R. T. Smith pointed out, "Schools and churches were held to be the best instruments for the transformation of a rebellious slave population into a peaceful and obedient working class."[25]

It will be seen later that the planter class not only enjoyed economic dominance in Guiana but also commanded nearly all political power up to 1928, and between then and 1945 considerably influenced the exercise of that power during the Crown Colony regime. The country had inherited the constitution of the former Dutch Colony, under which the British were, by treaty, expected to continue to administer the colony. This ensured that the plantocracy would con-

---

[24] See Dalton, p. 453.
[25] Smith, *British Guiana*, p. 145.

tinue as the strongest political force in the country. Franchise qualifications were very restricted and only the wealthier individuals— mainly the whites who were nearly all planters or heavily dependent on the plantation—became voters. Up to 1850 there were only 916 registered voters in a population of nearly 128,000. Clementi, from his study of the electorate, concluded that "it appears to be highly probable that in 1850 the electorate consisted almost exclusively of the adult male population of the European race, which formed 11% of the total adult male population of the Colony."[26]

It was the political dominance of the planter class in the legislature which made it possible for them to use public funds to subsidize the immigration of indentured labourers instead of paying reasonable wages to the ex-slaves. Between 1841 and 1848 the number of immigrants imported into Guiana was 46,514, at a direct cost to the Government of £336,685 plus the indirect costs of providing hospital services, etc. Total expenditure on immigration during those years was about £500,000. The fact that the planters could, through the exercise of their political power, have these expenses paid out of the public coffers was an important factor in their continued efforts to control the wage demands of the labour force by bringing in new supplies of cheap, unfree labour.

In addition, the plantocracy, through its position in the Combined Court, which controlled colonial revenues and expenditures, could enforce civil servants' acquiescence to its views simply by refusing to vote their salaries at budget time. For example, in 1887, Dr. Williams, Medical Inspector of the Colony, submitted a report describing the unsanitary conditions among the labourers of the sugar estates; in retaliation the Combined Court in December, 1887, struck his salary completely from the estimates.

The control of expenditure also gave the planters a chance of operating a police state or at least a state in which heavy emphasis was placed on its visible control mechanisms—the police force, the prisons, etc. For example, one finds that even though a compulsory education act was passed in 1876, partly through the influence of the British Government, the expenditure on the police force remained considerably greater than that on education—at least until the 1930s, as can be seen in Table 3.

However, from the 1850s on, there were infrequent constitutional reforms which broadened the base of the franchise, the most important one occurring in 1891 when property qualifications for entry into the Combined Court and the Court of Policy were modified and the suffrage extended by a lowering of the annual income qualification. The effect of these changes was a gradual redistribution of the

---

[26] Sir Cecil Clementi, *A Constitutional History of British Guiana* (London: Macmillan, 1937), p. 366.

Table 3   *Expenditure on the Police Force Compared with*
            Expenditure on Education in Guyana,
            1851-1938

Year	Expenditure on education	Expenditure on the police	Ratio of expenditure on education to that on the police force
1851	£ 3,212	£20,924	1:6.5
1901-02	27,527	55,699	1:2.0
1914-15	37,977	55,244	1:1.5
1938	101,817	95,290	1:0.9

Source: Computed from various Annual Reports and *Blue Book of Statistics on British Guiana by the Government of the United Kingdom* (London: H.M.S.O., 1851-1938).

political power in the country even though the influence of the planter group continued to be dominant.

By 1915, the total number of registered voters had risen to 4,321; the largest percentage of these (62%) were Africans. The East Indians, mainly because of their lack of literacy in English, then represented only 6.4% of the electorate even though they formed about 51% of the adult population. This disparity in the voting strength of the major ethnic groups was one of the chief arguments used by the British Government to suspend the constitution in 1928, placing the country under full colonial rule. The planter class was afraid that the Negro population would use its new-found political power in the interest of the working masses—as was indicated by previous actions—and as a result raised little objection to the British Government's complete abrogation of political power from the elected representatives. In fact, this "rape of the constitution" was actively supported by the sugar interests who were in a better position to influence political decisions made by the Colonial Office or by its local representative, the Governor, and his nominated members of the Legislative and the Executive councils.

The Dominance of European Culture

As previously indicated, a major characteristic of Guyanese and West Indian societies was the pervasiveness of the influence of European culture. The indigenous Amerindian population was completely wiped out in many of these colonies, with the result that the societies which later developed were almost completely influenced by European culture. Some of the cultural elements of other groups were in fact assimilated into the dominant European culture, resulting in what has often been referred to as "creole culture." But the dominance of European culture in West Indian societies remained and led one anthropologist to note that "the societies in the Caribbean are only superficially 'non-western,' taking on their particularity precisely because they are in some ways, and deceptively, among the most 'western' of all countries outside the United States and Western Europe."[27]

The influence of the European was seen in dress, language, and in many of the values which were idealized in Guyanese and West Indian societies. In 1836, Joseph Sturge and some of his fellow Quakers reported that during their visit to the West Indies it was not uncommon "to see *ladies* who had toiled under a burning sun during six days of the week attired on the seventh in silk stockings and straw bonnet with parasol and gloves and the *gentlemen* in black coats and fancy waistcoats."[28] Incidentally these ladies and gentlemen were black. This influence of the European on the dress of most West Indians has continued until today though in more recent times, following political independence, concerns have sometimes been expressed about the need for a national dress. Even the famous black liberator of Haiti, Toussaint Louverture, was not only passionately devoted to France but often appeared in the trappings of a French general.

Frantz Fanon was quite aware of the difference between West Indians and Africans in terms of their European acculturation, and writing about the West Indian Negro he observed:

> The West Indian was a European... a quasi metropolitan... not a Negro. Until 1939 the West Indian lived, thought, dreamed... composed poems, wrote novels exactly as a white man would have done.... Before Cesaire, West Indian literature was a literature of Europeans. The West Indian identified himself with the white man, adopted a white man's attitude, was a white man.[29]

R. T. Smith, in writing about the creole society in Guyana and the West Indies, which he saw historically as replacing slave society, observed that "the basic facts about creole society are that it was rooted in the political and economic dominance of the metropolitan power, it was colour stratified, and was integrated around the conception of the moral and cultural superiority of things English."[30]

[27] Sydney W. Mintz, "The Caribbean as a Socio-Cultural Area," in *Peoples and Cultures of the Caribbean*, ed. by M. M. Horowitz (New York: American Museum of Natural History, 1971), p. 18.

[28] J. Sturge and T. Harvey, *The West Indies in 1837* (London: Hamilton, Adams and Co., 1838), p. 84.

[29] Frantz Fanon, *Towards the African Revolution* (New York: Grove Press Inc., 1967), p. 26.

[30] Raymond T. Smith, "Social Stratification, Cultural Pluralism and Integration in West Indian Societies," in *Caribbean Integration*, ed. by S. Lewis and T. G. Matthews (Rio Pedras: University of Puerto Rico, 1967), p. 234.

Other Employment Opportunities Outside the Plantation System

It was already noted that the plantocracy wielded enough political power and influence to ensure that they always had an adequate supply of surplus labour at relatively low wages to meet the needs of the sugar estates, especially during the busy season. However, certain other economic developments took place even from the early years of the twentieth century and while most of these did not affect the labour needs of the plantations they did open up alternative avenues of employment for the masses who were outside the control and jurisdiction of the plantations.

Following emancipation, the great majority of Africans moved off the sugar estates although some had remained mainly as skilled workers in the factories. Those who settled in the rural villages were eking out a meagre existence by "ground provision" farming interspersed with a fortnight's work with the Public Works Department. The Government later established cooperative credit banks specifically to aid agricultural development outside the plantations, and by 1918 there were 28 such banks with some 5,815 shareholders.[31] While it is true that the total capital available to these banks was relatively small and their effect on peasant agriculture minimal, in some cases the money was crucial in aiding the efforts of the more progressive farmers.

Some of the Africans who moved to the urban areas were often able to secure skilled, semi-skilled, and unskilled jobs in the public and private sectors along with occasional employment on the docks. Later lower-level, white-collar jobs for positions such as primary school teachers, postmen, policemen, messengers, and junior clerks also became open to them.

The discovery of gold in 1882 and the flourishing of the diamond industry in 1922 accounted for about a quarter of the value of all exports from the country. These two fields also spasmodically attracted Africans as private entrepreneur "pork-knockers" or diamond seekers, though some of them also worked for the larger mining companies. The Demerara (now Guyana) Bauxite Company began its mining operations in 1916, and about four to five decades later was producing alumina locally. This industry largely attracted African workers, but most of the jobs which they were able to secure were at the lowest levels of the occupational hierarchy and required recruits with no more than a primary education.

With the expansion of the civil service and the further development of small private industries—most of which were associated with

[31] See, for example, Walter Rodney, "Masses in Action," in *New World, Guyana Independence Issue*, ed. by G. Lamming and M. Carter (Georgetown: New World Group of Associates, West Indies, 1966), for some account of more recent historical developments in Guyana.

the sugar companies—there were increasing numbers of lower-level, white-collar jobs and middle management positions that were open to the coloured population. This group had easier access to secondary education which was needed for entry into the more prestigious "classified" branch of the civil service. Those who did not obtain the necessary secondary school certificates were still able to find employment in private industry or in the "unclassified" public service such as the Transport and Harbours Department. These jobs in the public sector were at first closed to Africans and East Indians but, as some of them, especially the Africans, began to obtain secondary education they were also gradually able to compete for these positions.

When the indentureship contracts of the East Indians expired, some of them moved out of the sugar estates and took up rice farming and market gardening as small independent farmers, while others entered the field of commerce. Incidentally, rice cultivation started only after the constitutional changes of 1891, which reduced somewhat the previous complete dominance of the Combined Court by the plantocracy. Those who remained on the plantations found that the employment practices of the management, up to the late 1930s, were not dissimilar from what they were a century previously and the highest position which a non-white could hold was that of a "driver"—one step above the position of field labourer. Jagan had observed that "the unwritten law (of the sugar estates) was that none other than a white man could hold a post of overseer."[32] The only important change in the employment situation of the plantations was the increase in the number of lower-level white-collar jobs in the bureaucracy of the sugar estates—such as bookkeepers and office clerks—which were open to East Indians under the supervision of white or coloured office managers.

Those East Indians who left the sugar estates but did not return to India were granted lands in lieu of their return passage and many of them began to develop the local rice industry. By 1905 the country was beginning to export rice, and in 1964 the contribution of this commodity to the Gross Domestic Product (G.D.P.) was almost half that of sugar, providing employment for 12,000 persons as compared with 16,900 in sugar-cane cultivation. By 1911 half of the East Indian population was living outside the sugar plantations, working mainly as independent rice farmers.

Jobs outside agriculture were at first virtually closed to East Indians, and up to 1931 they were poorly represented even in such lower-level, white-collar jobs as primary school teachers and junior clerks in the public sector. There were many factors which restricted the physical, social, and occupational mobility of East Indians outside

[32] Jagan, p. 20.

the plantations. These included the geographical location of the sugar estates, the operation of "pass laws" which forbade the movement of East Indian labourers from the estates without management permission, strong family ties, a high rate of illiteracy, and a low representation on the voters' list. The result was that at this time "the East Indians clearly constituted the bottom rung of the colonial social ladder, which continued to be dominated by the European ruling class."[33] While this observation did not apply to all East Indians, it was certainly true of the great majority of them, and up to 1931 about 72% of the East Indian population was still engaged in agriculture as compared with 76% in 1891.

However, the opportunities for occupational and social mobility which were beginning to emerge, particularly for the two major ethnic groups in the society—the Africans and the East Indians— must be seen in perspective. They were, on the whole, very limited indeed and a majority of the members of these groups still earned their living in what Lewis refers to as the "low wage" sector of the economy—in rice farming and other forms of peasant agriculture or as seasonal agricultural labourers on the sugar estates with marginal incomes and little opportunity for their children to move out of this sector. The economically depressed state of the traditional sector in which most of them worked also provided limited opportunities for regular wage employment. Even the incomes of their craftsmen were very low, often no higher than those of their unskilled or semi-skilled co-workers. A few of the skilled workmen who received on-the-job training in the traditional sector later secured jobs in the modern sector of the economy, usually on the sugar estates or in the public service. But while their incomes were somewhat higher than those of peasant farmers, they were considerably lower than the incomes of white-collar workers, especially those with secondary education. Also, promotion prospects for these workers were virtually nonexistent, since the larger companies, like the Demerara Bauxite Company, for years imported nearly all supervisory staff and sometimes even skilled workers from the metropole.

Commerce and the Professions

Prior to the 1940s the limited opportunities for upward economic or social mobility open to the non-whites were usually in commerce and the independent professions because entry into these fields was not legally prohibited. However, an individual's success in commercial activities was heavily influenced by his relationship with the European business community, which dominated the import and wholesale trades and virtually controlled all credit facilities. The Africans were

[33] Mitchell *et al.*, p. 40.

the first to enter this field but, because of the lack of access to credit facilities, they were soon eclipsed by the Portuguese.

While this latter group began as peddlers and small shopkeepers, eventually ousting the small African traders, they did exceedingly well for themselves and soon entered the field of wholesale distribution. By the early twentieth century, they were not only retailers and wholesalers but also diamond merchants and owners of jewelry and pawnbroking establishments and insurance firms. Of the first fifty-five Guyanese businesses listed according to size in the *Red Book of the West Indies for 1922*, twenty-seven (54%) were identifiably owned by Portuguese.[34]

Until recently, preference in the recruitment of personnel for these Portuguese-owned business enterprises was given not only to family members but to others in the Portuguese community. In fact, most of the senior posts were virtually restricted to Portuguese and other persons of light complexion. Only the lowest positions were open to Africans, preferably those who were Roman Catholics; later some East Indians also joined these lower-level workers. Recruitment patterns among the European-owned firms were incidentally similar to those of the Portuguese except that with the former, their most senior positions were usually reserved for whites from the metropole.

The Chinese who entered the retail business owned laundries, restaurants, and other small business enterprises. Many of their ventures were family concerns and provided employment primarily for members of their own families who often performed a whole range of activities, from managers to labourers.

The East Indians began to engage in commerce mainly as rural shopkeepers, though some of them later moved into the urban centres and entered the distributive trades. Like the Portuguese, many East Indian businessmen later operated fairly large enterprises, including both wholesale and retail businesses. The smallest of these ventures were, as in the case of the Chinese, family enterprises and provided little opportunity for the employment of others outside the family group. In their larger business enterprises, the employment practices of the East Indians were somewhat similar to those of the Portuguese who owned firms of comparable size, that is, they preferred to employ East Indian workers. This practice was not restricted to supervisory and other senior positions but extended to all the available jobs. However, unlike the Portuguese, the rates of remuneration paid by East Indian businessmen were not only low but exploitative. This was largely because most other sectors of the job market were closed to East Indians and hence the supply of such labour was much greater than the demand. In addition, these workers were not usually

---

[34] *The Red Book of the West Indies 1922, Historical, Descriptive, Commercial and Industrial* (London: W. H. Collingridge, 1922).

allowed by the firms to organize themselves into trade unions for bargaining purposes.

Those Guyanese of the different ethnic groups who took up commerce were often highly motivated towards improving their economic position in the society through the only avenue that was at first open to them. Their long hours of hard work and their frugality, along with the sweated labour of their families and their employees, helped them to develop quite prosperous businesses. Names like D'Aguiar, Fernandes, J. P. Santos, Gajraj, Hack, Kawall, Kissoon, Toolsie, Persuad, Gafoor are well known for the economic success of an earlier member of the family.

Many of these businessmen earned enough profits to allow them not only to give their sons a secondary education but also to send them overseas to study for one of the independent professions, through which their acceptance in the higher levels of the social hierarchy became possible. The African population was, for reasons indicated earlier, not usually represented among these businessmen, and this is largely why, prior to the 1940s, they tended to be under-represented in such professions as law and medicine in comparison, for example, with East Indians despite the fact that a much higher percentage of their children attended primary and secondary schools.[35] Students of law and medicine studied mainly in the United Kingdom where the work-and-study practice which was characteristic of American universities was not in vogue. This meant that the earlier members of the independent professions who were Guyanese came from the somewhat economically better-off families. However, as qualifications in dentistry obtained in the United States became more acceptable in Guyana, and as U.S.-trained doctors were allowed to practise locally, an increasing number of students from the lower socio-economic groups, especially Africans and East Indians, began to enter universities in the U.S.A. They expected to help pay for their education by part-time or summer jobs. Similarly, as elitism in higher educaton in England began to erode, more Guyanese went to London to study for legal careers while working for their own upkeep.

The increasing number of Africans and East Indians who were entering the independent professions was of great significance to political developments in the country after the 1940s. Because of the economic independence which these professionals enjoyed they felt safe in taking up leadership roles in national politics and successfully challenged the authority and legitimacy of the small, white, ruling elite to continue holding positions of dominance in the country— usually with limited or no support from those whose interests they

[35] See M. K. Bacchus, *Education and Socio-Cultural Integration in a "Plural" Society*, Occasional Paper Series No. 6 (Montreal: Centre for Developing-Area Studies, McGill University, 1970).

were supposed to represent. Their efforts resulted in the constitutional reforms which started in 1943 and culminated in the achievement of self-government and independence about two decades later.

Effect of the Plantation System on Education

The influence of the plantation economy on education was profound, affecting not only the major function of education in Guyanese society, but also the rate of increase in the provision of educational services, the type of institutions that were developed, and the content of education offered in the schools. These points will be raised later in the study but some of them are briefly indicated here.

First, the plantocracy and other members of the dominant group obviously had a vested interest in retaining the essential features of the plantation society with its rigid system of stratification. This fact was reflected in their early efforts to prevent the extension of education facilities to the children of the slaves. They believed that a literate slave population could not be easily kept in bondage and generally blocked the efforts of early missionaries to teach or often even to christianize the black population. However, when it became obvious that the British Government was irretrievably committed to the legal abolition of slavery, the planters accepted the suggestion made by some of the early missionaries that education could become a valuable instrument for the "proper" socialization of the children of the ex-slaves, a means by which they could be taught to accept their roles as "hewers of wood" and "drawers of water" in a white-dominated society.

This resulted in the rapid expansion of a church-controlled system of primary education, followed by the introduction of the Compulsory Education Act, as early as 1876. The curriculum content of these schools consisted basically of the three Rs and religion, with the latter also inextricably interwoven in the teaching of reading and writing. The focus of these early efforts was to transmit those values which would make the ex-slaves voluntarily accept their position of subservience and become more productive labourers—values such as honesty, hard work, obedience, respect for authority—all of which were interpreted as developing a Christian attitude to life.

But while these efforts were to some extent successful in pacifying the black population, they did not succeed in keeping them as a servile labour force on the sugar plantations. Most blacks left the plantations and established independent villages along the coast. So when the East Indians later arrived on the sugar estates as indentured labourers, the planters were no longer as convinced about the role of education in producing docile labourers who would remain on the plantations after they had received an education.

In the case of these new labourers, the planters worked at frustrating the full implementation of the Compulsory Education Act by getting the Government, through an executive decision, to exclude from the provisions of the Act the children of East Indians. The major objective of the planters was to ensure that this new labour force would remain as general labourers on the sugar estates largely because they would find it difficult to secure employment outside the plantations due to their lack of education.[36] The dominant position of the planters over almost every aspect of life in the country made it possible for them to achieve this objective for a very long time. Similarly, the general unavailability of secondary education for the masses up to the 1940s, despite the passing of a Compulsory Education Act in 1876, was largely due to the interest of the planters in ensuring an adequate supply of manual labour in the country. They were very reluctant to see education becoming an instrument of upward social mobility for the children of the lower orders. This fact was reflected in their attitude to education for the children of the slaves, the ex-slaves, and later the East Indian workers on the sugar estates.

The continued dominance of the planters or their agents in the society was due not only to their political power and influence but also to the general acceptance by the non-whites of the cultural and moral superiority of the whites. The schools in Guyana and in the West Indies in general played an important part in passing on to the population a belief in the superiority of all things "white," especially all things English. The culture of all other groups was considered barbaric or superstitious, with the result that, prior to the 1960s, no attempt was made to familiarize pupils in schools with aspects of the cultural heritage of the various ethnic groups comprising Guyanese society. The acceptance of the superiority of the English culture was also reflected in the fact that the curriculum content of the schools was often an exact replica of that of the schools of England, especially at the secondary level. While this phenomenon existed in African and Asian colonial territories, such educational content was considered less alien to Guyanese and West Indian societies.

The social structure of the plantation society also had a direct influence on the educational aspirations of the population. It will be recalled that plantations approximated total institutions, and as a result, social and occupational mobility for the children of plantation labourers both within and outside the plantations was very difficult. This lack of mobility opportunities for Indo- and Afro-Guyanese both on and off the sugar estates, had a negative influence on their educa-

[36] My colleague Dr. R. S. Pannu has suggested to me that the decision might also have been influenced by the increased caution which was being taken by the British against intereference with the cultural traditions of the East Indian population following the Indian Mutiny of 1857.

tional aspirations for higher education outside the independent professions. It was then almost impossible for an African or East Indian who obtained a university degree which did not qualify him for entry into one of these professions to find an appropriate job either in the public or the private sector. This helped to increase the attractiveness of law and medicine for non-white Guyanese who wanted to pursue higher education prior to the 1940s.

The status and wage differentials which characterized the occupational structure of the plantations later also spread to all other fields. A major feature of this wage structure was that the white-collar jobs held by the coloured and white population were relatively high paid while those held by such low-status groups as Africans and East Indians—mainly manual, included skilled work—were poorly rewarded. The result was that white-collar jobs became even more prestigious than skilled jobs.

Further, since better educational facilities were more available to the coloured and white population, the possession of a secondary education was used to legitimize the status and income difference between the holders of these different types of jobs. This was one of the reasons why the masses began to value education even when it failed to teach them any useful and job-related skills. In fact, they rejected the idea that they should be given the type of formal education which could improve their efficiency in their low-status, manual occupations such as farming. Instead, they saw education as an instrument through which their children could obtain the certificates necessary to qualify them for those jobs which enjoyed higher prestige and greater economic rewards—the white-collar jobs.

Education in Other Economic Enterprises

The emergence of the gold, diamond, and bauxite mining industries, the production of rice, and the expansion of the urban labour force engaged in service type occupations, created demand for more unskilled, semi-skilled, and skilled jobs among the African and the East Indian population—jobs for which a primary education was considered a sufficient qualification. As happened on the plantations, white-collar jobs in these new industries, especially those requiring a secondary education, were at first held mainly by the coloureds, the Portuguese, and other Europeans. It was only much later, and more specifically after the 1940s, that the more prestigious jobs which required a secondary education became available to children of the lower-status groups in the society.

And even here there were two noticeable strands in this development: First, some of the jobs thrown open to children of the lower-status groups were not those which originally required a secondary education. They were, in fact, jobs which traditionally required only a primary education, but as the competition for them increased with the larger numbers of secondary school graduates entering the job market, the entry qualifications were in effect raised. The best example of this was the primary school teaching, which over time began to secure its recruits from the secondary school graduates. Second, a number of higher status positions, which traditionally required a secondary education, were also thrown open to Africans and East Indians. This began in an extended way after the 1940s. From then on, due to the steady shift in the locus of political power, increased pressure was exerted on the elected representatives to ensure that such jobs were thrown open to all sections of the population. In addition, the masses began to demand the more widespread provision of secondary and later tertiary level educational facilities to enable poorer students to acquire such an education. In fact, the rapid quantitative expansion of educational services occurring after the 1940s can be seen as a political response to this increasing popular pressure for greater opportunities for occupational and social mobility as the dominance of the plantation system began to weaken. This substitution of academic achievement for ascription based on ethnicity in the allocation of jobs was largely instrumental in raising the level of educational aspirations among the Africans, East Indians, Chinese, and other previously disadvantaged groups. And as the political system became increasingly "democratic," that is, more responsive to the demands of the masses, the pressure on the Government to expand the educational services increased.

From Table 4, which shows the occupational and ethnic composition of the major sectors of the Guyanese economy, one sees the overall relationship between colour and occupation which existed in the society prior to the 1940s.

Table 4 *Ethnicity of Employees by Occupational Levels in Guyana Prior to Self-Government*

THE PUBLIC SECTOR		THE PRIVATE SECTOR					
			BY WHOM HELD				
			IN COMMERCE			IN INDUSTRY	
POSTS	BY WHOM HELD	POSTS	European firms	Portuguese firms	Large E.I. firms	The sugar industry	The bauxite industry
Senior administrative and professional posts	Whites including some local Portuguese	Managerial, senior administrative, and professional posts	Whites from the metropole	Portuguese (usually family members); other whites	East Indians (usually children of proprietors)	Whites from the metropole	Whites: usually from North America (Canada)
"Key" supervisory post: Supt. of police, prisons, etc.	Whites from the metropole	Middle-level supervisory and executive posts; e.g., office managers	Whites, local Portuguese, and Coloureds	Portuguese; Coloureds	East Indians	Whites, including some Portuguese, Coloureds (overseers were white)	Whites: usually from North America
Middle-level supervisory and executive posts	Portuguese and Coloureds	Junior clerical posts and sales personnel	Coloureds	Portuguese; Coloureds; some Africans; few East Indians (E.I.)	East Indians	East Indians	Whites (skilled); Africans (semi-skilled workers and general labourers)

Table 4 *Continued*

THE PUBLIC SECTOR			THE PRIVATE SECTOR				
	BY WHOM HELD		BY WHOM HELD				
			IN COMMERCE			IN INDUSTRY	
POSTS	BY WHOM HELD	POSTS	European firms	Portuguese firms	Large E.I. firms	The sugar industry	The bauxite industry
Junior clerical posts: Police-men, postmen, messengers	Mainly Africans; later some East Indians	Skilled/semi-skilled workers; general labourers	Africans	Africans (mainly in semi-skilled and unskilled jobs)	East Indians (mainly in semi-skilled and un-skilled jobs)	Africans (skilled workers); East Indians (field labourers)	Coloureds

Notes:

Nearly all jobs in the smaller commercial enterprises owned by East Indians and Chinese were done by members of the family. Peasant agriculture was predominantly carried on by Africans and East Indians.

2. Post-1945 Developments in Guyana

Studies of educational systems have traditionally been conducted in isolation from other major institutions in society. This treatment of education, as an autonomous social institution, makes difficult any attempt at a meaningful assessment of its contribution to national development efforts. Furthermore, such studies result in evaluation of educational developments being focussed on quantitative expansion in educational services such as the increasing percentage of school-age population attending school, the range of new courses or programmes offered in primary, secondary, and tertiary level institutions, the rising level of education and training among teachers, and the growing per capita expenditure and percentage of the Gross National Product spent on education.

This study takes a somewhat broader approach. While quantitative increases in educational services will be examined, an attempt will be made to assess the effect of these educational developments in helping the nation meet its development goals. In order to do this, it is necessary first to provide a background description of the social, economic, and political changes in Guyanese society since 1945.

Economic Development, 1945-1972

Structure of the Economy in 1972

Before tracing developments in the economy from 1945 to 1972, it will be useful to refer briefly to the structure of the economy in the latter year. The picture which emerges (see Table 5) shows that up to 1972, only about one quarter (24%) of the country's G.D.P. was derived from agriculture, including the processing of the two main agricultural commodities—rice and sugar. But despite this, there was a marked lack of diversification in the economy which depended mainly on three products—sugar, rice, and bauxite including alumina. In 1972, bauxite was responsible for 44.1% of the total value of all exports, sugar with its by-products of molasses and rum for 34.3%, and rice for about 7.1%.

Economic Developments Since 1945

In looking more specifically at the economic changes since 1945, considerable use has been made of the figures provided in three national income studies done during the period, the three censuses (1945, 1960, and 1970), and two major surveys of unemployment

Table 5   *Industrial Origin of G.D.P. at Current Factor-Cost in $ Millions (Guyanese) in 1972*

	$ Millions	Percentage
Agriculture	104.3	19.7
Mining and quarrying	89.7	17.0
Manufacturing	106.6	20.2
Services	228.7	43.1
Total	529.3	100.0

Note: All reference to dollars will be Guyanese dollars; unless otherwise stated, $1 G = 45¢ U.S.
Source: Author's compilation from the Government of Guyana, *Economy Survey of Guyana, 1972.*

(1956 and 1965). Although the data from these different sources were not exactly comparable, they nevertheless gave a general picture of changes in the economy over the period.

1942-1972—The study by Percival and D'Andrade[1] indicates that the national income at current prices rose from $50 millions in 1942 to $100 millions in 1948 and then to $136 millions in 1951—an increase of 172%. However, in real terms the increase was about 25% between 1942 and 1948, and 15% between 1948 and 1951. Further, after population growth was taken into account, it was found that *per capita* income rose by just over 20% during the nine-year period, that is, about 2.3% per annum. As will be seen later, these last years of the war and the immediate postwar period were times of relatively high economic growth.

Between 1948 and 1960, net income, according to Kundu,[2] rose by just over 53%, or about 4.4% per annum, but when inflation and population increases are taken into account, there was very little real improvement in per capita income. In presenting a picture of the economic development of Guyana between 1953 and 1960, Newman also noted that the value of the national income at current prices increased by 51%. "But," he added, "this does not allow for the falling value of money—prices rose by about 12%—nor the increasing population—a rise of 23.5%. Hence, the real income per capita did not rise nearly so much, and indeed the household net income per capita hardly rose at all during this period." He therefore concluded

[1] D. A. Percival and W. P. D'Andrade, *The National Economic Accounts of British Guiana 1938-51* (Georgetown: The Daily Chronicle Ltd., 1952).
[2] A. Kundu, "The Economy of British Guiana 1960-75," *Social and Economic Studies* Vol. 12, No. 3 (September 1963), pp. 307-80.

that, "We can say that the economy grew just fast enough on average to maintain real incomes intact."[3] Kundu also came to the same conclusion:

> On the whole, there is a very slight upward trend in *per capita* net income over the period 1948-60. When one takes into account the high rate of population growth in British Guiana, it may be said that the economy is expanding at a rate just fast enough to match the increase in population, but can contribute nothing towards any significant economic growth or improvement in levels of living.[4]

The period 1960 to 1965 was one of the most difficult in recent Guyanese history, characterized by great political and social unrest following the granting of self-government. Local groups assisted by international organizations, including the Central Intelligence Agency, attempted to prevent the locally elected Government from "going socialist," resulting in riots in February 1962, a prolonged general strike in 1963, and several months of civil disturbance in 1964. This culminated in a change in the electoral system by the British Government at the insistence of the U.S.A. Since then, although physical violence has diminished, there exists an atmosphere of suspicion and distrust, especially among the two major ethnic groups of the country.

During this period, the G.D.P. increased by about 26%, or 5.2% per annum at current prices; but with price adjustments, the increase in real terms was only about 14%, or 2.8% per annum. When the population increase of 2.4% per annum is taken into account, the figures indicate that the per capita income hardly rose at all. The 1973 United Nations Mission to Guyana indicated that the per capita G.N.P. only rose from $643 to $644 (at 1971 prices) during these five years. There was some increase in the real per capita income between 1960 and 1963, but this was followed by an outright decline in 1963, brought about by the strikes and political disturbances of that year. In 1964, there was a slight upswing in the economy again, although the per capita G.D.P. in real terms did not reach the 1962 level by 1965. O. J. Francis,[5] after reviewing the economic position of the country between 1963 and 1965, concluded that one could best describe the economy as "static," with indications that the distribution of wealth had become more skewed than in previous years.

During the late 1960s, the rate of growth of the G.D.P. was reported to be quite favourable. Between 1965 and 1970, it was estimated that the G.D.P. increased in real terms by about 20%, or about

---

[3] Peter Newman, *British Guiana, Problems of Cohesion in an Immigrant Society* (London: Oxford University Press, 1964), p. 56.

[4] Kundu, pp. 312-13.

[5] O. J. Francis, *Report on Survey of Manpower Requirements in the Labour Force, British Guiana 1965*, Vol. 2: *Human Resources in Guiana* (Georgetown: Government of Guyana, 1966), p. 10.

4% per annum, but when population increase is taken into account, the per capita G.D.P. rose by less than 1% per annum. Since then, the growth rate has slowed down substantially. Dr. Clive Thomas observed that the Bank of Guyana Report, 1972, "shows the fall in the physical out-put of sugar and bauxite/alumina was 15% each; while the fall in rice production was of the order of 20%."[6] The world market price for bauxite/alumina also began to fall in 1970 while the price of rice was depressed since about 1965. In addition, Thomas pointed out that the domestic purchasing power of the Guyana dollar had fallen nearly 13% between January 1972 and August 1973. The total result was that there was a zero increase in real production in 1972, and when population increase is considered, the per capita G.D.P. at constant (1971) prices actually fell between 1970 and 1972 from about $719 to $666. The service sector was the only one to expand, with Government services—especially the army—growing fairly rapidly, i.e., about 15% in value in 1972, which was about 50% more than its average rate of growth over the previous five years.

From Table 6 can be seen how slowly the real per capita G.D.P. was increasing in the period from 1960 to 1972.

Table 6 *Per Capita G.D.P. at Constant (1971) Prices between 1960 and 1972*

Year	G.D.P. per capita, 1971 prices
1960	$643
1962	653
1964	597
1966	646
1968	643
1970	719
1972	666

Source: "Report of the UNESCO Educational Survey Mission to British Guiana" (Paris, UNESCO, 1973). (Mimeographed.)

Changes in the Structure of the Economy and Employment

An examination of the figures given by Kundu and others on the industrial origin of the G.D.P. in Guyana indicate that there had been no major change in the structure of the economy during the period

[6] Clive Y. Thomas, "Inflation, Shortages and the Working Class Interests in Guyana" (Turkeyen, Guyana: University of Guyana Library, November 1973), p. 15. (Mimeographed.)

under review, except that the contribution of agriculture to the economy was declining, and that mining, due to the development of the bauxite industry, was increasing. Up to 1956, O'Loughlin had noted:

> The structure of the economy still follows very closely on the "old colonial pattern" in which capital is concentrated and a few firms of mainly expatriate origin carry much of the productive and distribution activities of the country.... Opportunities for local investment of savings are limited and although capital is urgently needed, there is believed to be an annual capital outflow of local savings seeking investment overseas.... There has not been, as yet, much interest taken by either local or overseas capital in processing and manufacturing local materials for export.[7]

After 1956 there were some slight changes in the overall structure of employment by industry, as can be seen in Table 7. But these changes were not due to any diversification of the economy.

While nearly 30% of the labour force was still employed in agriculture in 1970, the proportion of workers engaged in this sector has been in steady decline since 1945. This was due largely to the increasing mechanization of sugar and rice production, with a resultant decline in agricultural employment at the same time that total agricultural production was still increasing. This explains, in part, why the prospects for additional employment in agriculture are not very bright especially if the same development strategies continue to be used. While the Government's policy of diversifying and further stimulating agricultural production might contribute to easing the balance of payment problem, it is not likely to be a solution for the unemployment problem.

Expansion of agricultural production is a real possibility for Guyana, but if the major orientation is to produce crops for export, a major constraint on such efforts will be the size of the market for agricultural products, especially since Guyana's main trading partners in the CARIFTA area are also essentially producers of agricultural products. In addition, as Dr. Phillips of the University of Guyana pointed out, "the growth rate in agriculture, despite large capital injections (25% of the Government capital expenditure) has been disappointing. Crop output has increased by less than 1% and yields per acres are showing downward trends for the major agricultural crops, rice and sugar."[8] Further, while Guyana is a large country by West Indian standards, the existing amount of cultivable land is limited and very heavy capital expenditure will be required for drainage and irrigation schemes to bring new land into cultivation.

[7] C. O'Loughlin, "The Economy of British Guiana 1952-56: A National Accounts Study," *Social and Economic Studies* Vol. 8, no. 1 (March 1959), p. 11.

[8] W. J. Phillips, "The Trade Unions and Guyana's Draft Development Plan 1972-76" (Turkeyen, Guyana: University of Guyana Library, September 1973), p. 3. (Mimeographed.)

Table 7 *Percentage of the Labour Force Employed in Different Industries between 1946 and 1970*

Industry	1945	1956	1960	1965	1970
PRIMARY PRODUCTION					
Agriculture, including livestock, fishing, hunting, and forestry	46.2	42.0	37.1	32.0	29.0
Mining	2.8	2.2	3.8	3.3	4.9
SECONDARY PRODUCTION					
Manufacturing, food processing, building and construction, fuel, and power	20.8	19.5	24.9	24.0	20.2
SERVICE					
Transport, communication, and distribution	12.5	18.0	16.1	20.0	15.7
Other services	16.9	18.3	18.0	19.9	28.1
NO INDUSTRY OR NOT STATED	.8		.1	.8	2.1
Total	100.0	100.0	100.0	100.0	100.0

Sources: Government of British Guiana, *Census of the Colony of British Guiana 9th April 1946* (Kingston, Jamaica: Government Printer, 1949); Government of British Guiana, *Census of the Colony of British Guiana, 1960* (Kingston, Jamaica); Government of Guyana, *Census of Guyana 1970* (Georgetown, Guyana); International Labour Organization (I.L.O.), "Report to the Government of British Guiana on Employment, Unemployment and Underemployment in the colony in 1956" (Geneva, 1957).(Mimeographed.); O. J. Frances, *Report on Survey of Manpower Requirements 1965*, Georgetown: Government of Guyana, 1966.

The 1972-76 development plans envisaged the very high growth rate of 8.5% per annum in agriculture, but the possibility of this happening and of making the agricultural sector capable of attracting vibrant young men into farming, seems doubtful.[9] For example, most of this development was planned to take place away from the established population centres, and as Phillips indicated, this is "the real problem." There is great reluctance by people to move into the more remote areas of the country to take up farming. Also, the Government seems keen, for political and social reasons, to attract more of the African population back to the land as farmers—an occupation which, for historical and psychological reasons, many of them have abandoned. The programme for agricultural development, therefore, involves both heavy capital investment and attitudinal changes to

[9] Government of British Guiana, "British Guiana Development Programme 1966-72" (Georgetown, 1966).

farming, particularly among the Africans—factors which are likely to reduce the rate of growth in this sector. Furthermore, the Government's financial position in 1974 caused a reduction of its development expenditure; this will certainly postpone the implementation of the agricultural development programme in view of the heavy capital investment required.

The percentage of the labour force employed in secondary production, which included manufacturing and food processing, increased slightly from under 20% in 1956 to nearly 25% in 1960. Since then, however, there has been a substantial drop in this figure, down to about 20% in 1970. This low rate of industrialization has been largely responsible for the relatively restricted employment opportunities for persons with post-secondary education, especially those with technical and craft training. In fact, the 1965 manpower survey revealed that "craftsmen and technicians" were experiencing an unemployment rate of 19.2% and were the second largest unemployed group in the country.

The service sector, on the other hand, was becoming increasingly important as far as employment opportunities were concerned. In 1945 over 30% of the working force was in this sector, but the figure rose to nearly 44% by 1970—an indication that the number of "white"-collar workers was increasing faster than any other occupational group. Between 1946 and 1960, the increase in the total labour force was just under 19%, while the increase among "clerical and sales workers" including those employed in commerce was about 50%. Similarly, between 1960 and 1970 the labour force again increased by about 20% while the numbers employed in the service sector rose by nearly 54%—from 29,102 to 44,772. Brewster, in commenting on the job situation between 1948 and 1960, observed that, insofar as new jobs were created, they were concentrated in the non-manual group.[10]

Two factors contributed to the increasing number of workers in the service sector. First, there has been an increase in the number employed in such public sector activities as the civil service, teaching, the police force, and the army. Second, more persons were being employed as domestic servants, a not uncommon phenomenon in poor countries where unemployment is worsening at the same time that the income levels of the employed are rising. It was also becoming more common for both husband and wife to be working outside the home while they employed paid domestic help.

Other Aspects of the Labour Force

Another aspect of the Guyanese labour force to be noted is its size and the relatively limited number of persons employed in each occupational group, as can be seen in Table 8.

[10] H. Brewster, "Some Factors of Guyana's Economic Development" (Mona, Jamaica: I.S.E.R. Library, University of the West Indies, 1965). (Mimeographed.)

Table 8 *Main Occupations of Persons in Employment in Guyana in 1965*

	Number	Percentage
Professionals	1,114	0.8
Non-professionals with specialized training	2,192	1.58
Administrative, executive and supervisory	5,823	4.21
Clerical and sales workers	23,616	17.09
Craftsmen and technicians	28,976	20.97
Service workers	23,661	17.12
Manual workers	52,416	37.94
Not stated	330	0.24
Total	138,128	99.95

Source: O. J. Francis, *Report on Survey of Manpower Requirements 1965* (Georgetown: Government of Guyana, 1966).

The small number of workers in each occupation itself poses a problem for the educational planner and calls for great flexibility in the development of new programmes. For example, the demand for draughtsmen at any one time might indicate the need for a full-time training programme for such personnel. But after a number of years of producing such workers, one is likely to find that the job market for them becomes saturated and the annual demand can no longer justify the retention of the full-time training programme. The usual result is that strong pressures develop from the tenured staff of educational institutions to lengthen the period of training required in order to justify the continuation of the course. The writer is aware of at least two training programmes in Guyana which are lengthened because the job market for these skills was becoming saturated.

The size of the Guyanese labour force makes for both a small demand for certain specific types of skills and for a miniscule vacancy factor. Yet, such vacancies as exist can adversely affect the economic development of the country. For example, the Government's 1960 Survey of Establishments noted that engineers and geologists figured significantly in the number of vacancies reported and pointed out that "if the exploitation of the mineral resources is to occupy an important position in the plans for the economic development of Guyana then ... the filling of these vacancies must be considered crucial."[11] The following list presented in the 1965 survey gives an idea of the limited number of vacancies that existed in certain crucial professional fields in Guyana.

Professional Fields	No. of Vacancies in 1965
Civil Engineers	13
Geologists	12
Mechanical Engineers	10
Land Surveyors	9
Chemists	3
Architects	2
Soil Physicists	1
Geophysicists	1
Petrologist/Mineralogists	1

The small size of the job market for such specialist skills poses a great dilemma for a country with its own higher-level educational institutions. Since it has been economically impossible to provide the specialist training required in these areas locally, efforts have been made to send Guyanese abroad for the necessary training. Also, overseas personnel have been recruited, usually on a temporary basis, to fill existing vacancies until trained Guyanese are available. But the problem which often arises is in the remuneration of such personnel. Those Guyanese who return home often expect salaries more in line with the international market for their skills. On the other hand, if they are paid such salaries, their remuneration is likely to be the reference point for new salary demands by other Government workers, especially those with a comparable length of training but whose skills are not in such short supply.

Unemployment

Since 1946 the unemployment rate has been growing, due mainly to the rapid increase of the labour force relative to the rate of growth of the economy. The figures in Table 9 compare the growth of the total labour force with that of the employed population between 1946 and 1970.

Between 1946 and 1960, the labour force increased by 18.6%, compared with a 6.8% increase in the employed population; and for the entire period 1946-1970, the total labour force increased by 42.4%, compared with a 21.8% increase in the numbers employed. In short, the size of the total labour force was growing nearly twice as fast as the employed population. While the labour force increased by

[11] Government of Guyana, Manpower Survey Office, Ministry of Labour and Social Security, *Report on Establishments Enquiry 1969* (Georgetown, May 1970), p. 76.

Table 9 *Increases in Population, Labour Force, and Total Employed Population between 1946 and 1970*

Year	Total population in 000s	Total labour force in 000s	Total employed population in 000s
1946	357.7	147.5	146.2
1960	560.3	175.0	156.1
1970	714.0	210.0	178.0
INCREASES			
a. 1946-1960			
Total in 000s	184.6	27.5	9.9
Percentage	49.1	18.6	6.8
b. 1946-1970			
Total	338.3	62.5	31.8
Percentage	90.0	42.4	21.8

62,500 between 1946 and 1970, only about half this number—31,800—were able to find employment.

The unemployment surveys of 1956 and 1965 confirmed this situation of increasing unemployment. The 1965 survey estimated that unemployment was about 18% of the labour force, while the figure in the 1965 survey was 20.9%. Brewster also noted:

> It appears from various sources that from 1948 to 1965, increases in employment must have averaged annually about 0.5% of the labour force. . . . The labour force . . . seemed to have been increasing by something like 1.2% a year. Thus, there has been an average annual residue of unemployed persons equal to 0.7% of the labour force. In other words, the economy has been able to provide for only approximately one-half of the net increment of the labour force.[12]

One factor responsible for the rising rate of unemployment in the country has been the increasing participation[13] of females in the labour force. In 1969 the ratio of males to females in the labour force was 3:1, but this figure represents a considerable increase over previous years. For example, between 1965 and 1969 there was a 59% increase in the number of female workers in the private sector compared with a 35% increase among males. The 1969 survey noted that "this indicated clearly that the rate of absorption of women into the work force was nearly twice that for males."[14]

[12] Brewster.
[13] Participation rates were based on surveys conducted on the non-agricultural sector of the economy which in 1970 employed 71% of the labour force. All public and private institutions employing five or more persons were surveyed.
[14] Government of Guyana, *Report on Establishments Enquiry*, p. 11.

Female under-representation has been more marked at the higher levels; the ratio of males to females in the professional and senior executive category was no more than 10:1 in 1971. But this situation is steadily changing and an increasing number of females are pursuing post-secondary education. This will put them in a better competitive position on the job market. One result of this increasing number of females entering the labour market is the high rate of unemployment among females—27.7% in 1965 compared with about 21% for the total labour force.

Government publications such as the Guyana Development Programme (1966-1972) have given a number of reasons for this continued rise in unemployment, which according to some calculations, was estimated at about 25% in 1975.[15] Among reasons listed is the "excessive mechanization" in the major industries and also in construction. In the sugar industry, for example, employment fell from 27,900 in 1954 to 17,800 in 1963, while output increased from 239,000 tons in 1954 to 317,000 tons in 1963.

The effect of this increase in mechanization was also reflected in improved school attendance. In the rice industry, production and cultivation were so labour intensive in earlier times that schools were literally closed at certain periods so children could help their parents on the farms. But by the 1960s, this situation had changed considerably, and in his manpower survey of 1965, Francis observed that "substantial importations of agricultural machinery had increased productivity with, of course, a lessening of the demand for labour."[16]

The increase in unemployment was also attributed to a "genuine dislike of young persons to pursue agricultural occupations" especially after they have received some formal education. But it needs to be pointed out that wages in the agricultural sector were substantially lower than those enjoyed by other workers; in fact all other indices would show that in Guyana, farmers probably occupied the lowest rung of the social and economic hierarchy. In such circumstances it was not surprising to find that youngsters who completed some years of primary schooling became somewhat "psychologically unfit" for low-status agricultural occupations, especially since education in the society has increasingly been looked upon as an instrument of upward mobility. Many preferred to remain unemployed, waiting for some suitable job to turn up rather than take a job for which they believed their schooling had made them "unfit."

A third factor contributing to unemployment, according to the 1966-1972 Development Plan, was the scarcity of cultivable lands for expansion of farming—in a country where the supply of land was

[15] M. K. Bacchus, "Manpower Implications of Guyana's Development (1966-72) Plan," *New World* Vol. 2 Crop Over Issue (1966), pp. 39-48.
[16] Francis, p. 42.

plentiful. This was due to the high cost of developing lands for agricultural cultivation, especially those outside the coastal strip, the lack of capital, and sometimes the lack of initiative.

Fourth, the economy has been characterized by the failure of existing industries to expand or new ones to develop. The manufacturing sector has not progressed very much, and, apart from the bauxite industry, there has been no significant industrial development. This was largely, though not entirely, due to lack of capital. As was already pointed out, despite the need for development, there has been an export of capital by local residents, and this was happening long before the 1963 political disturbances.

Lastly, there was the problem of rapid population increase which, at 1965 rates, was expected to double itself every twenty-five years. Providing employment opportunities to cope with such a rapid population increase must in itself be a heavy strain on the economy

The Structure of Unemployment

The unemployment situation in the different industries was described by two unemployment surveys and is summarized in Table 10. From these figures it can be seen that the "inexperienced unemployed"—those who had never worked—formed the largest single group in both of these surveys. In addition, their numbers increased between 1956 and 1965 by about 30%, rising faster than the overall rate of increase in unemployment. This indicates that it was becoming more difficult for young school leavers to find jobs. The agriculture sector employed the largest number of workers and had one of the highest rates of unemployment both in 1956 and 1965, the third highest rate in 1956 and the second highest in 1965. The service sector, which includes a large number of domestic servants, had a high percentage of unemployment in 1956 (18.3%), but by 1965 the situation here had improved considerably with the unemployment rate falling to 8.3%.

There were some other aspects of the structure of unemployment to which attention should be directed. One of these, as can be seen in Table 11, was that unemployment increased markedly down the occupational scale. In 1960 Kundu had already observed that "by occupation the percentage of unemployed persons in the labour force was rather high everywhere except for white-collar workers and professional people."[17] The economically more disadvantaged groups suffered most from unemployment.

An interesting offshoot of this was the fact that in a developing country like Guyana, unemployment among "craftsmen and technical workers" was about three times as high as that among clerical and sales workers, and 80% higher than for service workers. Commenting

[17] Kundu, p. 320.

Table 10 *Unemployment in the Different Sectors of the Economy in 1956 and 1965*

Sector	1956		1965	
	No. unemployed by sector	Percentage of labour force unemployed by sector	No. unemployed by sector	Percentage of labour force unemployed by sector
Agriculture	7,300	11.3	7,900	15.2
Mining and quarrying	100	5.3	270	5.5
Manufacturing, fuel, and power	1,800	9.4	2,086	7.3
Building and construction	2,400	20.8	2340	25.6
Transport and communication	900	11.0	900	9.0
Distribution	1,400	7.6	1,500	7.8
Public, professional and financial services	1,000) 6.5) } 18.3			
Recreational and other services	4,600) 28.6)		2,450	8.3
Never worked (inexperienced unemployed)	10,100		13,150	

Table 10 *Continued*

Sector	1956		1965	
	No. unemployed by sector	Percentage of labour force unemployed by sector	No. unemployed by sector	Percentage of labour force unemployed by sector
No industry	—		4,970	
Not stated	—		1,000	
Total	29,600		36,600	

Sources: International Labour Organization, "Report to the Government of British Guiana on Employment, Unemployment and Underemployment in the Colony in 1956" (Geneva: I.L.O., 1957). (Mimeographed.) O.J. Francis, *Report on Survey of Manpower Requirements in the Labour Force, British Guiana 1965* (4 vols.; Georgetown: Government of Guyana, 1966).

Table 11 *Percentage Distribution of the
Experienced Unemployed by Usual
Occupational Group, 1965*

Occupational group	Percentage unemployed
Professional	0.0
Non-professional with specialized training	0.3
Administrative, executive, and supervisory	0.1
Clerical and sales workers	6.4
Service workers	10.7
Craftsmen and technical workers	19.2
Manual workers	39.9
No special occupation	17.5
Occupation not stated	6.9

Source: O. J. Francis, *Report on Survey of Manpower Requirements in the Labour
Force, British Guiana 1965* (4 vols.; Georgetown: Government of
Guyana, 1966), p. 60.

on this situation, the 1965 report on unemployment observed, "It was
of some interest to note the high proportion of craftsmen who were
unemployed for long periods."[18] About 38% of the unemployed
craftsmen in the city had not worked for a period of three to six
months, and about 25% were out of work for six to twelve months. In
these days when there is increasing emphasis by the Government on
technical education, the high rate of unemployment among
"craftsmen and technical workers" hardly provides an incentive for
youngsters to aspire to become technical and skilled workers rather
than clerks.

Another factor in the unemployment situation revealed by the
1965 survey is that the previous urban/rural differential in employment levels had changed direction; in 1965, the unemployment rates
in urban areas were lower than those in the rural areas, whereas in
1956, the opposite was true. This was due somewhat to increasing
mechanization of agriculture and was also partly a reflection of the
increase in educational opportunities in the rural areas unaccompanied by increased job opportunities.

Unemployment Among the Young
The unemployment situation among the more recent school
leavers also presented an interesting picture. In 1965, about 43% of

[18] Francis, Vol. 2, p. 62.

the unemployed were under 21 years of age, and nearly 60% of these were below 18 years. Viewed from a slightly different angle, about 41% of the total age group under 19 in the labour force were unemployed. The intensity of the problem will be further appreciated when it is noted that 63% of the unemployed young persons under 21 years of age had never worked since leaving school. And the situation has shown no signs of improvement since 1965. In the unemployment survey done that year, it was revealed that nearly 40% of all unemployed persons were under 19, and about 53% of the 14-19 group who were in the labour force were unemployed.

A look at the educational backgrounds of the young unemployed in 1956, i.e., those under 21 years of age, revealed that they had, by and large, made full use of the educational facilities available to them. Over 13% had some secondary education and an additional 68% had between seven and eight years of "primary" schooling.[19] In 1965, Francis also observed that nearly all the "inexperienced" unemployed had enjoyed a "fair" amount of schooling.[20] About 20% of them did have some secondary education and nearly all the remainder had completed their "primary" school careers. The median number of years of schooling completed by the "inexperienced" unemployed in the capital city was 8.0 years for males and 8.5 years for females. In the rural areas, the figures for males and females were 7.4 and 7.7 years of schooling, respectively.

The question which arises next is whether the unemployed persons would have been able to find jobs in the existing economic structure if they had had more education and training. It is true that there were a number of vacancies reported in some fields in which heavy unemployment existed, e.g., among "craftsmen and technicians." The manpower survey of 1965 noted that this was to some extent an indication that the levels of skills or training among the unemployed in these fields might not have been sufficient to enable them to fill the existing vacancies. But this situation was true only to a limited extent. The 1965 manpower survey revealed a total of 1,086 effective vacancies which no one filled and which represented a real shortage of suitable manpower. If this is compared with the unemployment figures at that time—36,600—it will be seen that the effective vacancies were very much below the number of unemployed, and, therefore, more training would not in itself have solved this problem. Further, if a comparison is to be made between the types of vacancies and the usual occupations, if any, of the unemployed, it will be observed that a large number of vacancies were for persons whose training could not

[19] International Labour Organization (I.L.O.), "Report to the Government of British Guiana on Employment, Unemployment and Underemployment in the Colony in 1956" (Geneva, 1957), p. 44. (Mimeographed.)

[20] Francis, Vol. 2, p. 51.

have been obtained locally or for whom more education alone was not enough; experience was an important consideration for appointment.

Table 12 gives the number of vacancies which existed in 1965, by occupational group and by the number of unemployed persons in each category. The total number of vacancies in each occupation was, with the exception of the first three, considerably lower than the number of unemployed in these groups. For example, the number of unemployed craftsmen was about twenty times as large as the number of vacancies for this category of worker. The vacancies in the first three occupational groups often needed persons with both specialized types of training and experience. Also, the majority of these vacancies were in the public sector and many of them were not filled because of the Government's attempt at the time to restrict its expenditure. Further, if we look at the number of expatriates employed in Guyana, we shall find that not only were the numbers small but their replacement by Guyanese would not appreciably have affected the local unemployment situation. In the public sector, there were only about 95 non-Guyanese employed; some were personnel obtained under bilateral aid agreements while others were persons who were, at the time, difficult to recruit on the world market: geologists, university professors, doctors, etc. In the private sector, there were 508 expatriates—defined as non-Guyanese who migrated to the country within the past ten years. Most of them held professional and senior administrative posts, especially in the sugar, bauxite and newly-developing minor industries. Apart from the fact that their specialized experience was valuable for the economy, there were no Guyanese in these job categories who were unemployed. So the presence of these expatriates did not adversely affect the employment situation among Guyanese personnel.

The manpower survey also revealed that while the overall number of job vacancies was limited, the ratio of "qualified" to "unqualified" personnel employed in certain occupations was low, possibly indicating a need for more trained personnel in these fields to reduce such disparities. For example, there were 939 persons "engaged in accounting work" in the public sector, while the actual number of professionally trained accountants was only 19. But while this ratio might indicate a need for more professional accountants, one cannot assume from the figures alone that this was necessarily so. The jobs done even by senior persons "engaged in accounting work" in Government departments might not need the skills of a professional accountant. In fact, in many developing countries the nomenclature of jobs can be misleading and it does not always mean that the skills required for them are the same as those needed for similarly named jobs in more economically developed countries.

Table 12 *Number of Vacancies and Unemployed*
Persons by Occupational Level in
Guyana in 1965

Occupational groups	Vacancies	Number of unemployed
Professional, including those with university degrees	120	0
Non-professional with specialized training	138	65
Administrative, executive, and supervisory	128	25
Clerical	198	1,512
Craftsmen	210	4,266
Service workers	206	2,524
Manual workers	86	9,362

Source: O. J. Francis, *Report on Survey of Manpower Requirements in the Labour Force, British Guiana 1965*, Vol. 1 (4 vols.; Georgetown: Government of Guyana, 1966).

The main point here is that the unemployment problem in Guyana was not due to the shortage of educated Guyanese personnel but stemmed essentially from the slow rate of economic growth, especially when population increase was considered. Therefore, contrary to the popular belief among local educators and politicians, this problem cannot be overcome merely by providing better education and training facilities for the population, which was the solution generally attempted over the years.

Emigration

Over the past decade, there has been a marked increase in the rate of emigration from Guyana. According to Sukdeo,[21] the departure index of 100 for 1960 moved to 135 in 1962 and to 252 by 1970. Most emigrants were from the professional groups, skilled craftsmen, and the entrepreneurial elements in the population.

The effect of emigration on the educational system was felt in two ways. First, it was partly responsible for the low rate of increase in the primary school population after the mid-1960s. While the total population was increasing at the rate of 3.5% per annum between 1946 and 1960, this figure dropped to about 2.6% between 1960 and 1970,

[21] Fred Sukdeo, "The Impact of Emigration on Manpower Resources in Guyana" (Turkeyen, Guyana: University of Guyana Library, December 1972). (Mimeographed.)

partly as a result of increased emigration. A large percentage of those leaving the country were in the younger age groups, possibly a reflection of the immigration policies of the countries to which they were migrating. In 1970, about 33% of the permanent emigrants from the country were under 15 years of age. Also, the parents of these young emigrants were themselves quite young, since another 37% of permanent emigrants in 1970 were between 15 and 30 years of age. Many of these were professional and technical personnel: doctors, accountants, lawyers, nurses, skilled artisans, etc.

It now seems likely that most of those who are studying abroad will not return home. The number of returning doctors has been declining with the result that the Government was forced to employ doctors from South Korea and the Philippines to staff the hospitals and other health services. Between 1968 and 1970, the numbers of nurses who left the country exceeded those who were trained locally during the same period. Skilled workmen have also been migrating and even the large private firms now find it difficult to retain for very long the craftsmen they train. In June 1974, the *Guyana Graphic*[22] reported a speech by Dr. P. Reid, Deputy Prime Minister, in which he "bemoaned the fact that although Bookers Sugar Estates (one of the largest firms then operating locally) had spent over $9 millions in providing skilled training for hundreds of Guyanese youths, most of them have migrated to developed countries after training."

Migration was always higher among the Africans than among the East Indians in Guyana, partly due to the extended and close-knit nature of East Indian families. In 1960, when the People's Progressive Party (P.P.P.) was in power, the overwhelming majority of emigrants, as Dr. Sukdeo pointed out, were still Africans; but since then, East Indian emigration has substantially increased. By the 1970s, with the People's National Congress (P.N.C.) in power, the majority of all categories of emigrants together—permanent, temporary and students—were East Indians. Many of them went abroad as visitors or students, but with the hope of staying away permanently. The changing ethnic composition of the majority of migrants gives one clue as to the factors responsible for this increased emigration. A large number of East Indians now experience difficulties in finding employment, especially in the rapidly increasing public sector.

Summary

The economic problems which Guyana faced in 1974 were quite similar to those of other free-enterprise, developing countries—a continued dependence on two main export commodities, a very slow and often non-existent per capita growth, a high and increasing rate of unemployment especially among the lower socio-economic and

---

[22] *Guyana Graphic*, 13 June 1974.

younger age groups, and as a result increasing inequality of income distribution. Left-wing economists have argued that such conditions, especially in the third world, are an inevitable outcome of capitalist economic development which focusses on maximizing returns to capital rather than labour—hence its penchant for capital intensive technology irrespective of its effect on unemployment. More recently the Guyanese government has attempted to relabel the economy "socialist." However, it has been pursuing capitalist development strategies, though with greater efforts to localize the ownership of the means of production. State capitalism—following the nationalization of expatriate firms—complemented by the private enterprise efforts of the "comprador" elements which support and are in turn supported by the leaders of the Government, has been taking the place of the expatriate firms. Essentially the same approach of the past has been used. This leaves the country with most of the same problems as other capitalist developing countries.

Further, the provision of more educational facilities within this socio-economic context has not been able to help the country. The increase in its educational services has been based essentially on the "missing component" theory which assumed that increasing the number of educated individuals would help the country overcome its economic problems—especially unemployment. But judging from the situation described above, this is a false assumption. In fact, the rapid expansion of the existing educational services was probably contributing to economic underdevelopment in two ways. First, as will be seen later, there was a siphoning off of more economic resources, which might have been used more directly on productive economic development projects, to support educational services. Secondly, graduates of the educational system were, quite naturally, looking for jobs in the high-wage or "modern" sector of the economy, which was not growing fast enough to absorb them, and increasingly turning their backs on low-wage level jobs in the more traditional sector in which their parents worked. The result was that the unemployment situation was worsening at the same time that the educational level among the unemployed was rising.

Demographic Changes

Population Increase

A most noticeable feature of Guyanese society in the post-1945 period was its rapid rate of population increase. Tauber estimated that "the average annual rate of natural increase was slightly above half of one per cent in 1921-1930, one per cent in 1931-1940, and 1.5 per cent in 1941-1945."[23] Between 1945 and 1960, this figure had

[23] Irene B. Tauber, "British Guiana—Some Demographic Aspects of Economic Development," *Population Index* Vol. 18, No. 1 (1952), p. 5.

reached 3.5 per cent, and Guyana was by then ahead of all the larger ex-British West Indian territories in its rate of population growth.

The increase since 1945 resulted largely from a rapid fall in the death rate, especially the infant mortality rate, and a slight, though steady, increase in the birth rate. Between 1946 and 1963, the crude death rate was halved, falling from 15.5 to 7.8 per 1,000 population. The infant mortality rates decreased almost as fast, from 86.1 per 1,000 live births in 1946 to 47.2 per 1,000 in 1962. On the other hand, the crude birth rate rose from 35.8 per 1,000 population in 1946 to 44.5 per 1,000 in 1957, where it remained until after 1959, when it began to fall, reaching 34.3 per 1,000 population in 1970. The diagram in Appendix 1 which was prepared by the 1962 UNESCO Education Mission to British Guiana, presents the rate of population increase between 1931 and 1960.

The East Indians were primarily responsible for the increase in the birth rate. From 1911 to 1940, the birth rate among the African population fell slightly. It moved from 29.46 per 1,000 between 1911 and 1920, to 26.91 per 1,000 between 1920 and 1940 though subsequently there was a slight increase noted, until the 1956-1960 period. The East Indians, on the other hand, showed a continuous and sizeable birth rate increase from the 1911-1920 period, when their rate was 29.8 per 1,000, until 1960, when the rate had reached 48.50 per 1,000—an increase of over 60%. However, in the 1961-1965 period, both ethnic groups experienced a slight fall in their birth rates. The relatively advantageous position of the East Indians in terms of their higher birth rate was to some extent negated by the lower death rates among the African population. But the mortality rates among the East Indians also began to fall, and this difference between the two ethnic groups was gradually eliminated.

Population of School Age

Of direct interest to this study was the increasing size of the population "at risk," that is, of those in a position to utilize the country's educational provisions. Since figures for each of the age groups are not available, attention will be focussed on the total 0-14 age group. While the overall population increased by about 48% between 1946 and 1960, the number of children between 0-14 years increased by 86%. The result was quite a marked change in the age structure of the population, with the age group under 15 years making up 46% of the population in 1960, compared with 38% in 1946. The situation has stabilized somewhat since then; in 1970, about 47.1% of the population was in this age group. It will be recalled that the total population was growing much faster than the employed population. Between 1945 and 1970, the overall population increased four and a half times faster than the total employed population, and as a result, a relatively smaller size work force has been called upon to provide a growing range of social services, such as education, for an increasingly larger dependent sector in the country.

Urbanization

The population of Guyana during the period of this study remained predominantly rural even though the rate of migration to the urban areas increased. According to the 1946 Census, 27.6% of the population then lived in the two main urban centres; by 1970 this figure fell only slightly to 26.5%. But the decline in the percentage of the population living in towns is somewhat misleading since there was a fairly heavy migration to areas surrounding the capital city of Georgetown. For the whole "Greater Georgetown" area urban growth was more marked than the above figures indicate. For example, according to the 1960 Census, 28% of the residents in Georgetown and its suburbs were immigrants, mainly from the rural areas, and about half of these arrived since 1950. By 1970 about 46% of the entire population of the Greater Georgetown area was born outside the area, and in 1969-70 alone, it was reported that the number of internal migrants was twice as great as the addition to the population due to natural increase. Nevertheless, despite these facts, the rural character of Guyanese society remained dominant.

Political Developments Since 1945

Constitutional Changes

Unlike most of the former British West Indian territories, Guyana experienced a most difficult transition to self-government and independence. Up to 1928 the colony was still administered under the old Dutch constitution—with its very restricted franchise—which gave the planters, through their heavy representation in the Combined Court, virtual control over both the political and economic life of the country.

A new constitution, which made Guyana a Crown Colony, was introduced in 1928, removing all power from the elected element in the Legislature and transferring it to the Governor and his Executive Council. The 1928 Constitution, with minor modifications, remained in force until 1943 when a new constitution was introduced, giving the elected members a clear majority in the new Legislative Assembly even though executive power remained in the hands of the Governor and the civil service. The franchise was also very restricted by income or property qualifications and the "ability to read and write some language." This resulted in the denial of the vote to a large percentage of East Indians, among whom, according to the 1946 Census, the rate of illiteracy was about 44%. However, the 1938 West India Royal

Commission had recommended the granting of universal adult suffrage to the British West Indies with no literacy qualification, but because of World War II, no constitutional change took place until 1947.

It was also around this time that political observers noted the emergence of political consciousness among the masses.[24] The People's Progressive Party (P.P.P.), which later became a major political force, was formed in 1950. It was able to unite for political action the major ethnic groups in the society, especially the East Indians and Africans. The result was that in the P.P.P. at the time "sentiments of national unity transcending race or class or religious affiliation predominated."[25] The Party aimed at getting rid of the colonial system and steering economic development towards a socialist society. These objectives, as R. T. Smith observed, "implied a complete social revolution" and "were really incompatible with a declared British policy of gradual advancement to self-government."[26]

In 1953 a new constitution was introduced with universal adult suffrage at 21 and a substantial reduction in the non-elected element in the Legislature. There were only three ex-officio members as against 24 elected members. At the elections which followed, the P.P.P. was, no doubt, popular with most sections of the society, especially the working class, winning 18 out of the 24 seats. Smith, who was then doing anthropological field work in Guyana, commented thus on this situation sometime later:

> Despite all that has been said subsequently about the gullibility of the electorate, anyone who was in touch with the ordinary people of British Guiana in April 1953 knows that they had accepted the PPP as the instrument of a new deal for the country, and they had voted for it as a party that would work for a better future for them and their children.[27]

The Majority Party took office in April 1953 under a modified form of Ministerial Government, but by October of that year, six months after the new Government was in office, the constitution was suspended. According to a statement released by Her Majesty's Government this was done to prevent "Communist subversion" of the Government and a "dangerous crisis" both in public order and economic affairs.[28] The pros and cons of the British Government's action have been dealt with elsewhere and there will be no comment on this matter here except to mention that, according to Dr. Rita Hinden, one of the members of the Constitutional Commission, the

[24] See, for example, observations in Government of Great Britain, *British Guiana: Report of the Constitutional Commission 1950-51*, Col. No. 280 (London: H.M.S.O., 1951).

[25] Smith, *British Guiana*, p. 71.

[26] *Ibid.*, p. 168.

[27] *Ibid.*, p. 171.

[28] Government of Great Britain, *Statement by Her Majesty's Government: Suspension of Constitution*, Cmd. 8980 (London: H.M.S.O., 1953).

more radical reform measures proposed by the elected Government resulted from the fact that political advance had traditionally been kept too far behind that of social reforms, including education. This can be interpreted to mean that, from her point of view, the spread of education contributed to the great dissatisfaction which existed in the country over its slow constitutional progress.[29]

While the suspension of the constitution was a great political setback to the country, it had other social consequences. With the P.P.P. out of office, internal conflicts developed within the Party, leading to a leadership split on racial lines and the consequent break-up of mass support. A new political party, later named the People's National Congress (P.N.C.) was formed with its support drawn mainly from the Africans, while the P.P.P. came to represent the East Indian sector. This split led to great political and social conflict between the two major ethnic groups in Guyana.

With the suspension of the constitution, the Legislature again became a wholly nominated body. In 1957, after nearly four years of political "marking time," a new constitution, which re-introduced an elected majority in the Legislature and a modified form of the ministerial government was adopted. The P.P.P. again won the majority of seats and held office until the next constitutional reform in 1961, when full internal self-government was granted to the country. The three main political parties which contested the 1961 elections were the P.P.P., the P.N.C. and the newly formed United Force (U.F.); the latter was supported mainly by the Portuguese and the business elements in the country. The elections were once more won by the P.P.P. which secured 18 out of the 24 seats, and an ex-headmaster, the Hon. C. V. Nunes, was appointed Minister of Education in the new Government.

Great political conflicts spurred on by external interests especially in the U.S.A., developed during this period, and since the political parties drew their support from different ethnic groups, these conflicts assumed racial overtones. A general strike by P.N.C. and U.F. workers in Georgetown lasted 80 days and was allegedly financed secretly by the U.S. Central Intelligence Agency but openly by the International Confederation of Free Trade Unions (I.C.F.T.U.) and its regional body O.R.I.T. and the American Institute of Free Labour Development (A.I.F.L.D.). The U.S. Government was strongly opposed to the P.P.P. Government under the leadership of Cheddi Jagan and used its influence on Britain to have the electoral system changed. The upshot was that the British Government amended the constitution and changed the electoral system from "first-past-the post"—the voting system used in countries like the United Kingdom and the

[29] Rita Hinden, "The Case of British Guiana," *Encounter* Vol. 2, No. 1 (January 1954), pp. 18-22.

U.S.A.—to proportional representation, which was likely to ensure a defeat of the P.P.P.

Elections under the new constitution were held in December 1964, but the P.P.P., while increasing its percentage of the popular votes, obtained only 45.8% of the votes cast. The result was that the P.N.C., with 40.5% of the popular votes, and the U.F., with 12.4% agreed to form a coalition Government which was granted independence in May 1966. Elections were again held in 1968 and 1973, and while the official figures indicate that the P.N.C. party had captured more than 50% of the votes (55.8% in 1968 and 70.1% in 1973), evidence has been advanced which strongly indicates a massive rigging of the elections. The Government, on the other hand, argued that there has been a heavy swing in favour of the ruling party and that the primordial attachments revealed in the voting behaviour of different ethnic groups in plural societies have been transcended in Guyana.

However, it will be obvious to any impartial observer that the Government is now less dependent on the popular vote for its ability to hold office. This does not necessarily mean the Government is no longer responsive to public opinion or to the articulated demands of organized interest groups. No government can survive long in office unless it is prepared to spend an inordinate amount of its resources to shore up the repressive mechanisms by which it exerts control over the population. Nevertheless, leaving aside the ethical issues involved, this reduced Government dependence on the popular vote enables it to make "technocratic rational" decisions about allocation of resources without having to resort to "vote-catching" programmes. This outlook can be seen partly in the appointment of a number of "technocrats" (people who are not interested in seeking election to office through popular vote but who, because of their technical expertise, are made Cabinet members) as Ministers in the Government. The recent Minister of Education, the Hon. Ceciline Baird, was one of these technocrats. In many ways this position is somewhat similar to that of the former senior colonial civil servants who had a great amount of political power without any direct responsibility to the populace.

Local Government

There was very little progress in the development of local Government in Guyana despite what was described as its "precocious start." In 1958 Dr. A. H. Marshall[30] reported that local Government bodies were not really playing an important part in the affairs of British Guiana. The main problem which the local Government units faced was lack of finance, and as a result they

[30] A. H. Marshall, *Report on Local Government in British Guiana* (Georgetown, Guyana: Government of British Guiana, May 1955).

have never been able to contribute to the social services necessary for the welfare of their communities. Throughout their history they have been forced to receive rather than to give, and, as far as social services including education was concerned, the principle applied in Guyana was "no financial responsibility, no financial control."[31]

Beckford[32] attributed the underdevelopment of local Government in plantation economies like Guyana to a more basic source. He argued that local Government development was largely constrained by the legacy of the plantation system, which left the villages with an insufficient supply of good, arable land and kept the peasant sector on the margin of economic existence. Hence, the dependency of local Government units on central Government funds and the failure of local authorities to develop as a dynamic force in the political system of the country. Whatever the source of this underdevelopment, there was, up to 1974, no local Government involvement in providing education; this remained the full responsibility of the central Government.

Some Social Effects of Political Developments

The political development in Guyana had many favourable and some unfavourable repercussions in the society. First, it resulted in a steady shift from ascriptive to achievement criteria in job selection, especially in the public sector and in the larger private companies. During the period there was an increasing demand by the political leaders for Guyanese with the necessary qualifications to be appointed to senior positions in the public service and for the cessation of the traditional preference given to expatriate officers. For example, in January 1948 one member of the Legislative and Executive Councils requested the Governor to assure the Legislature that "sons of Guiana would be considered first when there are new appointments to be made provided . . . they have the necessary qualifications."[33] He also urged the private sector to follow the same recruitment policy which he was proposing for the public sector. Later, the Hon. T. Lee introduced a specific motion in the Legislature for the Government to "take steps to adopt the policy that British Guianese should be given first preference on all occasions in the filling of vacancies in the public service of British Guiana provided that candidates for vacant posts possess the requisite qualifications and experience."[34] The motion carried unanimously.

[31] Allan Young, *The Approaches to Local Self-Government in British Guiana* (London: Longmans, 1958), pp. 195-96.
[32] Beckford, see, for example, pp. 18-29.
[33] J. A. Nicholson, reported in *Hansard*, 6 January 1948.
[34] T. Lee, reported in *Hansard*, 9 November 1956.

The acceptance of this general principle proved a great stimulus to the educational efforts of Guyanese, especially at the higher education level, and resulted in an increasing diversification in the field of study they pursued. Instead of qualifying only for legal and medical careers, Guyanese students in the post-1945 period began to take up studies in engineering, agriculture, science, geology, economics, etc. Scholarships in these fields, granted under the Colonial Development and Welfare scheme, further aided this change.

Private industry also began to recruit Guyanese for senior positions in their firms. The Booker Group of Companies, then the largest single group of companies in the private sector, was probably the first to begin a training scheme for potential Guyanese executives. This group also established a trade school which conducted formal apprenticeship training programmes for its lower-level staff. The Demerara Bauxite Company, now the Guyana Bauxite Company, which controlled the second largest industry in the country, eventually, even though somewhat reluctantly at first, followed a similar policy. This opening up of job opportunities at the senior level in the public and private sectors because of political changes was quite marked; by 1965, one year before Guyana became independent, only 18% of all administrative, managerial, and senior executive posts in the capital city of Georgetown, in both the private and public sectors, were held by expatriates.[35]

Political developments also resulted in the creation of many new posts in the civil service. This meant more opportunities for promotion among Guyanese, a fact which provided further stimulus to their education efforts. To get some idea of the increase in opportunities for promotion in the civil service, an examination was made of salary increases of all civil servants on the Senior Staff list between 1953 and 1958, a period during which there was no salary revision. This revealed that over 90% of these civil servants had salary increases which could not have resulted from normal annual increments only, and which no doubt came from some form of promotion. Incidentally, nearly 75% of them experienced a salary rise of 50% or more during the five years.

Another fact was that with the achievement of self-government and independence there was not only more involvement of the people in the political process, but also an increasing feeling of responsibility among them for solving their own social problems. They began, though slowly at first, to realize that they could no longer lay all the blame on the metropolitan power if things went wrong. It was partly this feeling which led to the success of the self-help school building projects, launched after the achievement of self-government. Such projects would not have had much support in the colonial days, when

[35] Francis, Vol. 1, Part 3.

the general belief was that the provision of social services was the responsibility of "the Government"—with which the people understandably did not often identify. These political changes also created greater public pressure on the Government to provide more and better standards of education throughout the country.

On the negative side, political development produced or was simply accompanied by a major social problem: increased conflict between the two major ethnic groups in the country. One view is that the two ethnic groups were originally united because of their common desire to get rid of their colonial rulers. But when it became evident that the British were leaving and the issue of succession arose, primordial attachments again became dominant and succession was seen in racial terms: whether it should be the East Indians or the Africans. This led to a deterioration in the relationship between these groups, resulting in increased racial conflict in the post-1961 period and developing into fairly large-scale open violence which reached its peak in 1964. During this period, it was reported that

> About 2,668 families involving approximately 15,000 persons were forced to move their houses and settle in communities of their own ethnic group.... Over 1,400 homes were destroyed by fire. A total of 176 people were killed and 920 injured. Damage to property was estimated at about $4.3m. and the number of displaced persons reached 3,342.[36]

Relationship Between the Major Ethnic Groups

As mentioned earlier, the East Indians originally came to Guyana as indentured labourers to replace the Africans on the sugar estates. This system of indentureship was started because "the planters believed that importations of this nature would serve to convince the Negroes that their services were not indispensable,"[37] and thus to get them to make very moderate wage demands as workers on the sugar estates. This "playing off" of one ethnic group against another was part of the strategy of control adopted by the ruling groups. Another example of this was seen in the fact that one group was often used to suppress the other when disturbances occurred. Such practices, without doubt, adversely affected relationships between these different groups. Since the East Indians and Africans emerged numerically as the largest ethnic groups, the racial conflict which developed in the post-1945 period involved mainly them.

The East Indians, who became the numerically largest group, at first experienced great difficulties in finding jobs above the level of agricultural workers and manual labourers, a fact reflected in their

[36] Jagan, p. 361.
[37] Smith, *British Guiana*, p. 43.

poor representation in such white-collar occupations as teaching and the civil service. These lower-level, white-collar jobs tended to be held by Africans while senior positions were usually held by Europeans. Prior to 1947 the East Indians also had little political power and it was noted by Despres that "in 1915 the people of African descent represented 62.7% of the total electorate while only 42.3% of the total male population was African. The East Indians . . . comprised 51.8% of the total adult male population but only 6.4% of the total electorate.[38] Despite their representation on the voters' lists, the amount of real political power then exerted by the masses was negligible, but the ethnic composition of the electorate was "indicative of the relative position which various cultural sections had come to occupy within the European-dominated power structure."[39]

These factors, along with the continued practice of the planters to "play off" one ethnic group against another in the matter of wage claims, did not contribute to amicable relationships between the East Indians and Africans. Many observers have noted that over time there has been an increasing degree of socio-cultural integration among these various groups although there is still the question of how much integration has already occurred.

There are two major theoretical positions which have been taken in analyzing the structure and dynamics of Guyanese society. Depending on the position one takes, one gets a different answer as to how much socio-cultural integration has taken place.

First, there is the plural society model which owes its origin to Furnivall[40] but has been more fully developed and elaborated on by M. G. Smith.[41] This model assumes that the different cultural groups in societies like Guyana make up "a number of sub-societies each of which is an integrated entity with its own culture" or, according to M. G. Smith, "pluralism denotes congruent cultural and social cleavages within politically unified aggregates." In such societies, therefore, "no peaceful change in the social system is possible because the sections have nothing in common except involvement in economic and political relations which are essentially antagonistic."[42] This model thus assumes the persistence of cultural difference and conflict between these sub-societies or ethnic groups. Applying this theoretical framework to a field investigation, Singer and Araneta concluded:

[38] Leo A. Despres, *Cultural Pluralism and Nationalist Politics in British Guiana* (Chicago: Rand McNally & Co., 1967), p. 39.

[39] Despres, p. 40.

[40] J. S. Furnivall, *Colonial Policy and Practice: A Comparative Study of Burma and Netherlands India* (London: Cambridge University Press, 1948).

[41] M. G. Smith, *The Plural Society in the British West Indies* (Berkeley, Los Angeles, and London: University of California Press, 1965).

[42] M. G. Smith, in the Foreword to Despres, p. xiv.

Following M. G. Smith's conception of pluralism we believe that Africans and Indians alike are characterized by (to the other) separate closed cultural systems resulting in separate basic personalities and group identities. The core of these two closed cultural systems lies in their separate institutional systems.[43]

There are two major criticisms of the work of these authors. The first is that the research evidence which they presented certainly does not support their claim of basic personality differences between these groups. The second is that since their field work was done in Guyana at a time when the ethnic conflict was at its height, this might have resulted in a stronger assertion and highlighting of differences that existed between the groups. As R. T. Smith put it, there was in this period, "a regression from the normative order of colonial creole society."[44]

While basically still using M. G. Smith's theoretical model, Despres, in his study, *Cultural Pluralism and National Politics in British Guiana*, found that it obscured cultural similarities which do exist between ethnic groups in a "plural" society. In view of this, he did not dichotomize societies into distinct types of "plural" and "heterogenous" but instead regarded these as "ideal" types on a common continuum of socio-cultural integration. It seems that implicit in this modification of the plural society model is the view that there can be some degree of integration among the different groups in a "plural" society. However, from his study Despres concludes that while the different cultural sections of Guyanese society have been increasingly involved in a common social, economic, and political life, there is as yet little evidence that any marked degree of socio-cultural integration has taken place.

The second model which was used is what has been referred to as the "reticulated" or structuralist-functionalist model. It has built into it the assumption that structural changes in multiracial societies such as Guyana can bring about a more unified social system or at least greater cultural integration stemming from an increasing commitment by all groups to a common set of values. R. T. Smith, in using this model to explain social changes in Guyana, found that there has already been remarkable progress in the integration of the various ethnic groups into a common culture—a process which he describes as creolization. "The really interesting thing about British Guiana," he wrote, "is not the extent of ethnic differences but the degree to which a common culture already exists."[45]

[43] P. Singer and E. Araneta, "Hinduization and Creolization in Guyana," *Social and Economic Studies* Vol. 16, No. 3 (September 1967), pp. 221-36.

[44] Raymond T. Smith, "People and Change," in *New World: Guyana Independence Issue* (Georgetown: New World Group of Associates, West Indies, 1966), p. 51.

[45] Smith, *British Guiana*, p. 136.

Many factors have contributed to this increasing acceptance of a common culture by the country's various ethnic groups. First, there is a common language, English, which is used by all with the possible exception of some Amerindians, and is the "normal everyday language" of the whole population. Its use has helped increase communication and understanding among different groups. This has had an important unifying influence. In addition, there is, as R. T. Smith argues, "a basically similar outlook and a common understanding" among the groups which developed partly from their common experience as plantation labourers and partly as a result of the loss of "real contact" with their various homelands, especially after 1917, when all immigration schemes ceased.

Education has also been a unifying force in many ways. Children of all ethnic groups attend the same schools and are taught by teachers using a common curriculum and a common language of instruction. Also, since the 1940s there has been an increasingly homogenous job market for all groups, especially in the public services and in the larger private companies, with salaries based essentially on qualifications rather than ethnic origin. While this practice of remunerating people on the basis of qualification was never rigidly applied to Europeans, there was no stated policy (as existed in some colonial territories) which allowed persons of different ethnic groups with the same qualification and holding the same kinds of jobs to receive different rates of pay. As the Europeans left the Government service and the European-owned companies, there was an increasing rationality in the allocation of jobs in these sectors with qualification becoming the main consideration in job selection. This gradual substitution of achievement for ascriptive criteria meant that the basis of job allocation became more acceptable to all groups and education became the major legitimating criterion for access to jobs. This practice helped reduce conflict in a very important area of life in the society, that is, on the job market, a problem which has not yet been solved in other "plural" societies (e.g., Malaysia). Another result, as this writer has indicated in a previous study, was that "there has been over time, an increasing similarity in the attitudes of the major ethnic groups to education, and their patterns of utilization of educational resources" indicating that "they are more and more sharing a common desire for upward social mobility by means of education." This meant "that they [East Indians and Africans] have been developing a similar or common perception of the social system, at least as far as its occupational structure is concerned, and of their own chances of occupying positions at different levels in the social hierarchy of the society."[46] Such a development has resulted in the dispersal of the various ethnic groups throughout the society and has militated

[46] Bacchus, *Education and Socio-Cultural Integration*, p. 32.

against their continued concentrating, on an ethnic basis, in separate occupational sectors and becoming further strengthened as sub-societies within the total social system. Their resultant dispersal throughout the main occupational spheres of the society has been another factor which contributed towards greater socio-cultural integration in Guyana.

While R. T. Smith might at first have overestimated the degree of integration which had already taken place in Guyanese society, the factors mentioned above seemed to have contributed towards movements in this direction. But despite this progress, recent events have indicated that fissionary elements between the two major ethnic groups seem to have been greater than the forces of fusion in the post-1960 period.

R. T. Smith interpreted these conflicts in a different way. He argued that within recent years the forces which make for unification and assimilation have become more rapid and effective in their operation. He saw the recent open conflicts as an indication that the society was passing through a transitional stage to a more integrated society. Therefore, to interpret what has happened as an expression of fundamental social division between the African and East Indian sections of the society, would, in Smith's view, be an inadequate and misleading explanation, especially if it was taken as an indication of future possibilities. He firmly rejected the idea that these conflicts represented inevitable clashes between sections of a "plural" society consequent upon a change in the relationship between them.[47] A similar point is sometimes made about the recent racial conflicts in the United States. These have been seen as a transitional phenomenon brought about largely by the breaking out by the disadvantaged ethnic groups from the psychological, occupational, social, and residential ghettoes to which they were virtually confined in the past, and as a step towards their increased integration in the overall society.

However, whatever theoretical framework one uses, it is obvious that, after a century of living together, socio-cultural integration between Guyana's major ethnic groups has not yet evolved to such an extent as to ward off fissionary forces which led to open conflict in the society between 1962 and 1965. Also, the absence of conflict since 1965 cannot be interpreted as evidence of increased harmony between the ethnic groups. To some extent it resulted from the increased geographical separation between East Indians and Africans which followed the riots in the 1960s. In addition, it reflects the efficiency with which the state control mechanisms are being used.

The major point of interest to the educationist is whether education is or has been contributing towards greater socio-cultural integration between these groups. If one accepts M. G. Smith's theory that

---

[47] Smith, "People and Change," p. 53.

conflict in a "plural" society is inevitable and that "no peaceful change in the system is possible," then it follows that education can in no way bring about greater socio-cultural integration in Guyana. This theory is essentially pessimistic and if one does not accept the view that aggression and conflict are "self-generated intra-psychic events," then one sees the possibility that education can make a contribution to increased harmony between the different ethnic groups. This does not imply that education can solve the problem. Unless the social structure is correspondingly changed to allow all groups a chance to meet their basic economic and social needs, education's contribution would be minimal or even negative.

Many aspects of the traditional structure of ex-colonial society would have to be changed before the influence of education on socio-cultural integration could be maximized. In this context, R. T. Smith has pointed out the dangers of "a relatively slow evolutionary process" in solving the problems of race relations in Guyana. He sees the need for an attempt "not simply to create a common will out of near chaos . . . nor to reshuffle the sections in a plural society, but to transcend the limitations of the structure imposed by creole colonial society and to swing the whole system in a new direction."[48] Although Smith did not specify what this "new direction" should be, it is obvious that any solution along such lines would need major changes in the existing economic and social structure of Guyanese society. And there is no doubt that the worsening economic situation over the years has itself contributed to increased conflict between these ethnic groups in the society. As previously indicated, education has already played an important, if indirect, role in removing the boundaries between these "sub-societies" and in creating a more unified Guyanese society. First of all, even though the Compulsory Education Act of 1876 was not rigidly enforced, Guyanese children were increasingly attending common schools, and by 1945 an estimated 90% of school-age children were already enrolled in the primary schools. These schools served both villages and sugar estates, which meant that children of all ethnic groups were brought together for schooling. The experience of studying and mixing in a common school for about eight years no doubt contributed to the integrative tendencies noted in the society. Teachers were originally drawn largely from one ethnic group, the Afro-Guyanese, and while, as Despres argued, this initially affected the willingness of East Indian parents to send their children to school, there was no doubt that most of these teachers—who had absorbed the dominant creole values of the society—were non-discriminatory in trying to transmit these values to their pupils.

The emergence of a single occupational structure in which recruitment was increasingly based on such rational factors as school

48 *Ibid.*, p. 52.

performance rather than ethnic origin, has helped to break down the traditional relationship between occupation and ethnicity. In the post-1945 period, as Africans and East Indians increasingly began to work at the same occupations, they began to develop common occupational interests which transcended purely ethnic considerations. Education, through which they were qualified to enter these jobs, was thus indirectly contributing towards further socio-cultural integration in the society.

But while the contribution of education in the evolution of a Guyanese as opposed to a specifically African or East Indian way of life has been real, it was almost accidental. There were no special efforts to use the educational institutions to help bring about more harmonious relationships among the different ethnic groups. This was partly due to the dominant concern for socializing the young population to accept the superiority of the European and his culture.

It needs to be pointed out here that the role which education was indirectly playing in creating greater socio-cultural integration in Guyana was, in some ways, experiencing a setback due to recent developments in the society. For example, with the great increases in the school-age population, the village schools which traditionally served both villages and sugar estates were no longer large enough to accommodate all the students. As a result, new schools were built on the sugar estates or in other areas where population increase was great. Partly because such increase was most marked in the areas where East Indians lived, and partly for political and historical reasons, the additional primary schools established in the 1945-1965 period have been mainly in areas with large East Indian population. The result has been that the village common school, which was attended by both East Indians and Africans and which in the past contributed so much to socio-cultural integration in the society, has become less common, with a resulting increase in the number of schools which serve mainly one ethnic group.

This situation was worsened by the recent racial disturbances during which parents of one ethnic group were afraid to send their children to schools located in districts in which the population was largely of another ethnic group. Since most of the existing schools were still in the villages, it meant that many East Indian parents were withdrawing their children from village schools. They demanded that schools be established in their own areas, and despite an initial period of reluctance on the part of the Government to accede to this request, parents in many areas provided their own primary school facilities on a self-help basis; in one case they even paid their own teachers. The political pressures for recognition of these schools increased and eventually they were taken over as Government schools. Although this could be viewed as a politically partisan decision, when a new Government came into power in 1964 with the support of the former

Opposition parties, it soon recognized the realities of the situation and had no alternative but to confirm the establishment of most of these as yet unrecognized "mushroom" schools. The only exception was in a few cases where the schools were too small and uneconomical to operate.

However, the net effect has been some movement away from the common school for all ethnic groups. This point merits consideration in the development of any future education plans for Guyana, because unless something positive is done, Guyanese children will increasingly be attending schools which will be largely characterized by the absence of either East Indians or African pupils.

Another factor to be considered is the existence of large numbers of denominational primary schools, which for religious reasons tended to exclude East Indians from their staff, especially at the senior levels. In the past, we have observed, children not only attended common schools but were taught and introduced into the culture of creole society by what was essentially a common group of teachers—those of African origin. But within recent years there has been an increasing influx of East Indians into the teaching profession, and by 1965 they comprised over 40% of the primary school teaching force as compared with less than 8% in·1931. Because of the system of denominational control over primary and all-age schools, East Indians could not find jobs in the village schools and so sought appointments in the Canadian Mission Schools which were originally set up to provide educational facilities for East Indian children, or in the Government primary schools. These schools, both Canadian Mission and Government (the former all became Government schools in 1964) were located mainly in areas populated almost entirely by East Indians. A side-effect of this was that East Indians and Africans were not only attending separate schools but essentially being taught by teachers of their own ethnic origin. It is true that some denominational bodies employed East Indian teachers, usually at the lower levels of the teaching hierarchy. But since promotion to senior positions was not normally open to them, except to the very few who belonged to the religious denomination which operated the school, they tended to gravitate to the Government schools where a greater possibility of promotion existed for them.

This tendency in Guyana for children of the major ethnic groups to attend separate schools and be taught by teachers of their own ethnic origin will certainly adversely affect ethnic relationships in the future. It indicates the need for a conscious policy in the planning of educational facilities to ensure that this valuable experience of playing, studying, mixing together, and making friends across ethnic lines will not be lost to Guyanese children.[49]

[49] In 1976, the Government took over control of all denominational schools and it

Another area of education in which a lack of concern for this problem is revealed in in the curriculum of the schools. The term curriculum is being used here to include not only the formal instructional programme but also the whole range of experiences and activities which schools often provide for their pupils. So far there has been an unwillingness to explore the contribution which the curriculum can make to this important social problem. This has been partly due to the fact that of the two major political parties, one refuses to recognize the existence of this problem and the other chooses to see it strictly in economic and social class terms. For example, the new curriculum for primary and all-age schools, introduced in 1967, like the draft curriculum of 1963, also steered clear of the subject. And the secondary schools, which are still geared to get their students through the overseas examination, remained untouched and unconcerned about such local issues.

The inclusion of "race relations" in the curriculum of schools is not what the writer has in mind when he comments on the failure of local schools to consider the contribution which they can make to this problem. Formal instruction in this area is not likely to be very effective. It is the opportunities which schools can provide for children to learn about different groups and about their contribution to the development of the country, which the writer sees as likely to be more effective than formal instruction.

The unwillingness of the schools and in this case of the education authorities to include in the curriculum current issues of major social importance to the society is traditional though rapidly changing. In a way it reveals a justifiable lack of faith in the possible reconstructive role of the schools in bringing about social changes or in grappling with social issues. The major impetus for such change lies outside the school and often political decision-makers attempt to "pass the buck" by suggesting that the schools should do something about the problem. This has been a major reason why schools have failed to live up to what were, in fact, unjustified expectations of what they can do. But at the same time, one need not underestimate the role of the school in bringing about a society-wide awareness of social problems and of the need for change, as well as in playing an important supportive role once the direction of social change has been charted.

Finally, it is sometimes observed that the expansion of educational services has resulted in each ethnic group being better equipped to compete for the limited number of jobs in the society; this has intensified not only the competition for jobs but also the rivalry

is as yet too early to assess the effect of this move. Reports indicate, however, that particularistic criteria such as political affiliation and ethnicity are becoming important in job selection and promotion in all schools and to the extent that this happens the advantages that might have been gained from such a move will be negated.

and conflict between these groups. While this has certainly happened in Guyana, the problem lies not with education but is indicative of the failure of the political and economic policies pursued so far which have led to the increasing deterioration of the economic conditions, especially among the lower socio-economic groups.

3. Primary Education

Early Efforts at Establishing Primary Schools

There was little attempt to provide schools for the children of the slave population of Guyana prior to the abolition of slavery. The earliest efforts at establishing a school in the colony date back to the Dutch in 1685, with the arrival of a religious teacher in Essequibo, and were primarily directed at the children of the white population. Even when the first privately endowed school was opened in Georgetown in 1789 to provide an education for "orphans and non-European children," those admitted were the children of the free coloureds and in some cases the free blacks.

However, with the proposed abolition of slavery by the Government of the United Kingdom, the planters were faced with a new problem which changed their attitude towards education for the black population. They wanted to maintain some of the basic features of slave society, especially the exploitative relationship between planters and workers, even after the legal props which supported the system were withdrawn. Here it should be noted that social control in slave society rested not on any normative consensus among the parties involved, but essentially on the legalized use of coercive power by planters against slaves. Abolition meant the removal of the legal foundations which underpinned this society and which, at least as far as the planters were concerned, gave legitimacy to it. It was obvious that after slavery was abolished the ex-slaves might begin to oppose their continued exploitation and be unwilling to concede any longer the social superiority of the white population. In this situation the planters realized the need to take steps to inculcate in the ex-slaves those values which would help to prevent the whole edifice of their society from collapsing. One of the actions was to attempt to build up voluntaristic support for this exploitative system by "educating" the children of the slaves to accept some of the major values premises upon which slave society rested.

There were, among others, two important commitments which had to be inculcated. One was the idea that hard work as an estate labourer was a social and moral obligation of the labouring classes. The second was the belief in the superiority of the European and his culture and a willing acceptance of the view that only Europeans, or those like Europeans in their values, had the right to occupy high status positions in the society. Schooling, and more important, the teaching of religion were perceived as major instruments by which this support for the existing social structure and its dominant value system might be inculcated among the black population.

There was another advantage in trying to use education for this purpose. It is unlikely that any group in a population would willingly accept its position on the lowest rungs of the social and economic hierarchy, especially if, as in the case of the blacks in Guyana, they were in the majority, unless they saw the possibility of later social advancement for themselves or their children, either in this life or the life hereafter. Even though social mobility was difficult, and for the majority of the black population well nigh impossible, education held out some promise of social advancement and gave its recipients the hope, unrealistic though it might have been for the great majority, of rising somewhat up the social and economic ladder. While this was not the purpose of education as conceived by the planters, it nevertheless became the most important one to the ex-slaves who came to value education mainly as an instrument of upward social mobility.

The role of education in producing a pliant and submissive work force for the plantations was affirmed even by the various Christian churches engaged in providing education for the children of ex-slaves. This point was strongly made by the Rev. J. Sterling, who, during the apprenticeship period, was appointed by the British Government to review the educational situation in the West Indies. In his report, he emphasized the importance of education as an instrument which would help the planters develop such "power over the minds of the labouring classes" that would ensure a continued supply of labour for the sugar estates. He noted that

> The peace and prosperity of the Empire at large may not be remotely influenced by their [the ex-slaves'] moral condition. . . . Their perform- ance of functions of the labouring class in a small civilized community will depend entirely on the *power over their minds* of the same prudential and moral motives which govern more or less the mass of the people there. If they are not so disposed as to fulfill these functions [as labourers] property will perish in the colonies for lack of human impul- sion. . . . The certain result of the new situation when the minds of people are all in movement will be a *consciousness of their own independent value as rational beings without reference to the purposes for which they may be profitable to others.* The law having determined and enforced their civic right the task of bettering their conditions can be further advanced only by education.[1] (Emphasis added.)

As can be gleaned from the above quotation, there were three major considerations which the planters had in extending education

---

[1] The Rev. John Sterling, "Report to the British Government, 11th May 1835," quoted in Gordon, pp. 20-21.

to the masses. First, as Sterling implied, education was to assist in producing the kind of labourers who would be docile, obedient, and willing to continue working on the sugar estates. This view of education was also strongly put forward in the *Colonist*—a Guyanese newspaper which on previous occasions had objected strongly to the education of the slaves. In supporting the proposals for extending primary educational facilities to the masses, this newspaper now argued that education

> should be directed to motivating the Africans to work and respect authority. . . . They should learn that idleness is a crime against a higher law as well as an infraction of the social duty and that command which tells them to keep holy on the seventh day is equally explicit in requiring them to labour during the sixth.[2]

This was the same attitude shared by the dominant groups in the other West Indian territories. For example, the *Agricultural Reporter* commented in January 1892 that

> in our elementary schools we are teaching Geography and Grammar and History and Singing and so forth. . . . We are neglecting studies which would teach the rising generation, not only the *dignity of manual labour* but how *to labour freely to get their living in that sphere of life into which it has pleased God to call them.* . . . The sons and daughters of the labouring classes have become impregnated with the idea that the education which is imparted to them makes them better than their fathers; and they have begun to look with disdain upon mere manual labour. . . . Unless steps are taken to put an end to this state the most disastrous consequences must ensue.[3] (Emphasis added.)

Even Her Majesty's Government, which provided money for the education of the children of ex-slaves, had hoped that "the labouring classes will be animated by the same spirit of steady and patient industry which ought always to accompany good instruction."[4] Latrobe, the Inspector of Schools sent out by the Imperial Government in 1837 to report on the results of the first two years of the Negro Education Act, used the same criteria in assessing the effectiveness of ongoing educational programmes. "I shall," he remarked, "be inclined to doubt the wisdom or real kindness of any system or mode of instruction which will lead either the parents or the child to reason falsely on the subject *by not strongly impressing upon their minds the necessity of submitting to labour.*"[5] (Emphasis added.)

A second objective of providing elementary education for the masses was to teach them to accept their place in society and not

[2] *The Colonist*, quoted in Daly, p. 264.

[3] *Agricultural Reporter* (January 1892), quoted in Gordon, p. 135.

[4] British Government, Circular Dispatch (1 October 1845), quoted in Gordon, p. 42.

[5] Latrobe, "Report on the Windwards and the Leewards" (1838), quoted in Gordon, p. 30.

attempt to upset the status quo. Again, the *Colonist*, in supporting the provision of education for the masses, argued that

> Education should break down false ideas of independence which teach the Negroes to disregard to diversities of rank and condition of life imposed for wise purposes. They should be brought practically to love honesty, sobriety, reverence to authority and a Christian respect for all whom Providence has placed in a superior condition.[6]

The first Inspector of Schools in Guyana, George Dennis, was quite aware of the fact that the ruling class perceived elementary education for the masses as an instrument of social control and he used this line of argument whenever he sought support for his compulsory education proposal or just to secure more funds for education. He impressed on the authorities that "money laid out for the encouragement of virtue and the removal of ignorance is a far more profitable investment than that spent on the repression of punishment and crime."[7] And arguing in the same vein, the editor of the local *Royal Gazette* expressed the view that "it would be justified in building schools and paying teachers to prevent crime."[8]

A third objective of extending primary education to the children of the ex-slaves was a concern for their "religious and moral condition." This could, for example, be seen in the efforts of the Colonial Secretary to get the West Indian assemblies to introduce compulsory education for the masses at least three and a half decades before such legislation appeared in England. In his correspondence to the West Indian Governments in 1835 he argued that

> Whatever objection may exist in more advanced societies to the principle of compulsory education they can have no place in reference to a colony in which the great mass of the people have just emerged from slavery but have not yet generally acquired any acquaintance with the principles and precepts of Christianity and are for the most part destitute of the first elements of learning. . . . The advantages [of education] are so great [for them] that if necessary the members ought to have it forced upon them by legislative process.[9]

It was these new roles which education was expected to perform in "civilizing" and "tempering the masses" which contributed to some change in the attitude of the planter class towards the provision of educational services for the children of the slaves. So, between 1825 and 1830 two free schools for Negro children, were established in the capital city of Georgetown, owing to "the keen interest evinced by the

[6] *The Colonist*, quoted in Daly, p. 264.
[7] Government of Great Britain, Board of Education, *Special Reports on Educational Subjects*, Vol. 4: *Education Systems of the Chief Colonies of the British Empire* (London: H.M.S.O., 1901), p. 754.
[8] Daly, p. 264.
[9] Secretary of States for the Colonies, *Circular Dispatch to Governors*, 15 October 1835, quoted in Gordon, p. 27.

British Parliament in the education of the Negro";[10] in 1830 the local treasury made a small grant of £150 to aid these early educational efforts. In addition, the Colony of Berbice voted 6,000 guilders in January 1827 for "the establishment of a free school" which would provide an education for "children of the lower ranks in the society."[11]

Through the efforts of Fowell Buxton, the Lady Mico Trust funds were made available for educating children of ex-slaves in the West Indies. This, along with money provided by the British Government under the Negro Education Act of 1838, was mainly responsible for the fairly rapid expansion of primary school facilities in Guyana and in the West Indies up to about the mid-1840s. In 1841 there were 101 denominational schools in the Colony and the total primary school enrolment was just under 5,000.

But in 1845 the funds provided under the Negro Education Act came to an end, dealing a severe blow to the further immediate expansion of primary school facilities. This withdrawal of funds could not have come at a worse time economically for the country, since, in the following year, the British Government also began to withdraw its preferential treatment of West Indian sugar on the British Market. However, despite these drawbacks, the Government of British Guiana still maintained its belief in the importance of primary education for the masses, and in 1876 introduced a Compulsory Education Ordinance along the lines of the British Education Act of 1870. The local ordinance not only required every child to attend elementary school but also made illegal the employment of children who did not have a certificate of proficiency from an elementary school. It is true that for financial reasons the enforcement of this law was lax, but its introduction indicated to some extent the importance which was being attached to the "education" of the masses— at least by some influential elements of the society.

The active efforts by the churches in providing schools throughout the populated areas of the country continued even though they were at times forced to reduce the rate at which their work was being expanded due to decrease in Government grants; but they were extremely reluctant to cut back on those educational services which they had already been offering to the population. For example, while the Government per capita expenditure on primary school children was reduced from $9.92 to $4.85 (at current prices) between 1880 and 1890, a drop of just over 50%, school enrolment during that period declined by only 15%.

[10] Government of Great Britain, Board of Education, *Special Reports*, p. 754.

[11] See "Minutes of the Proceedings of the Colony of Berbice in the Year Ending 30th June 1827, A Proposal to Grant 6,000 Guilders Out of the Ordinary Revenue of the Colony to Establish Free Schools," 10 January 1827 (London: Public Records Office), p. 25.

The free Negroes were themselves very interested in education, but saw it mainly as an instrument for their own mobility into the middle and possibly even the higher level occupations, then filled by Europeans. However, when it became obvious to them that educational achievement was of much less importance for upward social mobility than such ascriptive critera as colour, there was a noticeable decline in their interest in schooling. For example, between 1869 and 1879 the average attendance in the elementary schools fell from 57% to 50%—a general indication of a falling interest in education. The same phenomenon was observed in Jamaica, where Patterson noted that by 1850 "the almost phenomenal success of missionary schools immediately after slavery had now been replaced by an almost complete lack of interest in education on the part of the Negroes."[12]

But with the persistence of the churches and the abolition of fees for primary education in 1918, educational facilities came more within the reach of the masses of the African population. Largely as a result of the type of education which was provided, this group soon began to share or accept, in practice or as an ideal, many of the values of the ruling European group. In this process of socialization they were taught that, as R. T. Smith[13] observed, all things European—and more specifically "English" and "white"—should be highly valued and all things African and black should be devalued. In fact, one of the factors which gradually influenced the admission of Africans into lower middle class positions was their growing acceptance of European values.

Another factor was the increase in the number of low-level, white-collar jobs such as primary school teachers, policemen, Government messengers, and letter carriers, relative to the supply of persons with a fair complexion to hold them. The primary schools played an important role in preparing them for those limited occupational opportunities.

Those Africans who moved into the white-collar occupations became the reference groups against which the younger Guyanese, especially those of African descent, attempted to pattern themselves. They not only regarded the European (English) culture as superior, but those who were successful often attempted to disassociate themselves from the masses, especially prior to the 1950s. These doctors, lawyers, and senior civil servants formed part of the local intelligentsia who, as R. T. Smith noted, "came to believe themselves qualitatively different from the other non-Europeans by virtue of their 'refinement'."[14] Incidentally, this was also true of some East Indians when

[12] Orlando Patterson, *The Sociology of Slavery: An Analysis of the Origins, Development and Structure of Negro Slave Society in Jamaica* (London: McGibbon and Kee, 1967), p. 287.

[13] Smith, *British Guiana*, p. 31.

[14] Smith, "Social Stratification," p. 237.

they began to rise up the occupational and social ladder. But the tendency was probably not as marked among this group largely because of the extended nature of the East Indian family which imposed greater obligation on those who were successful to help poorer members of the family and not to sever all connections with them.

The social and economic incentives which such white-collar jobs offered resulted in the development of quite favourable attitudes to education by the Africans, and they therefore began to make increasing use of all the educational facilities available to them locally. The report of the International Commission of Jurists, which dealt with the question of the racial composition of the public service in 1965, summarized the position of the Africans thus:

> Consequent on the abolition of slavery the African, wherever possible, turned his back on plantation life. Education in the mission schools provided them with the means of improving their social and economic standing while the growth of the public service on central and local government levels gave them opportunities for new careers. As the English tended to withdraw from the colony . . . and as the activities of the central Government spread, the Africans moved gradually into new ways of life, the civil service, the police, the teaching profession, medicine, and the skilled trades, etc.[15]

One of the strategic white-collar jobs open to the African was primary school teaching, and eventually the members of the teaching profession came to constitute the rural African elite. In their role as school teachers, the educated Africans played an important part in transmitting the norms, values, and beliefs of what is often called "creole society" to future Guyanese, and this included not only African children but those of other ethnic groups—East Indians, Chinese, and Portuguese. They naturally passed on to their students those values which they themselves had come to accept, and as a result, the cultural patterns of all non-English groups were viewed as inferior and ignored by the schools. This also applied to remnants of African customs which existed at the time. Despres[16] thinks that this was a special source of tension between African teachers and East Indian parents, contributing to the development of the negative attitude to primary education by the latter group which was especially noticeable before 1945.

Education Among the East Indians

The experience of the East Indians was somewhat similar to that of the Africans in their early efforts to secure an education. For years

[15] International Commission of Jurists, *Report of the British Guiana Commission of Enquiry: Racial Problems in the Public Service* (Geneva: I.C.J., 1965), p. 25.
[16] Despres, see pp. 101-102, 126-27.

after they first arrived in the colony they were not readily accepted within the dominant sector of the society in which European norms and values dominated. This was reflected in their poor representation in all white-collar occupations which helped to strengthen their early unfavourable attitude towards primary and even secondary education. It is true that the main idea among many of these early immigrants was to accumulate as much money as possible and return to India. So for them the cost of sending their children to school was considered too high, since nearly all of them, including quite young ones, could find odd jobs on the sugar estates. But over time, their desire to return to India diminished considerably and their continued and persistently negative attitude to education could be explained largely in terms of the hurdles they faced in moving out of their social and occupational roles as estate labourers.

A major reason for this was that the planter class, one of the most influential groups in the plantation economy of Guyana, opposed all efforts to get East Indian children to attend school. They reasoned that this was likely to result in their migration from the sugar estates, thus eventually causing a reduction in the size of the labour force available to the plantations. In addition, since most of these children were already working on the sugar estates, sending them to school would have meant an immediate loss of labour.

The influence of the planters was reflected even in the attitudes of senior civil servants on this issue. For example, Charles Bury, whose responsibility it was, as Immigration Agent General, to look after the general welfare of East Indians, was against the enforcement of the Compulsory Education Ordinance as far as the children of the sugar estate workers were concerned. He argued that "on most estates big gangs of little children under that age [school-leaving age] are employed in light work such as carrying earth, ashes and manure and this is not only a benefit to their parents but a source of pleasure to themselves."[17] Another Immigration Agent General was more pointed in his objection to the enforcement of compulsory education for East Indian children. He argued that "when a child was educated he looked down upon his father, got beyond control and after that rarely settled down on the land"[18]—a fact which could have adverse consequences for the supply of relatively cheap labour for the sugar estates.

In addition, there was a general reluctance by the authorities to enforce the Compulsory Education Act to include the East Indians. This could be seen, for example, in the introduction by the Govern-

[17] Government of British Guiana, Immigration Department, *Report of the Immigration Agent General for the Year 1880* (Georgetown, 1880), p. 18.
[18] Reported in Dwarka Nath, *A History of Indians in Guyana* (rev. ed.; London: Butler and Tanner, 1970), p. 188.

ment of the Swettenham Circular of 1904, which specifically exempted East Indian children from the Compulsory Education Ordinance during the first ten years of their parents' residence in the colony. The Governor-in-Council further expressed the view that no penalty should be inflicted on the parents if they objected to schools on account of the religion taught there or if they preferred not to send their daughters to school. This was, in fact, an invitation for East Indian parents to keep their children out of school, since these were all run by various Christian denominational groups and the East Indians were either Hindus or Muslims. Until 1933, when the Circular was withdrawn, the Government virtually closed its eyes, under pressure from the planters, to this non-attendance of East Indian children.

J. Ruhoman, a well-known East Indian journalist of the 1920s, argued this point, noting that the failure of the Government to extend the Compulsory Education Ordinance to East Indians was due to the pressure exerted by the planters who wanted to ensure an adequate supply of field labourers for the sugar estates. Writing on the position of the East Indian in *Timehri* in 1921 he observed:

> The educational interests of his children received but scant attention—so scant indeed as to have implied culpability in a high degree on the part of our education authorities. . . . What must we think of a so-called paternal Government which tolerates, if not encourages, a state of affairs in which we find that of some twenty thousand children of Indian parentage who should be attending school, only about six thousand do so, and this despite the presence in the Education Ordinance of the compulsory attendance clause? The only reasonable explanation for this is that the Government does not wish to see literate Indian population; or it may be that the interest of a certain class of employers of labour recognizes the expediency of keeping these people at such a mental standard as to make them incapable of extending their outlook beyond the field of agricultural labour. Even at the present moment many of us are painfully aware of an atrociously iniquitous movement on foot to conserve and utilize the Indian child life of the Colony for labour purposes on sugar plantations; and a supine and conniving Government is supposed to be looking on quite complacently.[19]

In addition to their lack of formal education, another factor responsible for the non-acceptance of East Indians into the European-dominated sector of the society was a marked difference between their culture and that of the dominant group. As Jayawardena observed:

> The language [of East Indians] was "outlandish." They knew no English, their clothes were strange and their religion was heathen. They lacked the cultural characteristics valued in the society and in return the society withheld its rights and privileges from them. Indian culture or

[19] J. Ruhoman, in *Timehri* Vol. 7, Third Series (August 1921) (Georgetown: Royal Agricultural and Commercial Society, 1921), p. 102.

"coolie" culture as it was called became a mark of low status in the eyes of the white upper status group.[20]

The total result of this was that East Indians experienced great difficulties prior to 1945 in their efforts to move up into even lower level, white-collar jobs and this affected their attitude to education. Primary school teaching is probably the most outstanding example of this. East Indians were virtually barred from becoming primary school teachers largely because they were not Christians. In 1925 and 1933, East Indians formed 3.3% and 6.6% respectively of the primary school teaching force despite the fact that according to the 1931 Census, they made up 41% of the total population. In the civil service, also, East Indians were heavily under-represented. The Immigration Agent General, in his annual reports, often drew attention to the fact that the number of East Indians employed in the public sector was far from proportionate to their numbers in the Colony. For example, as late as 1940, only about 12% of all civil service jobs were held by East Indians, as compared with about 36% held by Africans.

This lack of opportunity for white-collar employment resulted in the development by East Indians of a much less favourable attitude to primary and secondary education than Africans, at least up to about the mid-1940s. For example, in 1921, while East Indian children made up about 41% of the population of school age (those between 5 and 14 years), they accounted for only about 24% of the pupils enrolled in the primary schools. Similarly, at the secondary level, only about 16% of the pupils who qualified for Government scholarships to secondary schools between 1930 and 1950 were East Indians. It was only after the mid-1940s, when East Indians began to share more of the political power, that they became increasingly accepted into the dominant sector of the society. As a result, their opportunities for securing white-collar jobs improved and they developed more favourable attitudes to education. After 1945, their patterns of participation in all education institutions became very much like that of other ethnic groups in the country.[21]

Developments in Primary Education Since 1945

Quantitative Expansion

By the 1920s the Government was making a greater effort to enforce the Compulsory Education Ordinance, except as it applied to East Indians; but even their situation began to change with the withdrawal of the Swettenham Circular in 1933. So by the mid-1930s, it was estimated that about 80% of the children of school age in Guyana

[20] C. Jayawardena, *Conflict and Solidarity in a Guianese Plantation* (London: Athlone Press, 1963), p. 17.

[21] Bacchus, *Education and Socio-Cultural Integration*, see p. 25.

were enrolled in primary schools. Also, the average attendance in these schools had risen from 60% of enrolment in 1922 to 67% in 1931. When a survey of primary school facilities was made in 1937, it was found that even though Guyana had a higher pupil/teacher ratio than most of the larger British West Indian islands, it also had a higher percentage of its children regularly attending primary schools.

Table 13 *Primary Education in the West Indies, 1937*

Territory	Primary school enrolment as percentage of chidren of school age	Average attendance as percentage of enrolment	Number of enrolled pupils per teacher
British Guiana	90.2	74.5	58
Barbados	88.0	74.2	43
Trinidad	82.0	69.8	55
Jamaica	80.0	65.0	57

Source: Government of Great Britain, *West Indian Royal Commission Report 1938-39* (London: H.M.S.O., 1945), p. 87.

Before looking at further developments in primary and secondary education, attention needs to be drawn to the fact that historically there developed in Guyana, as in many other ex-British colonial territories, two almost independent but somewhat parallel educational sub-systems: the primary school system and the secondary school system. Primary schools were originally intended to provide education for the masses and the secondary schools education for the children of the elites and potential elites. While the latter normally provided education for children between 11 and 16 years of age, and up to 18 years for those intending to go to universities, many of them had "preparatory division" for younger children. These offered primary education to a select group of middle-class children who, on completion of their primary grades, normally proceeded to the secondary division of the school.

There was, at first, very little "meshing in" between the primary and secondary schools. Up to 1945, the only bridge between these two educational sub-systems in Guyana was the limited number of Government scholarships (twelve annually) allowing a few of the primary school pupils to enter the Government secondary schools. This stratification of the school system, with the children of the masses attending the primary schools while children of the middle class attended secondary schools (with their preparatory departments), was a further reflection of the rigidity of the stratificatory system of the whole society. In 1929 the Government spent $113.28(G) per annum for each student attending its secondary schools and $7.68(G) for those attending its primary schools.

However, the later establishment of low-cost private secondary schools, whose numbers increased after 1945, helped to widen the bridge linking the two sub-systems (primary and secondary schools), even though it did not at first result in any greater mixing of the social classes. This was due to the fact that children of parents from the higher socio-economic groups attended the elite secondary schools, while those from the lower socio-economic groups who attended the primary schools continued their education in the "non-elite" secondary schools.

The structure of the two sub-systems in education, the primary and the secondary, in and prior to 1945, are illustrated in Chart 1.

Primary Education in 1945

In 1945, there were 251 primary schools in the country, with an enrolment of 90% of all children of compulsory school age (6-14 years) and an average attendance of 74.2%. Enrolment and average attendance were lowest in the remote areas where school facilities were not within easy reach. For example, in the more remote areas like the North West District, average attendance in 1973 was under 70%, while in the other areas the figure reached over 80%. But the point was that despite physical hurdles which the children faced, e.g., many paddled themselves to school in open canoes, the attendance figures were still relatively high in these remote areas.

Another observable fact was that although there was no rigid enforcement of the Compulsory Education Ordinance, there was very little tendency, after 1945, for pupils to "drop out" during the compulsory attendance age. This phenomenon is noticeable in the 1945 figures of school attendance in Table 14, and since then, as will be seen later, the percentage of pupils staying on in the primary schools after reaching the upper age of compulsory attendance, i.e., 14 years of age, was increasing annually. Therefore, as early as 1945, the great majority (about 90%) of Guyanese children of school age were not only enrolled in primary schools but were staying on at school for a full period of eight years. In addition, nearly two-thirds of the age group five to six was starting school one year earlier than was legally required and about 15% of those in the age group fourteen to sixteen were staying on for two years beyond the compulsory attendance age.

Primary Education in 1973

Before discussing the developments in primary education between 1945 and 1973, it will be useful to look briefly at the structure

Chart 1 *Relationship between Primary and Secondary Schools in 1945*

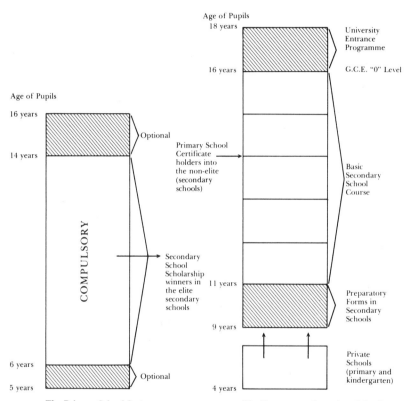

The Primary School System

The Government Secondary School System and its relationship to the Private Schools (primary and kindergarten)

Table 14   Age Structure of the Primary School
Population in Guyana, 1945

	Age group	1945
	5 to under 6	4,222
	6 to under 8	13,603
Compulsory attendance age	8 to under 10	15,723
	10 to under 12	13,861
	12 to under 14	10,264
	14 years and over	4,061

Source: Government of British Guiana, *Annual Report of the Director of Education or the Ministry of Education* (Georgetown, 1945).

of primary education in the country in the latter year. The comparison of the system at these two points will allow the reader to identify more readily the major changes which occurred during this period.

While education was compulsory from the age of six, there were, in 1973, quite a number of children below this age attending nursery schools, especially in the urban areas. The Government was not directly providing pre-primary educational facilities, but it nevertheless gave active encouragement to private bodies and local government agencies (town and village councils) to establish nursery schools. By 1972, there were, according to the Ministry of Education, about 300 such schools in the country, as against 400 primary schools. But even though the enrolment in each school was relatively small, they provided education for a substantial percentage of those under six years of age in Georgetown, the capital city. In 1976, the Government took over the full responsibility for nursery education.

Primary education was tuition-free and compulsory between the ages of 6 and 14 years. Up to the mid-1940s, children between the ages of 5 and 6 years were usually admitted to the primary schools. But with the pressure on school accommodation which developed since then, the admission age was set at 5 years and 9 months. Here it should be noted that, as was indicated previously, "primary" schools, despite their names, were in fact "all-age" schools and provided education both at the primary and secondary levels. After about five or six years of primary schooling, students took the Secondary Schools Entrance Examination, and those who were selected proceeded to the separate secondary schools. The others remained in the "primary" schools for an additional period of about five years, during which time they were likely to enter for the Preliminary Certificate of Education (P.C.E.) and then the English College of Preceptors (C.P.) Examination. The latter, which was usually written around the age of

15+, provided a second chance of entry into a separate secondary school. If at this stage a pupil was successful, he spent another two to three years in a secondary school, after which he entered for the General Certificate of Education (G.C.E.) "O" Level Examination.

In 1973 a large percentage of the population between the ages of 7 and 11 years was attending primary schools, as can be seen from the following involvement ratios, giving the percentage of children in each age group in the total population attending Government or Government-aided primary schools. If to these figures are added those children attending private primary schools, it is evident that nearly every child in Guyana, at least from the age of 7 was receiving a primary education in 1973.

Table 15   *Involvement Ratios of Pupils in Primary Schools (Government and Government-aided) in Guyana in 1973*

Age group	Involvement ratio of population in primary (Government and Government-aided) schools (percentages)
6 to under 7	57.46
7 to under 8	87.39
8 to under 9	92.46
9 to under 10	92.36
10 to under 11	96.79

Source: Government of Guyana, *A Digest of Educational Statistics 1972-73,* Ministry of Education, Guyana.

Primary schools are co-educational, and while there were still Government and denominational schools, there was not much difference between them except in the appointment of their teachers. Both types were almost totally financed by the central Government, and almost on the same basis. They were, however, all taken over by the Government in 1976.

Chart 2 indicates the flows which took place up the educational ladder and the relationship between the primary and secondary school sub-systems in 1973.

Increase in Primary School Enrolment Since 1945

There was a marked increase in primary school enrolment since 1945, as can be seen in Table 16. The numbers moved up from

Chart 2 *Progress up the Educational Ladder in the Primary and the Secondary Schools in Guyana, 1973*

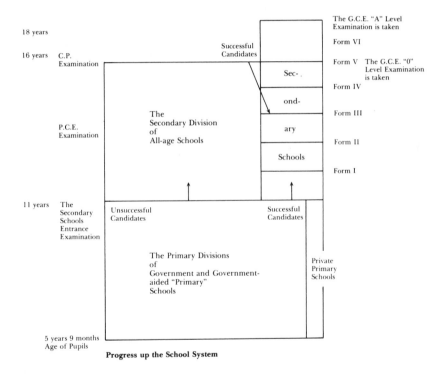

Progress up the School System

61,734 in 1945 to 146,494 in 1965, an overall increase of 137% over two decades, or an average increase of 6.85% per annum. This increase was largely due to more students staying on in the "primary" schools after they had reached the upper limit of the compulsory school attendance age, that is, 14 years.

Table 16   *Number of Pupils Enrolled in Primary Schools in Guyana and Average Attendance,* 1946 to 1972*

School year ending July	Primary school enrolment	Average attendance* as percentage of enrolment
1945	61,734	74.2
1950	74,153	80.4
1955	94,536	81.8
1960	125,348	81.8
1962	132,404	82.8
1965**	146,494	80.1
1968	171,469	78.6
1970	162,842	78.2
1972	168,954	77.7
1973	169,939	77.4

* In calculating average attendance, the twenty worst sessions in a school year of just over 400 sessions were excluded by the Ministry of Education.

** From 1965 average enrolment figures were used.

Source: Annual Report[s] of the Director (later Ministry) of Education, Digest of Educational Statistics (Guyana, 1945 to 1973).

Since 1965 there has been a rapid expansion in secondary school facilities throughout the country, with the result that "primary" school enrolment rose much more slowly, since large numbers of pupils over 11 years of age were attending these separate secondary schools, rather than remaining in the secondary divisions of the "primary" schools. So between 1965 and 1973, the percentage increase in "primary" school enrolment was only 16%, or about 2% per annum. For the entire period, therefore, between 1945 and 1973, the average increase in "primary school enrolment was 6.26% per annum. In addition, average attendance moved up from 74.25% in 1945 to 82.8% in 1962, falling to 77.7% in 1972 as an increasing number of brighter and possibly keener students were being drawn off into the secondary schools.

Several factors contributed to this increase in primary school enrolment and average attendance. First, between the two censuses of 1946 and 1960, there was a 72% absolute increase in the age group six to fourteen, or an annual increase of 5.2%. And between 1960 and 1970, there was an additional increase of about 30%, or roughly 3% per annum. Further, there was an improvement in the health of the child population during the period under study. Malaria, which prior to 1945 had been one of the major causes of morbidity and mortality among school children, was virtually wiped out by the mid-1950s, after a massive country-wide D.D.T. campaign. In 1947 there were 15,490 notified cases of malaria in the country, but ten years later this figure had dropped to four. Child welfare services were also improving, and according to the Ministry of Health reports, the number of children attending health clinics had increased from 28,107 in 1948 to 47,930 in 1958, a 70% increase in ten years. A school feeding programme was also started, and by the mid-1950s, with the assistance of UNICEF, about 20% of all school children were receiving a daily snack consisting of skimmed milk, fish liver capsules and "fortified" biscuits. Those selected for this programme were usually the malnourished children.

Another, and probably more important, contributing factor was the increasing competition for white-collar jobs to which most of the population aspired. The Primary School Certificate, which could be obtained by external examination after about eight or more years of primary school attendance was becoming a minimum entry requirement to any type of white-collar job—even that of a messenger—in the Government service.

There was also a marked change in the attitude of East Indian parents to primary education; They were now actively encouraging their children, especially their daughters, to attend schools. It was previously noted that in 1920, East Indian children made up 41% of the population of school age but only 24% of the primary school enrolment. By 1945, they comprised 51% of the school age population and 41% of the primary school enrollment, while by 1955 their enrolment in school had virtually caught up with their representation in the population of school age. This change in the attitudes towards primary education among East Indian children coincided with their increasing acceptance in the dominant sector of Guyanese society, as can be seen in their growing representation in white-collar jobs. For example, while in 1935 only 6.6% of the primary school teachers in Guyana were East Indians (despite the fact that they then made up about 41% of the total population), by 1965 they comprised 54% of the primary teaching force. Also, in 1942, East Indians held only about 12% of all civil service posts, but by 1965 this figure had reached 33%. In a previous study of the subject done by the author it was observed that

> Many non-economic factors contributed to the low primary school enrolment among East Indian children—their parents' own low level of

education, the fact that there were very few schools on the sugar estates, the conflict between the values shared by the [East Indian] parents and those shared by the teachers who were largely Negroes, the Christian religious education which was [taught] in the schools, etc. But these were only subsidiary problems. The main reason for the low enrolment among East Indian children [before 1945] seems to have been that [primary and secondary] education had little instrumental value in helping them to achieve their goals of upward social and economic mobility.[22]

Still another factor which contributed to the increased primary school enrolment and average attendance was the expansion of secondary education facilities and the democratization of entry, especially into the "elite" secondary schools. In the mid-1950s, the Government abolished the preparatory divisions of the Government secondary schools, and by 1960, having brought all the better secondary schools under its influence through the offer of financial assistance, it instituted a common secondary school entrance examination. This meant that the chances of entering the secondary schools were now more open to primary school pupils on the basis of their ability, and primary schooling became more valued by all. This fact is reflected in the number of entries for the examination on which scholarships, free places, and later even admission to Government or Government-aided secondary schools were based. The actual title of the examination changed since 1945, but in the twenty-seven years between 1945-46 and 1972-73, there was a twenty-fold increase in the number of entries for these examinations, or more precisely an average increase of about 68%. This can be seen in Table 17.

It should be noted that over 90% of students entering for the secondary school entrance examinations were from the public primary schools, and increasingly from the lower socio-economic groups. One study[23] revealed that while there was an absolute increase in the number of entrants from all socio-economic groups, the percentage of total entries from children whose parents held manual occupations has been increasing. As a result, primary education was being perceived more and more by the masses as a stepping stone to secondary education.

Yet another factor contributing to the increase in primary school enrolment was that the primary school leaving examination became more valuable not only in facilitating students' entry into the private secondary schools but also in securing for them partial exemption from the usual five year secondary school course. Prior to the introduction of a common secondary schools entrance examination, students who obtained the Primary School Certificate could receive from

[22] *Ibid.*, p. 22.
[23] M. K. Bacchus, "Social Factors in Secondary School Selection in British Guiana," *Social and Economic Studies* Vol. 15, No. 1 (March 1966), pp. 40-52.

Table 17 *Number of Entries for the Secondary Schools Entrance Examination, 1945 to 1974*

School year	Number of entries to the Government County Scholarship Examination, the Common Entrance Examination, or the Secondary Schools Entrance Examination
1945-46	732
1950-51	765
1955-56	1,173
1961-62	3,734
1965-66	11,135
1970-71	12,609
1971-72	14,283
1972-73	14,183

Note: Figures for 1960-61 were unobtainable.
Source: Government of British Guiana, *Annual Reports of the Director of Education or the Ministry of Education* (Georgetown, 1945 to 1973).

the private secondary schools a reduction of about two years in the secondary course and were allowed to take the senior Cambridge examination after about three years' attendance in these schools. So the extra time spent in primary school was seen as economically very worthwhile for those who wanted to proceed to the private secondary schools, since it often resulted in students having to take fewer years of the relatively costly private secondary school education. In 1964 the Government even allowed the "primary" schools to enter their students for the English College of Preceptors (C.P.) Examination, which was previously taken only by third-form pupils in the private secondary schools. All these developments helped to increase the importance of a successfully completed primary school course.

The changing value of the Primary School Certificate was reflected in the fluctuations of its annual number of examinations entries. For example, between 1946 and 1953, when the examination became a steppingstone to the secondary schools, entries rose markedly. In 1962 the entries numbered 8,377. By 1963 it was 12,157, a 45% increase over the previous year, and in 1972 the figure had reached 19,659. Within ten years, from 1962 to 1972, the entries for this examination had increased by 135%.

Those who were successful at the C.P. examination, which later could be taken in the "primary" schools, were able to enter the G.C.E. "O" level programme at one of the secondary schools. The influence of this decision to allow "primary" school students to write the C.P.

examination was also reflected in a marked rise in the number of pupils remaining in these schools after they had reached the upper limit (14 years) of the compulsory attendance age. Between 1945 and 1965, the number of pupils staying on in the "primary" schools after 14 years of age climbed from 3,981 to 17,758, an average increase of just over 17% per annum during the two decades, a rise which was more than double the overall average increase in primary school enrolment during the same period.

Meeting the Demand for Primary School Accomodation

The increase in primary school enrolment in the post-1945 period put a great strain on existing educational facilities, especially on accommodation. The churches, which in the past had provided most of the primary school buildings, were not only finding it financially difficult to provide additional accommodation at the rate that was being demanded, but were unable to maintain properly their existing schools. As early as 1945, the Director of Education, commenting on the state of these buildings, observed that "old unsuitable buildings, badly lighted and unsound from termite depredation from which the original coat of paint has frequently disappeared are the rule rather than the exception."[24] In addition, using the legal requirement of ten square feet of floor space per child, primary school enrolment in 1945 already exceeded available accommodation by 10%.

The Government, though aware of this situation, felt it was not in a strong enough financial position to devote more of its resources to building primary schools. Improvement in this situation started only when Colonial Development and Welfare (C.D. & W.) grants from the United Kingdom became available from about the mid-1940s. And because the school accommodation problem was growing, successive Governments between 1945 and 1964 spent a sizeable proportion of their education development budgets to provide more primary school accommodation. Table 18 shows the proportion of the educational budget which was allocated to building primary schools between 1945 and 1972.

The total number of additional primary school places provided between 1945 and 1964 resulted in a doubling of primary school accommodation during this period, but despite this substantial effort, the overcrowding increased tenfold. In the 1966-72 Development Programme it was noted that in 1964, 58% of the all-age schools were overcrowded.[25] The situation would have been worse had the public

---

[24] Government of British Guiana, *Annual Report of the Director of Education 1945* (Georgetown, 1945), p. 32.

[25] Government of British Guiana, "British Guiana Development Program 1966-72" (Georgetown, Guyana, 1966). (Mimeographed.)

Table 18 *Percentage of Development Budget Spent on Primary Schools, 1945 to 1972*

Period covered by the development budget	Percentage of development budget for education spent on primary school buildings
1945-48	60
1949-53	44
1954-55	94
1956-59	87
1960-64	70
1966-72	20*

* This is only an estimate. It was difficult to identify all the capital expenditure on primary schools alone for this period. The figure was arrived at by estimating the total cost of all primary school places provided during the period (the total number of places provided times the average cost of one primary school place) and calculating the percentage which this figure represented of the total capital expenditure on education.

Source: Government of Guyana, *Development Budgets* (Georgetown, 1945 to 1966).

health authorities officially condemned as unsuitable the more dilapidated school buildings.

Apart from the inadequacy of funds and the increase in enrolment, other factors contributed to the overcrowding. Among these was the uneven geographical distribution in the increase of the school population. The greatest increases occurred among the East Indian population which lived mainly on the sugar and rice estates, areas often geographically separate from the rural African villages. So when new schools were built in East Indian areas, parents transferred their children to them, often creating instant overcrowding and leaving vacancies in the old ones. For example, despite the overall accommodation shortage, in 1964 there were about 5,000 vacancies in the schools.

Another fact which bedevilled the school accommodation problem was the consistent request by educators for improvements to the existing facilities. This resulted in a substantial increase in the per capita cost of school accommodation, and with limited funds, meant a reduction in the number of places that could be provided. The 1945 design for primary schools comprised a relatively simple structure without windows, but with great overhanging eaves, semi-open sides and no classrooms. While in 1946 the Director of Education described these schools as "cool, airy and well lighted,"[26] by 1952 there was a strong demand for a change in the design. As a result, a new type of building was introduced with separate classrooms and corridors, subject rooms for home economics and woodwork, teachers' staff rooms and later even septic tanks instead of pit latrines.

In addition to the accommodation problem there was the increasing shortage of school furniture. In 1953 the Director of Education observed that most schools in the colony were short of desks and benches and much of the furniture in use needed repair or replacement. It was then estimated that 30% of the pupils had no desk space and 20% had no seats. This was the situation on which the UNESCO educational mission of 1963 commented when it noted that "four-seater benches packed as closely together as possible often had to seat six to eight children."[27] The overcrowding was partly relieved by the fact that attendance on any one day rarely reached 100%.

One result of the increase in enrolment, which brought about the overcrowded situation in most schools and a drop in the percentage of trained teachers from 19.4% in 1946 to 16.2% in 1957, was a possible reduction in the quality of education provided in the primary schools. The shortage of accommodation itself imposed severe restrictions on the methods of teaching. In 1949, a journalist from the *Daily Chronicle* gave a vivid picture of the constraints which overcrowding imposed. He reported that

> in some schools elbow space is hardly obtainable on the desks and a visitor can scarcely find his way to the head-teacher's table. It is difficult for pupils in any class to give individual attention to their own lessons and the conscientious teacher will admit that no matter how interesting he may endeavour to make a subject to his pupils they will sneak glances at the blackboard of a neighbouring class where colourful maps, pictures, diagrams, and sketches may be mounted or where children of another class are engaged in some form of dramatization.[28]

The author himself recalls a not too untypical incident resulting from the overcrowded situation in which a teacher was giving a mathematics lesson. When the teacher called on one student in the back row to present her work, he found she was writing a story. The pupil explained that she was carried away by the interesting English lesson being given by the teacher in a nearby class.

1964-1973

Overcrowding was markedly reduced between 1964 and 1973, during which time the rate of increase in the primary school population had slowed down considerably. It fell steadily from about 22% in

---

[26] Government of British Guiana, *Annual Report of the Director of Education 1946* (Georgetown, British Guiana, 1946), p. 24.

[27] UNESCO, "Report of the UNESCO Educational Survey Mission to British Guiana 1963" (Paris: UNESCO, 1963), p. 49. (Mimeographed.)

[28] *Daily Chronicle*, 2 May 1949.

1965 to just over 10% in 1973. But there was still a shortage of over 17,000 school places in 1973, when a UNESCO mission gave the following description of a typical Guyanese primary school:

> The normal situation is a long open room in which children are sitting cheek by jowl with only a portable blackboard separating them, the individual class consisting of children crowded together on benches, with little room to move their elbows for writing purposes. Any hope of using modern open methods is nullified by this grossly overcrowded situation, and the din is such that sometimes children at the back of the class, perhaps no more than 15 feet from the teacher, cannot hear her. When school broadcasting is used the whole room is dominated by the sounds emanating from the radio.[29]

There is an interesting point here to which attention needs to be drawn. The physical condition of schools had deteriorated quite substantially, especially prior to 1964, and overcrowding was a common feature in most primary schools. This was accompanied by a drop in the percentage of trained teachers in these schools. Yet these conditions did not seem to dampen the desire of the children for an education, judging both from the rising enrolments and the improvement in their attendance. Also, their performance at the local examinations was not adversely affected, though this is a more difficult matter to assess. However, it appears that the motivation for education, which increased as more job opportunities became available, helped counter some of the hardships created by the deteriorating physical conditions.

At the end of 1964, the Government decided not to provide additional primary school accommodation in the traditional way, i.e., entirely by Government funds, but on a community self-help basis instead, with Government providing materials and technical assistance and the community the necessary labour. These efforts were very successful, and later when the World Food Programme (W.F.P.) decided to grant assistance to the scheme by providing certain items of foodstuff for families who had worked voluntarily on the project, this gave an added incentive for community participation. The accommodation costs provided through the self-help schemes were, at first, 25-30% of the normal cost, which the Ministry of Works incurred in providing somewhat similar accommodation. The quality of the work on these earlier projects was not as high as that of Government-constructed buildings; later, as quality improved, the cost of providing self-help accommodation, including new buildings, rose to about 50% of the cost normally incurred by the Ministry of Works.

After a change of Government in 1965 there was a partial reversal of this policy of providing all new primary school accommodation

[29] UNESCO, "Guyana—Suggestions for Reform and Improvement of Education" (Paris: UNESCO, January 1973), pp. 7-8. (Mimeographed.)

on a self-help basis largely because most of the new primary schools built by the former Government were in areas where that Government had its greatest support. Incidentally, most of these were also the areas where the largest population increases were occurring. The new Government felt that it had an obligation to its own supporters, who also lived in areas where the school accommodation was inadequate, to provide them with up-to-date buildings. It, therefore, began to build or rebuild some primary schools in the traditional way, i.e., through the Ministry of Works. However, the cost factor could not be ignored, and the new Government continued to give support to the self-help school building projects. The result was that of the 10,768 new school places provided between 1965 and 1967, about 88% were built by self-help. This soon became the basic method by which primary school accommodation was provided.

Curriculum Changes in Primary Schools

It was already pointed out that when slavery was abolished in 1834 the planters became interested in the education of the masses as a means of socializing them to accept the basic features of plantation society. The content of the curriculum, therefore, had a very strong religious and moral emphasis, since it was felt that this type of education was important in the efforts to build up the needed support for the system.

Religion thus dominated the curriculum of the primary school from its inception and this subject was taught not only during periods formally set aside for it, but pervaded the entire programme of instruction in the primary school, which at that time consisted mainly of the three Rs. Despite the limitations of the statistics, some direct evidence of the pervasiveness of religion in the primary school curriculum in the West Indies at the time can be gathered from the report of the Inspector of Schools in Barbados, which then had educational goals similar to Guyana. In 1872 about 68% of the 3,709 examinations in reading conducted there were based on the Old and New Testaments, while about 60% of the dictation examination passages were drawn from the same source. In the "higher subjects," which included grammar, geography, etc., this influence was even more dominant. Of the 7,913 examinations in this area, about 88% (7,022) were in "Catechistical Religious Knowledge" (6,625) and "Bible History" (397).[30] In addition to formal religious instruction, the virtues of humility, obedience to and reverence for one's superiors and contentment with one's position in life were among the moral qualities most heavily stressed in schools.

[30] "Report by Elliott, Inspector of Schools for Barbados, 14th May 1872," quoted in Gordon, pp. 83-84.

Although the need to get the non-white masses to accept their subservient and conformist roles did not change (with the result that moral and religious education continued to be the focus of the primary school curriculum), there were other developments in the society which resulted in curriculum changes at the primary level. First, education costs were rapidly rising with the quadrupling of primary school enrolment between 1839 and 1879. Because of this, the ruling groups strongly urged that the education of the masses should prepare them to contribute more directly to their productivity in the economic system.

The early efforts at educating children of ex-slaves were not focussed on giving them lower level job skills, since this would have turned them away from school. The Rev. John Sterling had warned that "the object must be to *encourage* and *tempt* the masses to send their children"[31] to school. It was only later, when education costs were rising rapidly, that the introduction of practical subjects like agriculture was stressed. Further, it was felt that these subjects would help to increase the "respectability" of manual work in the eyes of the ex-slaves, and be one way of "strongly impressing upon the mind the necessity of submitting to labour."[32] This objective became very important for the planters, because after the abolition of slavery many ex-slaves were no longer interested in labouring on the sugar estates, creating a serious manpower shortage. With the same type of problem in Jamaica, the Governor there urged the inclusion in the school curriculum of "a course of instruction which promises both to connect the vocation of the husbandman with subjects of intellectual interest" in order to "render his labour more valuable to himself and his employers."[33]

The skills and knowledge required in these practical subjects were considered necessary for the improvement of the economy. The Colonial Office, in a circular dispatch, had pointed out the need for agricultural knowledge to prevent "the exhaustion of virgin soils" which was taking place in many tropical dependencies. In addition, it urged the establishment of industrial schools in order "to render the labour of the children available towards meeting some part of the expenses of their education."[34] Also, in Guyana, the need for "skilled mechanics" and the surplus of "unskilled labour" were often cited as reasons for including more practical subjects in the primary school curriculum.

Thus, in time, the role of religion in primary schools was less heavily emphasized, while the arguments for producing youngsters

[31] Sterling, quoted in Gordon, p. 63.

[32] Gordon, p. 30.

[33] Elgin, "Dispatch Covering Blue Book of 1855," 7 May 1845, quoted in Gordon, p. 59.

[34] Government of Great Britain, Colonial Office Library, *Miscellaneous Pamphlets* Vol. 1, No. 1.

with skills, knowledge, and attitudes more relevant to their future economic roles in the society increased. One observer of the educational scene argued in 1898 that the schools were increasingly turning out "lads and lasses whose memories are well-stocked with fundamental knowledge but who found it difficult to find a job because of the lack of any skills" and were thus becoming "pests to the society."[35] Practical training was to be included in the curriculum, since this "would teach the rising generaton not only the dignity of manual labour but how to labour freely to get their living in that sphere of life in which it had pleased God to call them."[36]

The result was that, with these pressures and the recommendations of the Secretary of State for the Colonies on the teaching of agriculture, practical subjects were included in the primary school curriculum even before the end of the nineteenth century. In 1900 the Inspector of Schools reported[37] the initiation of a scheme whereby schools were paid several grants if they gave two hours "technical instruction" a day, and by 1907, the two subjects, agriculture for boys and needlework for girls, were among those for which payment on results were made.[38]

The continued emphasis on the importance of practical subjects in the primary schools was reflected in the recommendations of every Government-appointed commission which commented on the country's educational system. The 1925 Educational Commission strongly criticized the primary schools for focussing attention on the "imparting of knowledge," even when that knowledge was not related to "the needs of the country."[39] It urged an increased emphasis both on "character building" and on practical subjects, the latter to be taught in every grade of the primary school. The aim of the latter was to direct children's interests and activities more towards the agricultural life of the society.

The West Indian Royal Commission of 1939 considered the curriculum of the schools in the West Indies and Guyana as illogical and wasteful, since, although these countries were predominantly agricultural, their system was based on a literary curriculum fitting people only for white-collar jobs in which opportunities were comparatively limited.[40] It further noted that the curriculum was not only irrelevant

---

[35] *The Echo*, 18 June 1898, quoted in Gordon, p. 137.

[36] *Agricultural Reporter*, January 1892, quoted in Gordon, p. 135.

[37] Blair, Inspector of Schools, "Paper Read to the Agricultural Conference in Barbados, January, 1800," quoted in Gordon, p. 146.

[38] Government of British Guiana, *Code of Regulations for Education* (Georgetown, 1901).

[39] Government of British Guiana, "Report of the Educational Commission, 1925" (Georgetown, British Guiana, 1925). (Mimeographed.)

[40] Government of Great Britain,*West Indian Royal Commission Report 1938-39*, 6607 (London: H.M.S.O., 1945), p. 120.

but dysfunctional to the society, since it made the pupils acutely dissatisfied with their future status as ordinary workers. The Commission recommended, therefore, that to counteract this tendency, practical subjects such as domestic science, woodwork, and agriculture, should be taught in the senior divisions of all primary schools.

The Government's efforts to introduce practical subjects were again seen in the "schemes of work" which accompanied the revised Education Code of 1940.[41] The subjects included a variety of activities, such as paper cutting, plasticine modelling, needlework, woodwork, gardening, hammock making, basketweaving, chaircaning, bookbinding, and leather crafts. They were to be introduced from the first grade and continued throughout the eight grades of the primary school. In addition, pupils in the remote areas of the country were expected to achieve a higher standard of performance in these subjects.

The 1942 Memorandum on Education,[42] prepared by the Colonial Development and Welfare Adviser, urged the reorganization of primary education to provide senior schools or departments which would focus on "cultivating a practical turn of mind and practical skills" among senior pupils. Special emphasis was to be placed on handicraft, agriculture, housecraft, and needlework, and in addition, 4H Clubs with their farm-oriented programmes, were to be encouraged. The Government's Education Development Committee of 1946[43] endorsed this recommendation with one of the sub-committees further urging that school gardening should be made compulsory in these schools.

In 1952, the Nicole Committee Report on Primary Education again recommended that practical subjects such as "housecraft, handicraft, and husbandry should be the chief means in the primary schools of giving reality to school work."[44] Later in the same year, the Technical Adviser to the Secretary of State for the Colonies also strongly urged the establishment of senior schools which would "give ample time and emphasis to practical subjects such as agriculture and horticulture, woodwork and metal work for boys and home-making for girls."[45]

[41] Government of British Guiana, *Education Code 1940* (Georgetown, 1940).

[42] Government of Great Britain, Colonial Development and Welfare, *Memorandum on Education in British Guiana 1942* (Georgetown: Government of British Guiana, 1942).

[43] Government of British Guiana, *Report of the Education Development Committee 1946* (Georgetown, 1946).

[44] Government of British Guiana, *Report of the Primary Education Policy Committee 1952* (Georgetown, 1952), p. 21.

[45] Government of British Guiana, *Memorandum on Technical Education*, by Dr. Harlow, Technical Education Adviser to the Secretary of State for the Colonies (Georgetown: 1 December 1952). (Mimeographed.)

The Government's 1957 Memorandum of Secondary Education once more pointed out the need for a new curriculum for senior pupils in the primary schools, one "more closely related to the environment and interest of the senior child and related particularly to the home, the farm and the workshop."[46] The thrust in this direction was to be achieved with the provision of new and improved facilities for practical work in home economics and woodwork. By 1962, a new curriculum guide[47] was completed. It again stressed the importance of practical work in the senior divisions of the primary schools, with the suggestion that teachers attempt to introduce these practical activities even when available facilities might not be quite adequate.

In addition, the important opinion leaders in the society, including legislators, educators, newspaper editors, and others, lost no opportunity to support the introduction of practical subjects in the primary schools, especially for the senior pupils. In August 1945, the Governor, in a public speech, declared that "many of us hold the view that the most important need in the colony is post-primary education given to children 12 to 16 with far greater facilities for vocational training, domestic science, agriculture and handicraft."[48] The editor of the *Daily Argosy*, which was then a very influential newspaper, also supported such practical training and continually urged that vocational education should start at age twelve in the primary schools. In August 1945 it lamented the fact that "vocational training does not occupy in the curriculum . . . the importance which is should" and urged that "youngsters must be given facilities for developing more practical skills—side by side with a sound but simple general education."[49] Also, in commenting on the inadequacy of the existing school gardening programme, it suggested that if "these young people are taken in hand at the earliest opportunity and given a thorough extensive training in the various vocational subjects there would be less unemployment and fewer cases of delinquency."[50]

A year later the editor reminded the public that "the hands in which the future of British Guiana lies should be trained in a much greater degree to *do* and to *make* things."[51] Again in 1952 the newspaper argued that the primary education offered by the schools "is far from suitable to a country which is (and is likely to remain) chiefly agricultural and in which the opportunities for a wholly academic training are few and far between."[52]

[46] Government of British Guiana, *Memorandum on Secondary Education 1957* (Georgetown, British Guiana, 1957), p. 12.
[47] Government of British Guiana, Ministry of Education, "Suggested Curriculum Guide 1962" (Georgetown, 1962). (Mimeographed.)
[48] *Daily Argosy*, 18 August 1945.
[49] *Ibid.*, 8 March 1951.
[50] *Ibid.*, 8 May 1948.
[51] *Ibid.*, 28 February 1949.
[52] *Ibid.*, 2 March 1952.

The interesting point is that the perception of the role of education by working class parents was quite different from that of the ruling elite. They saw education mainly as an instrument for upward social mobility of their children into white-collar jobs and not as a means of increasing their efficiency as farmers, semi-skilled or even skilled workers. In their view, which they transmitted to their children, the emphasis on practical subjects in schools only diminished one's chances of entering white-collar occupations, while academic subjects increased these chances.

In 1890 the Inspector of Schools reported that attempts to introduce woodwork and agriculture in the primary school curriculum proved abortive because of parental opposition to these subjects, an observation made on many other occasions. In 1900 Blair, the Inspector of Schools, commenting on the failure of two agricultural schools established by the Government, observed that "the more ambitious of them [the students] considered working in the field degrading and they were anxious to attain what Mr. Gladstone described as the supposed paradise of pen and ink."[53] Most parents felt that the practical subjects taught in schools were something their children had to endure in order to receive an education, and the value of the skills taught was considered unimportant. This could be seen in some of the observations made by school inspectors. For example, the 1948 Annual Report noted that "gardening is looked upon ... as something having no particular connection with the rest of the curriculum and therefore a somewhat wearisome necessity."[54] Similarly, it was observed that other practical subjects did not have "a strong carry over effect to the pupils' homes" and as one inspector of schools reported "one would like to see more home gardens, more home-made hats and better repaired books as a result of the training received at school."[55]

The Venn Commission of 1949 criticized the view of many parents that "an office job is more to be esteemed than the carpenter's bench";[56] and the *Daily Argosy*, which championed the case for including practical subjects in the primary school curriculum, observed in 1949, "It cannot be a source of comfort to right thinking people to reflect upon the alarming degree to which Guianese have latterly become prepossessed with the idea of placing their children in white

[53] Blair, quoted in Gordon, p. 146.
[54] Government of British Guiana, *Annual Report of the Director of Education 1948* (Georgetown, 1948), p. 13.
[55] Government of British Guiana, *Annual Report of the Director of Education 1946* (Georgetown, 1946), pp. 10-11.
[56] Government of Great Britain, Colonial Office, *Report of a Commission of Enquiry into the Sugar Industry of British Guiana*, Chairman J. Venn, Col. 249 (London: H.M.S.O., 1949), p. 132.

collar employment."[57] Also, in 1952, the editor, again reacting to this growing concern by parents to have their children enter white-collar jobs on completion of their education, felt it necessary to issue a call to youths "to forget the so-called white collar jobs and turn to the factory, the machine shop, the timber grants, the mines, the mills and the land."[58]

Probably the most striking evidence pertaining to the strong preference by parents for "academic" education came after self-government in 1962. The new Minister of Education attempted to make available to a greater degree the type of education—the "academic" type—the public was demanding for its children. As part of this policy, the primary schools were reorganized into primary and secondary departments, and the latter allowed to offer some programmes similar to those in the "academic" secondary schools.

The result was, as previously pointed out, a massive increase in the number of pupils staying on in these newly-restructured "primary and all-age" schools beyond the school leaving age of 14 years. During the two years following the introduction of this more "academic" programme in the primary schools, their enrolment of pupils over 14 years increased on the average by about 24% per year. The greater "irrelevance"[59] of the courses which the students were now taking was of little concern to the parents and even the pupils.

The general lack of enthusiasm for practical subjects resulted in the fact that no steady progress was achieved with their introduction in the schools, despite the many recommendations which were made. Whenever a new report on the subject appeared, the Department of Education was jolted into doing something about it and there was a flurry of practical activities in the schools. But these were never sustained. Already in 1901 it was reported that although "agriculture has now been one of the extra subjects [in the primary school curriculum], yet it is disappointing to find so few children present for examination." The possibility of revising the grant structure by raising the payment made for a pass in agriculture was even mooted so that "schoolmasters might be induced to pay more attention to this subject."[60]

The same indifference to these subjects continued until about the 1940s, when the new schemes of work appeared, with heavy emphasis

[57] *Daily Argosy*, 1 September 1949.

[58] *Ibid.*, 24 November 1952.

[59] The term "irrelevance" here refers to the value of the skills and knowledge for increasing the productive efforts of the pupil in the Guyanese economy. But from the individual's point of view, these subjects were highly relevant since they led to increased opportunities for upward mobility, which was seen as the main objective of an education.

[60] Government of British Guiana, "Report of Inspector of Schools, 1902-03," quoted in Gordon, p. 150.

on practical subjects. During this period, immediately following the release of these new schemes, the primary school inspectors reported increased attention to subjects such as bookbinding, straw work, needlework, woodwork, and leathercraft. School gardens, which were further stimulated by the Government's Grow More Food campaign during the latter years of the war, also flourished. But despite the reported increase in practical activities, there was no falling off in the teaching of "academic" subjects. In fact, in many schools practical subjects were taken in the late afternoon and sometimes continued long after official school hours. But by the late 1940s and the early 1950s, this reported enthusiasm for practical subjects began to wane. By 1948 the Director of Education noted that teachers were again treating "practical subjects in the curriculum as of minor importance."[61] There was some rekindling of interest in the 1950s when a number of home economics and woodwork centres attached to existing primary schools were set up and the Government launched a new school gardening programme with the appointment of an agricultural education officer. Although the teaching of home economics and woodwork continued to expand, though very slowly, by 1960 the teaching of agriculture or school gardening in the primary schools was virtually non-existent.

And as can be seen, this was not due to any change in government policy, but stemmed more from lack of enthusiasm for these subjects by parents, students, and even teachers. This is strongly supported by the fact that when, in 1962, the Government gave permission for the all-age schools to enter their pupils for the English C.P. examination, the response was massive. The 1962 curriculum guide, which was prepared with great effort by educators and teachers, and the local primary school certificate examination syllabus were in many ways found to be irreconcileable with the syllabus of the English C.P. examination. As a result, the former was abandoned and schools concentrated their efforts on the more "irrelevant" C.P. syllabus.

The report of the UNESCO Mission, which visited the country around this time, gave a vivid description of what was happening to the primary school curriculum as a result of the new policy:

> Forgotten were the exhortations to make the curriculum vital and realistic by introducing local flavour and content and by taking into account the needs of the community; agriculture and technical subjects were virtually unknown in the grammar schools, why therefore should the secondary departments [of the all-age schools] devote any time to these humble subjects?[62]

Another point is that this strong preference for academic subjects continued despite the fact that these subjects, and especially those

[61] Government of British Guiana, *Annual Report of the Director of Education 1948* (Georgetown, 1948), p. 4.
[62] UNESCO, "Report of the UNESCO Educational Survey Mission," p. 47.

taken at the English C.P. examination, remained divorced from the pupil's life experience. Evidence of this emerges from a study of the school inspector's reports. In the field of arithmetic, the inspectors were constantly suggesting to teachers that the mathematical problems given to pupils should be related to the pupils' everyday experiences. For example, they were urged to substitute local currency (dollars and cents) for sterling (pounds, shillings, and pence) which appeared in the British textbooks that were being used in the schools.[63] In nature study it was noted that "the pupils are not taught to observe Nature around them . . . and then see how they [these observations] fit in with the facts given in the textbooks."[64] The success of a health education programme launched by the school medical officer was adversely affected by "the traditional bookish approach to all education"[65] with the result that the pupils crammed the principles of hygiene without paying much attention to the unsanitary surroundings of their schools, homes, and communities. The readers used in these schools were also "Victorian in content and outlook and bear no relation to the life which children have to live"[66] in British Guiana. In areas such as language arts, it was reported that English textbooks were used "without discrimination between material which is suitable for our schools and which is not."[67]

This was the general situation which existed when the Director admitted, as he did on many occasions, that "the present curriculum has a tendency to rest upon books rather than life itself."[68] In addition, he kept suggesting to teachers, apparently with little success, that "book knowledge must be related to events in the pupils' environment" and criticized their practice of following "too slavishly textbooks which are written for entirely different environments."[69]

It was obvious that the members of the dominant group in society saw primary education for the masses as a means of improving their expertise in those jobs which they were most likely to hold. Since most of them would inevitably return to farming or be engaged in skilled, semi-skilled, or even unskilled work, the ruling groups felt that some practical training would be of greatest value to them. One senior

[63] Government of British Guiana, *Annual Reports of the Director of Education 1945-50.*

[64] Government of British Guiana, *Annual Report of the Director of Education 1946,* p. 9.

[65] Government of British Guiana, *Annual Report of the Director of Education 1948,* p. 12.

[66] Government of British Guiana, *Annual Report of the Director of Education 1945,* p. 12.

[67] Government of British Guiana, *Annual Report of the Director of Education 1952-54* (Georgetown, 1956), p. 26.

[68] *Daily Argosy,* 23 August 1950.

[69] Government of British Guiana, *Annual Report of the Director of Education 1952-54,* p. 25.

educational administrator summarized these views, when, in supporting the establishment of senior schools with emphasis on practical
training, he argued that since "British Guiana raises its revenues prin-
cipally from agricultural, mining and forest industries . . . our schools
must produce youths who [working in these industries] would ulti-
mately be useful and efficient contributors to our revenue."[70]

This difference in attitude between the ruling groups and the
masses in their perception of the role of education, even at the primary level, is typical of most developing societies. Writing on the
subject, Beeby has observed that in these societies

> Parents . . . often have a clear idea of what constitutes education, it is the
> kind of schooling their European rulers had. . . . However unfitted it
> might be to the life of the primitive village or farm this was the type of
> education which gave the European his material superiority, that of-
> fered the local boy a hope of release from the poverty and tedium of life
> on the land.

Hence, "a practical form of education better suited to the needs of
farm or factory is liable to be regarded as a subtle attempt to fob
children off with something inferior."[71] Similarly, Foster, in writing
about Ghana, reported that "European educators were very much
concerned with the development of alternative forms of educational
institutions while African . . . demand . . . took the form of pressure of
'academic' instruction."[72]

One of the main reasons for this preference for an academic
education was the great difference in wages and employment opportunities for white-collar jobs as compared with manual occupations.
This fact was documented for the period 1945 to 1965. Not only was
the percentage of the labour force employed in "agriculture, forests,
and fishing" falling rapidly, dropping from 46.3% in 1945 to 32% in
1954, but unemployment in this sector was high and increasing with
mechanization. It rose from 11.3% in 1956 to 15.2% in 1965.

On the other hand, the numbers employed in the service sector
rose from about 29.5% of the labour force in 1945 to near 40% in
1965, while the rate of unemployment in this sector fell from 18.3% in
1956 to 8.3% in 1965. The increase in service sector employment was
mainly in the field of "clerical and sales" workers, an increase of about
50% between 1945 and 1960, pushing up their figures from 8.5% to
11.5% of the labour force. It will be recalled that Brewster estimated
that between 1948 and 1960, "insofar as new jobs were created they

[70] Government of British Guiana, Memo by the Principal, Government Training
College, "Proposals for the Establishment of Senior Schools for British Guiana"
(Georgetown, 13 January 1953). (Mimeographed.)

[71] C. E. Beeby, *The Quality of Education in Developing Countries* (Cambridge, Mass.:
Harvard University Press, 1966), pp. 29-30.

[72] Philip Foster, *Education and Social Change in Ghana* (London: Routledge and
Kegan Paul, 1965), p. 53.

were concentrated in the non-manual workers,"[73] while for 1960, Kundu observed that "by occupation the percentages of unemployed persons to the labour force were high everywhere except for white-collar workers and professional people."[74]

The structure of unemployment by occupation in 1965 also revealed that of all occupational groups the rate of unemployment was highest (39.9%) among the manual workers. In this group there were about 109 unemployed persons for each job vacancy that existed. Even among "craftsmen and technicians" the unemployment rate in 1965 was 19.2%. In view of this it was quite understandable why parents were so anxious to have their children receive the type of education that would most likely lead them to the white-collar jobs.

The ruling groups were quite concerned about the growing pressure for white-collar employment in a situation in which the overall unemployment rate was rising steadily. In fact, recent school leavers formed about 35% of the unemployed population in 1965. With a deteriorating unemployment situation, there was increasing concern to get the youngsters back to or prevent them from leaving the farms. It was felt that this was possible if youngsters had the agricultural knowledge and proper attitudes to farming and manual work in general. And it was here that they expected the schools to make their most important contribution. The structural constraints which farming imposed, the unavailability of land or capital to purchase land or bring new land into cultivation, local drainage and irrigation costs for new lands, etc., not to mention the low average income of farmers as compared even with messengers in the Government service, were often ignored.

This concern for providing an education which would keep people on the land, and possibly increase their productivity there, exists in many other developing countries. In 1947, the Development Committee of Kenya strongly expressed the view that education should remove "the exaggerated and dangerously misleading values"[75] placed on literacy as the first road to salaried employment, a point which was reported in the Guyanese press. The general assumption which underlies this view is that the educational system can, through the curriculum offered in schools, influence students to shift their interests to and prepare for occupations which, though necessary in a society, are not attracting enough recruits largely because the monetary and social rewards are considered inadequate. Foster and others have indicated that students are usually fairly well oriented to the economic and social realities of the job market, tending to prefer those occupations in which the economic returns are greatest. Thus,

[73] Brewster.
[74] Kundu, p. 320.
[75] *Daily Argosy*, 30 June 1947.

any attempt to use school curriculum changes to get pupils interested in jobs which are inadequately rewarded in the society is simply farcical. To bring about such changes, it is first necessary to change the existing reward structure and thus put the jobs into which it is desired to attract people in a more relatively favourable position. It is only after this is done that the educational system can, through curriculum changes in schools, help to stimulate the interest of students in these occupations.

Summary

It is obvious from the above analysis that changing popular attitudes to education, even at the primary level, were closely related to changes occurring in the opportunity structure in Guyanese society. After the mid-1940s primary education became even more functional as an instrument of upward mobility, either to the lower level white-collar job market or to further opportunities for education at the secondary level. As this happened, the desire for education even at this level increased and was one of the important factors contributing towards the increase in enrolment in the primary schools between 1945 and 1973. This could partly be seen in the fact that, during these years, the actual enrolment in the primary schools was increasing about one and one quarter times faster than the total population of primary school age. Also, average attendance in these schools rose from 69% in the 1930s to nearly 80% in the 1960s.

Further, it was noticed that students revealed a great perspicacity in their educational decisions, and whenever educational opportunities likely to lead to increased occupational mobility were introduced, the students exerted great efforts to utilize them. For example, when the bridge linking the primary and secondary school system was widened with the introduction of a national secondary schools selection examination, the result was a tenfold increase in fifteen years in the number of students taking the examination. Similarly, as the value of the Primary School Certificate declined on the job market, the number of entries to this examination began to fall, dropping by about 12% between 1945 and 1950. When, however, this examination again became valuable, e.g., as an acceptable qualification for secondary school entry and later as a prerequisite for the College of Preceptors Examination, it was noticed that the number of students entering for it increased about 135% within a decade. Also, when the Government decided to allow pupils to do part of the course normally offered in secondary schools within the primary and all-age schools, the response was massive. In short, as one "primary" school examination became of little value for occupational selection or for entry into a secondary school programme, the students raised their aspirations even higher to more "useful" examinations. When the College of

Preceptors Certificate superseded the Primary School or Preliminary Certificate as the minimum qualification for most white-collar jobs, students were staying on in the primary and all-age schools, even until they were 17 years old, to try to obtain that certificate.

The important changes that were taking place in the country, and which were largely responsible for the increased opportunities available to Guyanese, were the constitutional ones. These allowed increased popular inputs in the political decision-making process, making it more difficult for the Government to ignore the increasing demand by the population for more or better educational services. One example of this can be seen in the way in which primary school overcrowding was tackled. Although the colonial administration was aware that this problem was getting worse, it made no firm policy decision on how to deal with it, despite the many recommendations by educational advisors and specially-appointed committees. The Director of Education had, in 1948,[76] clearly pointed out the two alternatives which the Government faced on this issue: it had either to allocate a larger proportion of its revenue to primary education or lower the standard or the scope of its existing educational services.

The first alternative posed its own problems. Educational expenditure was rising as fast as, and sometimes faster than, the increase in the total Government recurrent budget, and already in 1951, the Financial Secretary had informed the Legislative Council that "it seems tolerably certain that revenue, without impinging on other essential services, will not be able to finance the needs of the large number of children seeking admission to the schools on the basis provided by the Education Code."[77]

The other alternative was a reduction in the quality or scope of existing educational programmes. S. A. Hammond, the C.D. & W. Educational Adviser, had suggested a lowering of the compulsory school attendance ages from 6-14 to 6-12 years, while the Director of Education had urged the exclusion from the primary schools of all children outside the statutory school attendance age on the grounds that "the course (in the primary schools) is designed for the great majority who begin at six and leave at fourteen."[78] The Nicole Committee proposed the experimental introduction of the double-shift system, which if successful, could gradually be introduced in other areas of the country.

But the Government was unwilling to accept any of these recommendations because of the strong popular opposition to them. The proposal to exclude from school all children who were outside the

[76] Government of British Guiana, *Annual Report of the Director of Education 1948*.

[77] Government of British Guiana, "Statement by the Financial Secretary in *Hansard*, 28th November 1957" (Georgetown, 1957).

[78] Government of British Guiana, *Annual Report of the Director of Education 1948*, p. 6.

statutory school attendance age—not to mention the reduction of the compulsory attendance age suggested by Hammond—would have raised a political hornet's nest. The Government did attempt, through administrative action on the part of the Director of Education, to restrict the entry of children under six years of age into the primary schools in accordance with the existing regulation which only allowed such children to be admitted if accommodation was available. However, the public outcry against the action prevented the Government from pursuing the other recommendation, which was to exclude those over 14 from the primary schools.

But the Nicole proposals were the most unpopular of all. The public expressed the view that Nicole's recommendation to experiment with the double-shift system was "part of the scheme by the Imperial Government" to ensure the continued oppression of the Guyanese people since it was felt that this proposal would not only lower the educational level of the population but would also give the Government justification to further postpone the political advancement of the country and its move towards self-government and independence.[79]

The unwillingness of the Government to make a clear policy decision on this obviously crucial issue indicates the increasing importance which popular pressures were having on educational planning decisions. The Colonial administration had already indicated its desire to grant political independence to the territories in the region, including Guyana, and preferred, where possible, to avoid political confrontation with the masses, something likely to occur if steps were taken to reduce the range or the quality of the existing educational services, even at the primary level. The result was that no formal policy was made and the Government took the "easy way out" by building more schools in the usual way, improving the design of the buildings as pressures accumulated and ignoring the worsening overcrowding situation.

It was not until a fully-elected Government came into power that a decision was taken in 1964 to depend on community self-help efforts rather than to provide more primary school accommodation in the usual way. The political atmosphere was by then more conducive to such a solution, partly because of a greater popular identification with the new Government and partly because of the hopes shared by the masses that self-government would create more jobs for their children—jobs for which their educational background would be the most important consideration.

But even though the public was prepared to help with the provision of school accommodation, it did not ease up its pressures on the

[79] J. A. Nicholson, reported in Government of British Guiana *Hansard*, 18 July 1952 (Georgetown, 1952).

Government to improve the range of primary educational services which it was offering. In fact, when the Government began implementing its self-help school building programme in 1963 to save on costs, it was "forced" to make other concessions, which entirely cancelled the savings that were being incurred by building schools on a self-help basis. For example, the Government agreed to admit more pupils under six years of age into primary schools, and between 1964 and 1968, the size of this group had increased by 32%. In addition, pupils were allowed to stay at school even beyond the legal age limit of 16 to take the College of Preceptors Examination. The result was that two years following this decision, the number of pupils over 14 remaining in the primary and all-age schools was increasing by about 24% per annum, as compared with the previous average annual increase of 6.5%. The P.N.C. Government, which took and held office continuously since 1964, continued the same policy of increasing and improving school accommodation, even though in 1968 it decided to restrict entry into primary schools to those who were at least 5 years and 9 months of age. On the other hand, local authorities were encouraged to provide kindergarten education for preschoolers, and in 1976 the Government accepted responsibility for this level of education also.

So, since the end of the colonial administration, the new Government, instead of attempting to control or reduce educational expenditure, found it necessary or desirable, partly because of increasing popular pressures and those from its own professional staff and partly because of its own belief in education as a major instrument of development, to continue providing more and improved educational facilities, even at the primary level. One result was that between 1960 and 1965 the expenditure on primary education had increased by 90.6% (18.1% per annum), which was considerably higher than the rate of increase in expenditure in the total Government budget for that period. However, all the efforts by the Government to make practical instruction an important part of the primary school curriculum were rejected by the masses who wanted their children to be given an education which would prepare them for entry into the secondary schools or directly into some white-collar occupation.

4. Teacher Education

Following the English pattern, teachers in primary and those in the secondary grammar schools in Guyana belonged to two separate sub-groups. Differences existed in their educational background, professional training, salaries, and status in the society. Secondary school teachers were ideally university graduates who received their professional training at institutions of similar rank while primary school teachers were usually trained in teachers' training colleges. In 1932 the ratio of the average salary of teachers in the fully-aided primary schools to that of teachers in the Government boys' secondary school was 1:75. This chapter will deal largely with the preparation of teachers for the "primary" schools, and will focus attention on quantitative expansion of teacher training facilities, the rate of output of trained teachers, and curriculum changes over time in the teacher education programmes.

Pre-1945 Attempts at Teacher Training

The first local training centre for teachers was opened about 1852, and after about thirty years of existence, was closed for financial reasons. Since then, and for the next half century, there were many half-hearted, unsuccessful attempts to re-establish a teacher's training college. The result was a constant decline in the number of trained teachers in the colony, from 200 in 1882 to about eighty-five in 1928 when a new college was eventually established. By this time, trained techers constituted only 6% of those employed in the profession.

Some attempts were made to send Guyanese teachers for training at Mico and Shortwood Training Colleges in Jamaica and the Rawle Training Institute in Barbados, but for many reasons, including costs, these efforts were not successful; only a few students benefitted from the arrangements. Therefore, when Bain Gray was appointed Commissioner of Education to the colony in the early 1920s, he placed the training of teachers as one of his priorities. Largely through his influence, a committee was appointed in 1924 to examine the possibility of training teachers locally. It recommended the immediate establishment of a non-residential Teachers' Training College with an intake of thirty students annually.

The plan which Bain Gray obviously had in mind was one which, as was mentioned elsewhere,[1] would eventually have resulted in a

[1] M. K. Bacchus, "Education and Development in Guyana since 1945 with Esti-

fully certificated teaching profession. At the time, teachers could obtain certification either by successfully completing a course of training at a recognized teachers' college or by passing the Teachers' Certificate Examination conducted by the Department of Education. Bain Gray attempted a two-pronged attack on this problem of teacher certification. The first was to increase the number of teachers from a recognized training institution, via the proposed Teachers' Training Centre, and the second was to provide facilities for better preparation of those who sought certification through the Teacher's Certificate Examination. These two measures were together aimed at eventually producing a fully certificated teaching profession in the colony.

Bain Gray also wanted to improve teaching competence in the schools, and for this he proposed that the existing system of preparing pupil teachers should be modified to allow them to attend a secondary school during the period of their pupil teachership. In addition, he sought to improve the expertise of practising teachers by organizing in-service training and refresher courses, and by providing facilities for them to read more widely in their professional field. As part of the latter effort, he was responsible for establishing a central teachers' library from which teachers all over the country could borrow books without charge, not even for postage.

This was the first real attempt at developing an overall policy for teacher education. But the then colonial Government did not provide the necessary funds, and the programme had to be considerably modified. The original plan for putting out thirty trained teachers annually was cut by half, and the newly established teachers' training college was not even assigned a full-time principal during its first ten years of existence.

The need for teachers with a secondary education was reiterated by the 1925 Commission,[2] on which Bain Gray sat, but one of the problems was to find potential recruits into primary school teaching from graduates of the secondary schools. The children of the middle and upper middle classes who were then attending the secondary schools regarded primary school teaching, with its relatively low salaries and status, as an occupation that, for them, was socially "infra-dig."

The other measure, i.e., providing pupil teachers with a period of full-time secondary education at an approved secondary school, also encountered difficulties. The rural areas had no secondary schools and, therefore, Bain Gray recommended the establishment of "pupil teacher centres," where an education similar to that provided in a secondary school could be made available to pupil teachers. But these

mates of Educational Needs up to 1975" (unpublished Ph.D. thesis, University of London, 1968).

[2] Government of British Guiana, "Report of the Educational Commission 1925."

recommendations were not yet accepted by 1939 when the Primary Education Committee[3] was established with Bain Gray as chairman. This new committee again drew attention to the need for improving the basic educational level of teachers and recommended that only part of the pupil teacher's time (seventeen hours per week) be spent teaching while the other part was to be devoted to study. It further suggested that, where possible, classes for pupil teachers should be organized at Government expense in certain centres.

The 1939 West India Royal Commission was also strongly critical of local efforts at teacher training and recruitment and felt that "too little effort was made to attract into the profession those who had received a secondary education."[4] In addition, it condemned the pupil teacher system which it observed as, "theoretically a means of training teachers but all too often simply a means of obtaining cheap staff,"[5] and recommended its gradual abolition, urging that reforms to ensure that all teachers receive systematic training be pushed ahead. The 1942 Memorandum by Hammond, the C.D. & W. Educational Adviser, also emphasized the need for reforms in teacher education. It suggested that the annual output of trained teachers should be increased five-fold, from twenty to one hundred, to ensure that eventually all new appointees to teaching would be trained teachers. Hammond also observed that "what is needed is not so much a better trained as a better educated teacher"[6] and suggested the implementation of a three-year secondary course for those between the ages of 15 and 18 who intended to take up teaching as a career. The Teacher Training Sub-Committee[7] of the Education Development Committee of 1948 agreed with nearly all of the proposals put forward by the C.D. & W. Educational Adviser, but felt that the educational background of intending teachers should be a normal five-year secondary school course. It, therefore, urged that efforts be made to attract School Certificate holders from the secondary schools, into primary school teaching, and recommended the granting of 100 scholarships to intending teachers to attend such schools.

These different reports all drew attention to the need to improve the quality of primary education through raising the academic and professional standards of the teachers by recruiting better educated individuals into the profession and by substantially expanding teacher training facilities. Although these needs were clearly and repeatedly

[3] Government of British Guiana, *Report of the Primary Education Committee 1939.*
[4] Government of Great Britain, *West India Royal Commission Report, 1938-39*, p. 122.
[5] *Ibid.*, p. 92.
[6] Government of Great Britain Colonial Development and Welfare, *Memorandum on Education in British Guiana 1942*, p. 35.
[7] See Government of British Guiana, *Report of the Education Development Committee 1946.*

identified since 1925, when an elected Government took office in 1957 it found that very little had been done to implement any of these recommendations. To understand what happened, one needs to consider the essential difference in operational style between a colonial and a non-colonial Government, or more correctly between a Government which did not have to depend very much on popular support for holding office and one whose accession to power and basis of legitimacy depended on the support which it received at election from the general populace.

In addition to the political there was the important financial aspect to the problem, ignored at first in the post-war euphoria for the expansion of educational services. Both the reports by the West India Royal Commission and the C.D. & W. Education Adviser were made without any assessment of the financial resources of the various countries in the region. But in 1945 Hammond did a study on the *Future Cost of Education in the West Indies*, and from his figures, he argued not only that the cost of providing free elementary education in these territories was already too high in relation to their budgetary resources, but also suggested that even "if the elementary school teaching service were developed along *existing* lines, the cost of a sufficient number of competent teachers would be substantially greater than the provision which most of the West Indian Governments can be expected to make for this purpose within the foreseeable future." He urged, therefore, that "any attempt at increasing costs by improving the teachers' salaries' bill should not be undertaken lightly."[8]

These recommendations completely contradicted his earlier report, but they were now based on his assessment of the potential economic resources of the region. Echoing a similar note in 1948, the Director of Education in Guyana indicated that it would be impossible for the country to afford all fully qualified primary school teachers, as was suggested by the Royal Commission. He saw that the employment of trained teachers would increase "the teachers' salary vote (now approximately $1.25 million) at a rate of $50,000 per annum, eventually doubling it; a prospect which cannot be faced."[9] Although the Director might have exaggerated the rate of increase in the teachers' salary bill, his concern over the rising expenditure on salaries was shared by most colonial administrators at the time.

To overcome the problem of cost, Hammond suggested, among other measures, that steps be taken to dilute the teaching force by returning to a modified version of the monitorial system. Pupils were to be divided into groups, with teaching done by a trained master

[8] Government of Great Britain, Colonial Development and Welfare, *The Future Cost of Education*, Bulletin No. 15 (n.d.), p. 28.

[9] Government of British Guiana, *Annual Report of the Director of Education 1948*, p. 8.

teacher who would be assisted by pupil teachers and senior pupils acting as "group leaders," a proposal which the C.D. & W. Controller even attempted to justify on educational grounds. In a communique to the Secretary of State for the Colonies, he wrote, "The use of pupils as group leaders is, I am advised, in accordance with advanced educational practice and it is worth recalling that in young people at least, having to teach is an effective incentive in learning."[10] Instead of abolishing the pupil teacher system, as was recommended by the Royal Commission, the West Indian Governments were now urged to extend the system "as a sound working instrument and as a means of continued education for the young people engaged in it."[11]

With this official seal of approval given to the Hammond recommendation, the hands of the Guyanese Government were virtually tied. But the Secretary of State and his advisers did not reckon with the changes taking place on the political scene. The population had become less passive and more demanding of social reforms than in the past. They had pinned their hopes to the belief that education was going to be one of the main instruments of social and economic reconstruction. The result was a massive public outcry against the proposed dilution of the teaching staff in Guyana and throughout the West Indies. The *Daily Argosy*, after noting the "pronounced tendency of the working classes to avail themselves, in the interest of their children and wards of the educational facilities existing" in the country, observed that "this section of the community looks askance at any proposal, the adoption of which can only result in the restriction of the educational facilities already existing and also at the lowering of the standard of teaching in the primary schools."[12] The Synod of the local Anglican Church, which was never known for its criticism of the colonial government, passed a resolution drawing attention to the need for an adequate supply of trained teachers in the primary schools and calling on the population to reject any compromise contained in the proposal for a dilution of the teaching staff.[13]

The local population was further strengthened in its opposition to the proposal when it learned that the other West Indian territories had made similar protests. The *Daily Argosy* reported that it was

> in a position to state that in certain of the West Indian colonies, the responsible sections of the respective communities have already determined that they would have nothing to do with the proposed Dilution scheme, the introduction of which, they maintain, will definitely not be in the best interests of the communities involved.[14]

[10] Government of Great Britain, Colonial Development and Welfare, Memorandum on *The Future Cost of Education*, p. 5.
[11] *Ibid.*, p. 4.
[12] *Daily Argosy*, 15 April 1945.
[13] *Ibid.*, 14 April 1945.
[14] *Ibid.*, 15 April 1945.

Even the *Times* of London came to the support of the protesting West Indian population, arguing that if the large use of pupil teachers was not educationally beneficial to the West Indies but was an expedient imposed by lack of funds, then sufficient money must be found to dispense with it. The newspaper went on to say that the granting of aid to the West Indies should not necessarily, as was suggested, prejudice their political development and self-sufficiency, for which education was needed. In the spirit of liberalism to the colonies, which pervaded post-war Britain, the *Times* concluded, "The reasons why the colonies cannot themselves pay for desperately needed reforms must be traced to an age darker and more distant. . . . The endorsement of that principle [of trusteeship] no less than honour requires the payment of a debt long owing to these people . . . and it can surely be paid without harm to the creditors' self respect."[15]

Finding itself between these two pressures—the financial costs involved in increasing the number of trained teachers and the mounting public pressure against further dilution of the quality of the teaching staff—the colonial administration in Guyana took no further action towards improving facilities for teacher education. In fact, by its inaction it brought about a reduction in the percentage of trained teachers in the schools and possibly also in the quality of primary education. This "policy" of inaction by the colonial Government when faced with rapidly rising educational costs on the one hand and with popular pressure on the other, was typical of this period of Guyanese educational history. The use of the same strategy was earlier observed in connection with the provision of primary school accommodation.

There was some gradual improvement in the quality of the recruits into primary school teaching, but this did not result from any planned effort by the Government. It occurred largely because of the rapid rise in secondary school enrolment since 1945, and the fact that the civil service, which was the traditional field of employment for secondary school graduates, was not expanding rapidly enough to absorb all of them. Also, female civil servants with only a secondary education who had to resign their jobs upon getting married, generally took up primary school teaching. The results were that:

(1) The percentage of pupil teachers without a secondary education began to fall, and between 1945 and 1955 their proportion dropped from 14% to 8%.

(2) The percentage of untrained teachers who had completed secondary school rose from 30% in 1950 to 45% in 1955, although this figure fell back to 40% in 1960, due to a rapid increase in the total size of the teaching profession.

(3) The percentage of trained teachers who had completed secondary school rose from 23% in 1950 to 60% in 1964.

[15] Reported in *ibid.*, 18 December 1945.

But in the area of professional preparation, the situation seems to have been deteriorating. Between 1945 and 1965 the percentage of trained teachers in Guyana was gradually falling and the number of students admitted to full-time training remained at twenty per year, even though the size of the teaching profession had doubled between 1945 and 1963. Despite this fact, the number of teachers seeking certification by the second route, that is, through the Teachers' Certificate Examination, fell by about one third during this period. Many of them became frustrated at the low percentage of passes (around 25%) at this examination, which was largely a reflection of their inability to secure competent help with their studies. The Department's refresher courses were usually concerned with passing on practical teaching skills and were of little use to those taking the Teachers' Certificate examinations.

The first improvement in this situation was brought about by the popularly-elected Government of 1953, when the then Minister of Education increased by 50% the intake into the Teachers' College, from twenty to thirty students per year. But with the suspension of the constitution in 1953 and a return to full colonial rule, no further step was taken to increase the output of trained teachers. The only progress that was made in this field was the training of a limited number of home economics and woodwork teachers and the provision of five scholarships annually for teachers to do a one-year course in the study of the United Kingdom. The latter course of action was in essence part of the political strategy of the colonial administration to win the support of the leaders of the teaching profession, who, it was believed, heavily supported the "errant" political party, the P.P.P., in the 1953 elections.

As a result of the general inaction by the Government, the percentage of trained teachers in the country fell from about 20% in 1945 to 16.2% in 1957, by which time, as can be seen from Tables 19 and 20, Guyana had one of the lowest percentages of trained teachers in the British Caribbean.

The return of an elected Government to office in late 1957 again saw another expansion of teacher education facilities in the country. In January 1958 the Government doubled the number of teachers in training by admitting thirty additional students to the Teachers' College on a special eighteen-month course. By 1959 it took a more radical step to increase the supply of trained teachers by temporarily suspending the two-year training course and introducing a one-year course for five times (150) as many trainees. The Potter Committee[16] of 1955 had previously suggested the introduction of a one-year programme for certificated, untrained teachers to be conducted alongside the regular two-year course. However, the Government de-

[16] Government of British Guiana, *Report of the Primary School Teachers' Salaries Structure Committee 1955* (Georgetown, 1955).

Table 19 *Percentage of Trained Teachers in Guyana, 1945-1957*

Year	Total number of trained teachers	Total number of teachers	Percentage of trained teachers
1945	N.A.	N.A.	20.0
1946	300	1,550	19.4
1948	321	1,604	20.0
1950	335	1,829	18.3
1952	352	1,775	20.0
1954	383	2,107	18.2
1956	426	2,548	16.7
1957	435	2,682	16.2

Source: Government of British Guiana, *Annual Reports of the Director of Education or the Ministry of Education* (Georgetown, 1946-1957).

Table 20 *Percentage of Trained Teachers in Primary Schools in the West Indies in 1957*

Territory	Percentage of college-trained teachers
Trinidad	45
Jamaica	44
Antigua	40
Barbados	25
Montserrat	21
St. Kitts	20
British Guiana	17
Dominica	9
Grenada	8
St. Vincent	6
St. Lucia	6

Source: Development and Welfare in the West Indies, *Report of the Regional Conference on the Training of Teachers in the British Caribbean*, Bulletin No. 39 (Bridgetown, Barbados, 1957).

cided against this more conservative step, and concentrated on a fairly large quantitative increase in teacher output by reducing the length of the training programmes for all trainees.

The British Guiana Teachers' Association opposed the one-year course because it felt that this move reflected the parsimony of the

Government in dealing with such an important area of education and partly because it feared that such a step might eventually result in a lowering of educational standards. But the teachers likely to benefit from the change responded favourably to it, and in 1959 there were 500 applicants for the 150 vacancies at the Teachers' College. The elected Government, confident of public support on this issue, in 1962 further increased by 50% the number of teachers accepted for the one-year training, from 150 to 225 teachers. These additional seventy-five teachers were even admitted on the condition that they would meet their own maintenance costs, though the cost of instruction remained free.

Despite the increase in the number of teachers in training, the UNESCO mission of 1962-63 considered the annual output of 225 teachers as highly inadequate and recommended a large-scale four-pronged attack[17] on this problem, a recommendation which was accepted in full by the Government. This total approach was to produce a fully trained primary school teacher population by 1975. The programme consisted of:

(1) Short Courses (lasting six weeks), especially in school administration and curriculum development for Class I and Class II certificated but untrained head teachers and senior assistants;

(2) A two-year Pre-Service Course for new recruits with a good secondary education background;

(3) A one-year (later two-year) Inservice Course for practising teachers. This involved the establishment of eight teacher training centres throughout the country;

(4) Pre-service courses for teachers of special subjects—mainly industrial arts and home economics.

By 1964, after it became obvious that the original target of pre-service trainees was not being fully met, the Minister of Education decided to establish a new rural training centre, which was closed by the new Government in 1965, mainly for political reasons.

It was amazing that the UNESCO proposals were so readily accepted by the Government, despite the cost implications, especially considering the fact that so little progress had been made over the past century in this field. But these bold steps enjoyed popularity among most sections of the population.

Developments Between 1964 and 1973

Up to 1963 the Government Training College for Teachers had trained only 1,296 teachers during its thirty-five-year existence, giv-

---

[17] UNESCO, "Memorandum to the Minister of Education, Teacher Education Programme" (Georgetown: UNESCO Educational Mission, 15 February 1963). (Mimeographed.)

ing an average output of thirty-seven trained teachers per year. But between 1965 and 1973 alone, as can be seen from Table 21, the total output was 1,076, or an average of 119 per year. A new Teachers' College was built in 1973 to accommodate 660 students and offered residential accommodation for 280. This has made it possible for the college to aim seriously at an annual output of over 300 teachers, which was the original target of the 1962 UNESCO recommendations.

Table 21   *Output from the Government Training College, 1965-1973*

Year	Output
1965	47
1966	153
1967	85
1968	105
1969	170
1970	127
1971	122
1972	130
1973	137
Total	1,076

As the enrolment in the pre-service programme increased, the annual output of trained teachers from the in-service course began to decline (see Table 22). This was the direct result of a 1966 policy change by the Ministry of Education, which attempted to steer younger teachers away from the in-service to the pre-service programme by raising the minimum age and the number of years of teaching experience required for entry into the in-service course. For example, in 1966, of the 571 persons who applied for entry, only 144 were eligible for admission under the new regulations. This resulted in the closing down of six rural training centres, and only the two located in Georgetown and New Amsterdam remained open. Nevertheless, between 1964 and 1973 the in-service programme still provided the largest number of trained teachers for the primary schools. Its total output of 1,725 teachers during these years was substantially greater than the output from the pre-service course.

Special emphasis was also placed on the training of teachers for the "secondary" grades of the all-age schools. In the late 1960s, the World Bank agreed to finance six multilateral secondary schools and a College of Education to train teachers for these schools. The annual

Table 22 Output of Trained
Teachers from the
In-Service Training
Programme, 1963-64
to1971-73

Year	Output
1963-64	457
1964-66	527
1966-68	103
1967-69	65
1968-70	128
1969-71	214
1970-72	144
1971-73	87
Total	1,725

enrolment at the College was between forty and fifty, and the length of the course was three years.

In 1969, the Government launched an additional programme for training teachers of agriculture, which was conducted by the Guyana School of Agriculture. From 1963 to 1973 the total number of specialist teachers trained was 223, with 51% in home economics, 23% in industrial arts, and 25% in agriculture.

The major administrative problem that faced the teacher education programmes in Guyana was the lack of coordination of the work of the various institutions engaged in this activity. The University of Guyana offered professional training courses not only for secondary school teachers but also for those in the secondary departments of the all-age schools, and even for some senior primary school teachers. The College of Secondary Education offered academic and professional training for teachers of the multilateral schools and the secondary divisions of the all-age schools, while the Government Training College offered training for teachers in the lower grades of these very schools. This division of responsibility has made a coordinated attack on the teacher education problem difficult.

In summary, there was an overall increase in the numbers and percentage of trained primary school teachers between 1945 and 1974; the following figures for selected years between 1948 and 1973 provides further evidence of this. It was already observed from Table 19 that the percentage of trained teachers fell from 20% in 1945 to 16.2% in 1957. However, after the policies of the elected Government began to have their impact in the early 1960s, this trend was reversed. By 1973 trained teachers made up just over 42% of the profession. In addition, the pupil/teachers ratio was nearly halved between 1948 and 1971, dropping from an average 44.8 in the former year to 22.7 in the latter. This lower ratio of pupils to teachers has remained fairly constant since then.

Table 23   *Numbers and Percentage of Trained Teachers and Pupil/Teacher Ratio in the Primary Schools of Guyana, 1948-1973*

Year	Total number of trained teachers	Total teacher population	Trained teachers as a percentage of the total	No. of pupils per teacher
1948	330	1,544	21.4	44.8
1951	356	1,839	19.4	42.4
1962	835	3,271	25.5	40.7
1964	937	4,348	21.5	34.0
1967	1,947	5,255	37.0	25.7
1969	2,028	5,441	37.3	24.0
1971	2,101	5,749	36.5	22.7
1972	2,263	5,754	39.3	22.7
1973	2,433	5,783	42.1	22.7

Source: Government of British Guiana, *Annual Report[s] of the Director of Education or the Ministry of Education* (Georgetown, 1948-1973).

The Curriculum of the Teachers' College

An examination of the curriculum of the teachers' college in the mid-1940s would reveal the expectation which Guyanese society had of its primary school teachers. The schools were expected to help solve the many problems which the society faced, and at the same time pass on the basic knowledge and skills which were considered (a) an instrinsic mark of anyone who had an education, and (b) useful to the society.

Since primary school teachers were general practitioners, nearly all the subjects taught in the primary schools had to be studied by the teachers in training. So at the end of their two-year course, teachers had to write twenty examinations in fifteen subjects, plus two examinations in Infant Teaching and Arithmetic, which they did in their first year. The subjects included Principles of Education, Mathematics, Geography, Hygiene and Health Education, History, Nature Study, Bookbinding, Hammock and Matmaking, Shoe Repairing, Agricultural Science, Physical Training, Art, Music, and Woodwork and Mothercraft for males and females, respectively. In addition, students were expected to take courses in West Indian Literature and Civics, which were offered in the evening, and Religious Education.

The effect of the drive to include agriculture in the primary school curriculum in the 1940s was also reflected in the Training College programme. When the Government launched its Grow More Food campaign during the 1940s, the teaching of agriculture at the college was given added push with the appointment of a full-time agricultural instructor, and for many years, ancillary activities such as poultry rearing and beekeeping were also undertaken by students. While optional subjects were gradually introduced and the students no longer had to take the full range of courses offered, the Government continued to exert pressures on the primary schools to teach new subjects considered important to "national development." As this happened, the training college had to prepare their students in these areas also. For example, when Guyana declared itself a "Cooperative Republic" in the late 1960s, the "Principles of Cooperatives" became a compulsory subject in the curriculum of the teachers' college.

Another important change in the Teachers' College curriculum was a shift in emphasis from "academic" to the "professional" subjects. During the 1940s and up to the mid-1950s, when few students had a good secondary education, emphasis was on raising the students' academic standards in the subjects which they had to teach. For example, in 1948 the Principal of the Teachers' Training College was still noting that "the training programme is traditional in being only partly professional, a considerable proportion of the curriculum being devoted to the attainment of higher standards of knowledge in the subjects they are to teach."[18] But by the late 1950s, as the academic background of students improved, there was a noticeable shift in emphasis towards the "professional subjects," such as the methodology of teaching. In his 1957 report the principal noted that "plans are under way to reorganize the curriculum even more drastically and to lay far more emphasis on the professional aspect of training as well as on the personal development of the students." In justification of this step, he argued that teachers were now entering the college with a higher level of education.

This shift to the "professional" subjects was even more heavily marked with the introduction of the one-year training programme in 1959. The older, two-year-trained teachers somewhat unkindly, though not entirely untruthfully, observed that those undergoing the new one-year course were being trained "to teach nothing beautifully." However, since 1963, with the reintroduction of a two-year course, and partly as a result of the discussions about teacher educa-

---

[18] Government of British Guiana, *Triennial Report of the Education Department 1954-57* (Georgetown, 1957), p. 12.

tion which followed the publication of the Conant Report,[19] there has been greater emphasis on the general education of teachers with the introduction of foundation courses in such areas as the social sciences.

The major motivating factor in recent curriculum changes at the teachers' college was the desire by the staff to develop a programme that was in line with "progressive ideas and practices" in teacher education overseas. Since most lecturers had themselves been trained abroad and were familiar with Western ideas about teacher preparation, this pressure became even more marked. The content of many of the courses still remained similar to that taught in training colleges overseas, especially in England, with two factors largely responsible for this. First, there was, among teacher educators, the assumption of a universally "good teacher education programme." Second, there was little research work on Guyanese society available to students, so that the texts used for subjects such as educational psychology had no references to growing up in Guyanese society or understanding behaviour patterns among students in Guyanese schools.

Another source of pressure on the curriculum of the Teachers' College was that imposed by the Government in its effort to get this institution to include subjects or activities which would give intending teachers those skills, knowledge, and attitudes valuable for the economic development of the country. The assumption was that such an orientation would better equip teachers to implement the new "development-oriented" curriculum being put out by the Ministry of Education, and hence would be more effective in transmitting to their pupils the type of skills, attitudes, and knowledge which were likely to foster development. Because of the new "socialist" policy of the Government, the role of the teacher was seen as crucial in its efforts to bring about economic and social change. This meant that teacher educators had come to assume even more importance, and in 1974 this fact had been directly acknowledged by a substantial increase in their salaries, placing them financially above those teaching in the elite secondary grammar schools and even above those in some other professions. The new salary scales for lecturers at the Teachers' Colleges were not influenced by supply and demand factors, but reflected the importance of the role which the Government considered that teacher educators ought to be playing in the development of Guyanese society.

The Changing Role of the Primary School Teacher

As was pointed out before, primary education was at first considered a major instrument for the "moral and spiritual upliftment" of

[19] J. B. Conant, *The Education of American Teachers* (New York: McGraw-Hill, 1963).

the Guyanese masses, and teachers were expected to play a crucial role in the achievement of this goal, not only by being moral exemplars but also by playing an active part in "raising" the moral standards of the community. As a result, both the "moral character" and the religious persuasion of individuals were considered important for their appointment as teachers. Standards of morality were identified with the practice of Christianity; hence non-Christians had very little chance of securing jobs as teachers, especially in the denominational schools. In addition, teachers were expected to play an active part in the religious activities of the churches, which controlled the schools, and the roles of the village schoolmaster and the village lay preacher were often inseparable. The headmaster's wife, too, made her contribution to these activities, and was often the chief bazaar organizer and fund raiser for the village church. In this context, it is easy to understand why Christian religious education was such an important part of the curriculum of the Teachers' College up to the mid-1950s. As late as 1947 the churches were able to obtain a formal commitment from the Government that Religious Instruction, which in fact meant instruction in Christianity, was to have a definite place in the curriculum of the Teachers' College and be taught "during normal instructional hours." And this, it will be recalled, was in a society where about half the population was non-Christian.

The village schoolmaster was also a very important figure in the rural community, often serving as a village councillor or even village chairman. In the earlier days, he was usually the chief draftsman of petitions to the Government and consultant on matters affecting the relationship between the village farmers and the central Government. But as politics became more "cosmopolitanized" and the centre of political activities moved from the local to the national arena, the political role of the village schoolmaster diminished considerably. One reason for this was that since political party affiliation and ethnicity have become closely linked throughout the country, those village schoolmasters who actively participated in village politics were likely to lose the confidence of at least one major ethnic group in the community.

Another factor which affected teachers' involvement in community activities was the fact that they traditionally enjoyed relatively high status in the villages. The local citizenry not only respected their position, but often sought and followed their advice on important issues. Today, primary school teachers no longer enjoy the same prestige in the villages. Their status has declined in the rural social hierarchy, stemming largely from the fact that they were no longer the most educated individuals in these communities. There were likely to be many others with higher levels of formal education to whom the local citizenry could turn for advice. This has affected the very nature of teacher involvement in community affairs. Previously, teachers who worked for rural communities developed an almost paternalistic relationship with the local community leaders and members. But more recently they have not automatically been enjoying high status in the villages, and instead had to learn how to work "with" the villagers rather than just "for" them. Since the psychological incentive for involvement in community work, which stemmed from the status superiority accorded to them by the villagers, no longer existed, teachers found it difficult working on community projects, as equals with the villagers, especially since they still felt that their higher level of education had made them culturally superior to the ordinary village folks.

The withdrawal of the teacher from such activities was already apparent in the 1940s when the *Daily Argosy* carried an editorial suggesting that teachers still had a very important role to play in rural development. The editor, after noting that in the past teachers took an active part in community work, urged that in the implementation of the new Government programmes aimed at raising the standard of life in the rural areas, teachers' participation should again be encouraged. "We are convinced" he wrote, "that an important share of this work, that of creating a new and improved community, depends on the lead given by and the active enthusiastic cooperation of our teachers."[20]

Some attempts had been made by the Teachers' College around the mid-1940s to get trainees more oriented towards working with the communities. Visits were arranged twice per week to youth clubs, and a formal course of instruction was held for female students on certain aspects of community work. But these efforts were regarded as peripheral to the total work of the college by the staff, which tended to see the teachers' sphere of operation only within the classroom. A good teacher was judged on how well he transmitted to the pupils in school the knowledge and skills outlined in the curriculum, and largely as a result of this attitude, the efforts at orienting students towards community work was dropped from the college curriculum. In 1962, a UNESCO Report urged that "the teachers' role in the rural community needs to be carefully considered within the framework of social development and economic plans and his training should take cognisance of this."[21] But despite these pleas, there was very little change in this situation until the 1970s. Then, with a desire to implement a socialist philosophy of development, the Government increasingly expected teachers to play a more active part as "change agents" and "change pushers" in the rural areas. As a result, the Teachers' College once again introduced a programme to teach skills that would

[20] *Daily Argosy*, 14 August 1947.
[21] UNESCO, "Memorandum to the Minister of Education," p. 3.

be useful for working on community projects. But the programme was still in its formative stage, and it was not possible to make any assessment of its success.

Summary and Observations

Reviewing the developments in teacher education during the 1945-1973 period, two major problems were noted in this area. The first was the need to expand the existing teacher training facilities, bearing in mind the cost implications of such a move. The second was the problem of recruiting into primary school teaching youngsters who had a good secondary education background. From an examination of the historical evidence, it can be seen that little was done directly by the colonial administration to grapple with either of these problems. On the latter issue, it was observed that the supply of secondary school graduates to primary school teaching increased during this period, but not because of any planned Government action; it was largely due to the increasing number of graduates from the private secondary schools who could not find employment in their usual job market—mainly the civil service. As a result, many began to take up primary school teaching, a field of employment which such graduates formerly felt was "infra dig" for them.

The colonial administration also took little action towards expanding the facilities for teacher education. In fact, every step made since the 1940s to increase the number of teachers in training was taken by an elected Government. This started modestly in 1953, with a decision to increase the annual intake into the Teachers' College from twenty to thirty, an increase of 50%, and culminated in the massive teacher education programme which began in 1963. Other efforts at increasing facilities for teacher preparation, such as the establishment of a College of Education and the introduction of various teacher education programmes at the University of Guyana, were made by subsequent elected Governments.

These actions highlight the differences between a Government which holds office as a result of popular support and one which does not. The former obviously has to be more responsive to popular demands. In addition, as the Guyanese masses became more involved in the political process, they came increasingly to realize the potential of their newly-gained political power. Therefore, unless their demands were met, they were likely to refuse support in the future and to transfer it to some other competing political group. This is why democratic regimes must have what is referred to as "higher responsive capability" to the demands of the general populace.

It was not that all policy makers in the elected Governments were necessarily more concerned than all colonial directors of education with raising educational levels in the country. The contribution of Major Bain Gray belies this assumption. But the major source of the difference between these two groups in their response capacity to public demands lay in the different source of legitimacy for their holding of office and in the limitations imposed or possibilities opened up to them by the nature of the system in which they were operating. For example, the ultimate source of authority among the colonial civil servants rested with the British Government and stemmed from the legal relationship between the metropole and the colony, between the "exploiter" and the "exploited." The civil servants who represented the metropolitan Government wielded much political power but had little political responsibility to the population. Their responsibility was to the colonial authority and therefore they could more easily ignore popular pressures or demands. Also, because of the more limited access to information, public opinion on some of these issues was not as widespread as it was in the post-independence period. In fact, if decisions made by civil servants were technically sound, they could usually count on the colonial authorities for support. This situation, in which the policy-makers were not usually accountable for their decisions to the populace, made technical, rational decisions more possible.

In short, when outputs from the political system in terms of policy decisions can be independent of inputs in terms of popular political support, then those who administer the system can more easily make decisions based on technical considerations alone. In the eyes of the colonial administrators, education costs in Guyana were rising too rapidly and were already out of proportion to the economic resources of the country. Hence, the technically right decision for them was to do nothing that would further aggravate the situation; hence, no action was taken to increase teacher training facilities in the country.

The Minister of Education in a popularly elected Government, on the other hand, had no similar haven in which to hide, no Colonial Office to offer him umbrage from the masses if he made a technically right decision but a politically unpopular one. And it was very difficult for his Government, if it wanted to continue receiving popular support, to remain inactive, especially if such inaction was likely to result in a further deterioration of the situation which triggered the demand. This is what happened with the output of trained teachers between 1945 and 1953, and again between 1953 and 1957, when colonial civil servants were responsible for formulating policies on such issues.

In developing countries, where the masses are not likely to have much experience in adjusting political demands to economic resources, it is often difficult, in the short run, to educate the population about resource limitation and still maintain popular support, especially when opposition parties are indicating that they will meet these demands if returned to office. In such a situation, the Government attempts to meet as many of the popular demands as possible. Their choice of priorities is often based on the strength of the pressure exerted and not necessarily on the economic wisdom of the decisions. In many ways, this is not altogether different from the workings of even more sophisticated democratic political systems.

A second factor was the nature of the political system in which the colonial administrators worked. Colonial Governments were essentially concerned with the economic exploitation of the resources of the colonies and not primarily with "educational development" of the colonized. In the context of latter-day colonialism, there were two principles that guided administrative action. The first was that only services which the colony could finance from its existing recurrent budget should be provided. This principle, it was felt, had assumed greater importance with the promise of eventual self-government to the territories in the region. The second was that if the population strongly opposed a measure, it should not be foisted on them unless it was necessary to support the structure of the colonial administration. In other words, since stability was a necessary precondition for successful exploitation, it meant that the colonial authority would not normally approve any step which would likely upset this stability.

An example of the application of the first principle was seen in the opposition of the C.D. & W. Educational Adviser to any subsidy from the Imperial Government to meet the recurrent costs of providing these needed teacher training facilities. In his report, Hammond remarked, "I consider that for wider reasons the meeting of a permanent recurrent expenditure on teachers' salaries should be regarded as an appropriate responsibility of the West Indies themselves. Self-government was incompatible with a permanent subvention from Imperial Funds."[22] His stand on this issue was firmly supported by the colonial Government. An example of the second principle was seen in the decision of the various colonial Governments in the West Indies not to proceed with Hammond's scheme for diluting the teaching staff of their primary schools any further, due to popular opposition to such a proposal.

The result was that the Directors of Education had to work within these policy parameters, and could not make any decision on the assumption that the existing structure would change. In fact, they accepted the premise that their role was not to change the existing structure. Eric Williams, commenting on the Hammond Report, which he observed was limited to the existing economic and social structure of a colonial society, made this the focal point of his criticism

---

[22] Government of Great Britain, Colonial Development and Welfare, *The Future Cost of Education*, p. 28.

when he wrote, "Mr. Hammond subtly gives the impression that the British West Indian revenues have reached saturation point and are fixed for all time . . . he accepts the existing structure."[23]

Ministers of Education in elected Governments could, however, through their membership in the Cabinet and the principle of collective responsibility, influence their colleagues to change priorities and introduce new tax measures to finance a service which the public was demanding. In short, elected Governments did not necessarily have to accept the structures imposed by an existing system, but where necessary could attempt to change these if such a change was considered desirable. This made it possible for Ministers of Education in an elected Government to be more responsive to popular demand. In Guyana, the masses were putting great faith in education as an instrument through which their children could better be prepared to enter the increasingly competitive job market with some chance of securing one of the desired higher income jobs. The primary school was the first step in this direction, and hence parents were becoming increasingly concerned about the quality of the primary teaching staff. They continuously mounted pressures on the various elected Governments to improve the facilities for teacher preparation.

It is difficult to estimate the relative importance of the popular pressure exerted on the Government in its decision to accept the massive teacher education programme of 1963 as against the amount of support which the Minister of Education anticipated in advance from the population if he were to introduce such a measure. But certainly both factors were influential; every measure to increase the number of trained teachers in the primary schools was to some extent stimulated by popular pressure and, more importantly, received considerable public support.

The growing importance of popular political pressure explains, to a large extent, why elected Governments cannot easily ignore educational problems on which the population is seeking action. It also throws light on the rapid expansion of educational services in many developing countries which have just achieved independence. In fact, in most cases these political considerations have become more important than economic ones in explaining the educational explosion occurring in most third world countries. And it must be remembered that even the autocratic regimes in some of these countries cannot continue to exist without some degree of popular support; they, too, must be responsive to increasing popular demand for services such as education.

[23] Eric Williams, "Education in the Dependent Territories in America," *Journal of Negro Education* Vol. 15, No. 3 (Summer 1946), pp. 534-51.

5. Secondary Education

The most outstanding feature of post-1945 developments in Guyanese education was the tremendous growth in public demand[1] for secondary school facilities and the efforts made, first by the private sector and later by the Government, to meet these demands. As a result, secondary school enrolment, especially in the post-1960 period, was increasing much faster than enrolment in the primary schools. A major reason for this was that primary education was already available in 1945 to nearly every child of school age and the possession of a secondary education was becoming the minimum qualification for entry to the more remunerative jobs—which happened to be the white-collar jobs—in the society.

In his 1948 Annual Report, the Director of Education noted that "a very large demand exists for the type of secondary education which is designed to lead to the professions, or failing that a 'white collar' job."[2] And two years later, commenting on the increase in the number of entries for overseas examinations (entries for the secondary School Certificate Examination rose by 27% between 1947 and 1950), he observed that "the very large demand for the (academic) type of secondary education ... shows no sign of abating."[3] In November 1949 the *Daily Argosy* reported that "recent years have witnessed an unprecedented urge after secondary education for their children, on the part of the masses of this country" with the result that "within the past decade such schools [private secondary schools] have sprung up like mushrooms all over the colony to satisfy this public craving for secondary education."[4] A few years later, in a more moderate tone, the editor again observed that "the great majority of parents in the com-

[1] The term "demand" is used by economists to refer to people's *willingness* and *ability* to purchase a commodity. Since education in Guyana was increasingly being provided as a "free" or highly subsidized commodity, the term "demand" is used here to refer to people's desire for education and their willingness to utilize the educational services provided. There is no essential difference in these two usages since when a commodity like education is provided "free" to the consumer the willingness to use it becomes a more important consideration than the ability to "purchase" it. Obviously, as the students get older the opportunity cost of education rises and even when it is offered as a "free" commodity, ability to sacrifice alternative earnings to receive an education becomes an important aspect of cost and affects the consumer's ability to make use of it, i.e., his demand for it.

[2] Government of British Guiana, *Annual Report of the Director of Education 1948*, p. 8.

[3] *Ibid., 1950*, p. 29.

[4] *Daily Argosy*, 11 November 1949.

munity are now deeply anxious, more than ever before, for their children to obtain the best possible education [i.e., academic secondary education about which the editor was writing] . . . which they see as the key to future economic and social status and individual happiness."[5]

Elected legislators and other interested groups also commented on this growing popular demand for more secondary education. In 1955 the British Guiana Teachers' Association (B.G.T.A.), which represented primary school teachers, passed a resolution calling on the Government to establish more grammar schools and to increase the number of scholarships available to them. The principal of St. Stanislaus College, probably the best private secondary school in the country, reported an increase of 115% in the number of those applying for entry into that school between 1949 and 1953.

One factor which contributed somewhat to the growing demand for education at the secondary level was the general improvement in personal incomes which occurred during the war years; with the then existing import restrictions, many lower middle class families began spending part of their incomes on secondary education for their children. In addition, the buoyancy of the job market for secondary school graduates, due to the increasing demand for teachers and junior level civil servants, also made parents more willing to invest in this level of education for their children.

Some indication of the rate of increase in the Government services can be seen in the fact that the nation's recurrent budget doubled (at current prices) between 1946 and 1952, and before that, between 1942 and 1946, the rate of increase was even higher. Inflation was a negligible factor in this increase, which stemmed largely from an expansion of Government activities. The capital budget fared even better because of the substantial flow of funds from the C.D. & W. grants during and after the 1940s.

The increase in demand for secondary education after 1945 was also a reflection of the fact that due to the war, there was an accumulated shortage of more highly educated personnel in the professions, preventing Guyanese students from pursuing studies in the United Kingdom, where they traditionally received their tertiary level education. In addition, a number of C.D. & W. scholarships were made available to all British colonial students after 1945 and candidates needed a good secondary education to qualify for them.

Lastly, with the political developments of the post-1940 period, the elected members of the Legislature began to exert greater pressure for Guyanese to be given preference in the recruitment of personnel for the public service and even for the private sector. All these factors, along with some of those mentioned previously as contribut-

[5] *Ibid.*, 12 July 1953.

ing to the increase in primary school enrolment, were responsible for the growing demand for secondary education. By 1952 the Director of Education was still commenting on the "great demand [which existed] for secondary education as this leads to the professions, the civil service and to teaching."[6]

Meeting the Demand

The response to this increasing demand for secondary education came at first from the private sector, mainly through the entrepreneurial activities of individuals. Some of these were formerly nongraduate teachers, other unemployed graduates from the U.S.A., whose qualifications were generally not recognized for employment in the public sector, and some who simply saw the provision of private secondary education as a very profitable field of activity. It was only after self-government and independence that the Government really became involved in providing additional secondary educational facilities to help meet this growing demand.

Table 24 *Comparison of Increase in Enrolment in Primary and Secondary Schools, 1945 to 1960*

Year	Secondary school enrolment	Primary school enrolment	Enrolment in Government secondary schools only
1945	4,858	61,734	625
1960	11,484	125,348	1,089
Absolute increase between 1945 and 1960	6,626	63,614	464
Percentage increase between 1945 and 1960	136	103	75

Source: Census, 1945 and 1960; Government of British Guiana, Annual Reports of the Director of Education or the Ministry of Education (Georgetown, 1945 and 1960).

Between 1945 and 1960, according to the census figures, the number of pupils attending secondary schools increased by 136% (about a 9% increase per annum), as compared with an increase of 103% (about 6.8% per annum) in primary enrolment during the same period (see Table 24). The small absolute increase in the enrolment at

[6] Government of British Guiana, *Annual Report of the Director of Education 1952*, p. 36.

the Government secondary schools during this period indicates that these schools did not respond readily to the increasing popular demand for this level of education. They took less than 9% of the additional secondary school population and the remaining 91% were enrolled in the private secondary schools.

However, after self-government was achieved in 1961, there was a steady increase in the number of and enrolment in Government-owned and Government-aided secondary schools, which together rose from 6,975 in 1960 to 24,897 in 1973. This represents an increase of 275% or about 19.8% per annum, which was over twice the rate of increase (9%) experienced during the previous fifteen years. The result was that Government-owned and Government-aided schools enrolled 80.4% of the secondary school population in 1972, as compared with 39.3% in 1960.

Government Response to Increased Popular Demand for Secondary Education

Prior to 1960 the Government's involvement in secondary education was minimal and up to the 1940s it owned and operated one secondary school. In the development plans drawn up just before the end of the war, it had proposed to take over and rebuild the Bishop's High School, which became the first Government-owned girls' secondary school, and to rebuild and enlarge Queen's College, the only existing Government boys' secondary school, to accommodate 50% more students. This was the full extent of the Government's commitment to secondary education in these years.

But by the mid-1940s the Government was already having second thoughts even on these modest commitments, when it became increasingly concerned about the ability of the economy to absorb the products of the grammar schools. The Director of Education commented on this point in his Annual Report, stating that job opportunities for secondary school graduates were limited, and therefore, "from an economic point of view, no expansion of the grammar school or academic type of education is called for, unless some other outlet for the ex-school pupils is provided."[7] This personal assessment of manpower needs, even within the structure of a colonial society like Guyana, was myopic since it failed to take into account the expanding civil service, the teaching force, and the opportunities which increasingly became open in the private sector for Guyanese with this level of education. Another source of error in the Director's assessment was his assumption that the existing relationship between education and occupation was fixed. He, therefore, did not envisage secondary school graduates moving into other fields of employment, notably

[7] *Ibid., 1948*, p. 8.

Table 25 *Increase in Secondary School Enrolment, 1960 to 1973*

School year ending August	(a) Enrolment in Government-aided secondary schools	(b) Enrolment in Government-owned secondary schools	Total	(c) Enrolment in private secondary schools	(a+b+c) Total enrolment in secondary schools
1960	5,889	1,068	6,975	4,509	11,484
1962	7,397	1,254	8,651	6,070*	14,721
1964	7,271	4,025	11,296	6,070*	17,366
1966	8,125	6,339	15,178	6,070*	21,248
1968	8,751	7,621	16,372	6,070*	22,442
1970	8,920	10,383	19,303	6,070*	25,373
1972	9,026	14,438	23,464	6,070*	29,534
1973	9,515	15,382	24,897	6,070*	30,967

* Enrolment figures were not collected for private secondary schools but the figure of 4,509 was calculated from the 1960 Census. The UNESCO Mission of 1962-63 reported an enrolment of 4,670 in the twenty-five largest private secondary schools but there were at least twenty others from which it was unable to collect figures. For these schools the author estimated an enrolment of 1,400, making a total of 6,070 for 1962. Further it was assumed that with the rapid expansion of the Government secondary schools since 1962 and the fact that secondary education of a standard possibly superior to that offered in the private secondary schools was obtainable tuition-free in the all-age schools, the enrolment in the private secondary schools has remained fairly static.

Source: Census, 1960; Government of British Guiana, *Annual Reports of the Director of Education or the Ministry of Education* (Georgetown, 1960 to 1973).

primary school teaching, which in the past they tended to look down upon as a possible field of employment. But another concern of the colonial administration was that a large number of educated unemployed at this level might also begin to pose an awkward political problem.

The Government, therefore, became interested in converting this additional demand for an academic secondary education into a demand for a more "practical" type of post-primary education in which such subjects as agriculture, woodwork, and home economics would be offered. In pursuit of this policy, it announced in June 1945 its decision not to proceed with its earlier proposal to build a larger boys' secondary school. But this announcement met with tremendous public protest, especially from the urban middle class whose children would have been the major beneficiaries of such an expansion. The *Daily Argosy* noted that "few Government announcements within recent times have produced in the community a reaction so fiercely and universally unfavourable" with "a frank and hectic condemnation of Government's policy."[8] Once again the heavy criticism of the colonial administration by the population indicated how strongly the Guyanese public at the time felt about any plans to reduce educational services, either those already existing or those promised to them. The result of this pressure was that the Government decided, without further delay, to proceed with its original plans to rebuild and enlarge the boys' secondary school.

But the Government was not prepared, at the time, to go beyond this modest increase in accommodation which was provided in the two elite secondary schools. It would have preferred to put a curb on the further expansion of private secondary schools, but the public reaction to such a proposal proved so strong that this step was never taken. So the provision of additional secondary educational facilities was left almost entirely to private enterprise until the political changes of the 1950s.

Aid to Private Secondary Schools

Although there were regulations since 1929 under which government aid to secondary schools could be granted, there was in 1945 only one private secondary school, the Berbice High School in New Amsterdam, which was receiving any form of Government aid. In 1952, on a Private Member's Bill, the Legislature approved financial assistance to a Catholic secondary school for boys—the St. Stanislaus College located in Georgetown. But the Financial Secretary, who voted against the bill, warned members that such a step "would cer-

[8] *Daily Argosy*, 12 June 1945.

tainly open the door for pressure being exerted for grants-in-aid from other secondary schools."[9]

Many other efforts were made by legislators and others to get the colonial Government to increase the secondary school facilities in the country, but these met with little success. In the Budget Debate of 1949, Dr. Gonsalves reminded the Government that its two secondary schools were not providing enough places and urged it to extend these facilities to other sections of the society by granting subsidies to private secondary schools. Some time later, R. Jailall, speaking in a Legislative Council debate about the absence of a Government secondary school in Berbice, argued that "there is a lack of vision in this respect," and again in 1956, he observed that he had been repeatedly trying "to get a promise of help (from the Government) in this field but failed."[10] After the Interim Government had announced its intention in 1957 to grant aid to the private secondary schools, Ramphal, a former principal of a private secondary school and then a nominated member of the Legislative Council, observed that "there has been a crying need for help to the secondary schools for a long time."[11]

Standards were low in most of the private secondary schools and, although the Government had been aware of the fact, it did very little to help, fearing the financial repercussions of any decision it might take. In 1945 the Education Committee pointed out the need for Government to exercise some supervision over the private schools, especially those at the secondary level, and as a result of this recommendation and other pressures, a draft ordinance for regulating the academic and public health standards of these schools was prepared. But this proposal met with very strong opposition from the Private Schools Union on the grounds that no financial assistance was being offered by the Government to help existing schools achieve the recommended standards. And so no further Government action was taken for some time, despite the fact that the *Daily Argosy* kept up a steady attack on the poor academic standards of these private secondary schools, observing that their owners had turned the business of imparting knowledge into one mad scramble for certificates. The editor noted that many youngsters with the Cambridge School Certificates who applied for jobs in his company could not even write a proper application and he suggested that "the kind of rush teaching which they received did nothing to develop their capacity to think." Further, he observed that the poor teaching techniques used "brought the private schools in the front rank of money-making concerns,"[12] and called upon the Government "to give the public some

[9] Government of British Guiana, Speech by Financial Secretary, *Hansard*, 16 November 1957.

[10] See Speeches by R. Jailall *et al.*, *Hansard*, 4 February 1955 and 2 February 1956.

[11] J. Ramphal, Speech in *Hansard*, 2 February 1956.

[12] *Daily Argosy*, 11 November 1949.

measure of protection from these cramming institutions."[13] As he saw it, the value of their teaching was "practically nil except to squeeze the pupils through an examination that will produce the longed-for certificate," a process which produced students "who remain blissfully ignorant of the *King's English*."[14]

But despite the efforts of many individuals and groups, including the *Daily Argosy*, the Government still did nothing to regulate the standards of these private schools. The factors responsible for the Government's inaction were the cost that would have been involved if it was forced to extend aid to these schools and, secondly, the likely public opposition to any measure which might have resulted in the closing down of some of these schools because they could not, on their own resources, reach the prescribed standards.

However, with continued pressure from some groups, the Government in 1949 again produced another draft ordinance with the same features as the earlier version. Once more the Private Schools Union opposed the measure on the same grounds, arguing that while Government was seeking to impose higher standards on the private schools, it was not prepared to help them financially to achieve these standards. And, as in 1945, the Government withdrew its draft ordinance after the Private Schools Union protested against it.

These private secondary schools were very popular with the lower socio-economic groups, despite their low standards and the fact that they were indeed "cramming shops," as the *Daily Argosy* dubbed them. They provided the only available opportunity for their children to secure a secondary education at a price they could afford. The Private Schools Union was fully aware of this and sought the support of the public by indicating to them that any effort by the Government to enforce their standards without financial assistance would result in a closing down of these schools, "depriving the masses of secondary education, retarding the progress of the people and increasing crime and lawlessness in the society."[15] The Union argued, further, that the private secondary schools were in fact helping to meet a need "which every progressive country realizes is the duty of the Government to satisfy."[16]

This appeal to the public for support by the Private Schools Union on its stand of "no control without subsidization" paid off. The schools were too popular for the Government to close. And since the colonial administration was not prepared to grant financial assistance, it dropped all efforts to introduce its proposed regulations.

But apart from the stated aim of the Government, which was to raise the educational and public health standards of these schools, a

[13] *Ibid.*, 11 July 1947.
[14] *Ibid.*, 6 November 1949.
[15] *Ibid.*, 16 November 1949.
[16] *Ibid.*

very important unstated objective was to reduce the number of students graduating from secondary schools because of the fear that an "over-supply" of secondary school graduates might later have serious implications for political stability in the country. This was partly why, as the Private Schools Union quite correctly observed, the Government "was seeking to impose upon schools unaided by public funds, standards which were far from being attained in schools [referring to aided primary schools] which were, and have been for a considerable period, supported by the Government."[17]

Even though the *Daily Argosy*, which was never on the side of the private secondary schools, supported them over the issue of financial assitance, the Government remained unshaken in its decision not to grant them aid. These are the words of the editor:

> We believe that the time is ripe for a general revision of private secondary education in the colony, but that, if it is to be carried out as it should be, the Government must be prepared to assist the deserving schools to raise their standards to the required level. The result will be greatly to the benefit of future generations of Guianese.[18]

But the Government soon dropped the whole issue with the result that the standards in most of these schools continued to remain low. In 1950 the Director of Education admitted that

> hardly any of the private [secondary] schools can afford the equipment or the accommodation for a science course, even of the simplest kind; their curriculum is therefore almost entirely "bookish," the courses are dictated by the external examination syllabus and an education for life is very difficult to realize.[19]

The Venn Commission of Enquiry into the Sugar Industry made similar observations. It reported that

> Several estate managers told us despairingly that they found very few of the [secondary school] certificate holders who were able to apply their knowledge; in fact it seemed to be a reward for memory rather than intelligence.... Although these children have a larger stock of knowledge than most of their school fellows, it has scarcely better equipped them for life and work.[20]

The *Daily Argosy*, in December 1950, commenting on the Cambridge School Certificate passes by private secondary school pupils, observed, "some schools recorded in the results published earlier this year a 10% or a 20% degree of success. Others had 100% failure." In view of this the newspaper again called upon the Government to

[17] *Ibid.*
[18] *Ibid.*, 8 August 1949.
[19] Government of British Guiana, *Annual Report of the Director of Education 1950*, p. 29.
[20] Government of Great Britain, *Report of a Commission of Enquiry into the Sugar Industry of British Guiana*, p. 13.

apply "some sort of brake to curb the over-enthusiasm [or plain avarice] of some of the Colony's secondary schools."[21]

Despite the obvious political motives of some of these critics, there was no doubt that, in most of the private secondary schools, standards were low, teachers were poorly qualified and poorly paid, and education often took the form of rote learning.

But since the Government, for financial and political reasons, did nothing to afford the public the "protection" which the *Daily Argosy* sought, these private secondary schools continued "directing all their energies towards getting the greatest number of pupils through certain examinations, by hook or crook, regardless of their true education."[22]

The political changes of 1953, which gave the popularly elected representatives an important voice in both the Legislative and Executive Councils, resulted in a different attitude by Government towards its role in secondary education. In August 1953, four months after election to office, the Minister of Education announced that the Government would increase the number of scholarships to secondary schools and was pushing ahead with plans to grant aid to private secondary schools. But with the suspension of the constitution in October 1953, the elected Government did not have the opportunity to fulfill these promises and the issue of aid to private secondary schools remained in abeyance until 1957, when the Interim Government introduced its *Memorandum on Secondary Education* in the Legislature.

In March 1955 a Private Member's Bill was tabled in the Legislative Council for the establishment of "fully aided" secondary schools; even the *Daily Argosy*, which was always critical of the amount of Government expenditure on education, again called upon Government to provide some financial assistance in this field. It argued that:

> The country of British Guiana, with its greater need lags behind the colonies in the Caribbean in providing secondary education. . . . There is evidently an excellent case for aid to schools which can, or could, attain certain standards. We feel, therefore, that urgent consideration should be given to a scheme of State aid for up to eight or more secondary schools.[23]

But the Government did not respond to these pressures.

Meanwhile, the public demand for secondary education continued to grow, as can be seen in the number of private secondary schools of varying standards which were opened all over the country, some in response to the efforts of industry to help provide secondary education for children of its workers. In March 1956 the cornerstone of a new Lutheran High School was laid; in September 1957 the

[21] *Daily Argosy*, 12 December 1950.
[22] *Ibid.*, 8 August 1949.
[23] *Ibid.*, 20 April 1955.

Demerara Company announced the award of secondary school bursaries to children of sugar workers. This was followed by a similar announcement by the Booker Group of Companies in 1959. In February 1959 a new science laboratory for the Hindu College was declared open; in January 1954 St. Stanislaus College announced plans for a new, three-stream grammar school, and by September 1959, a new high school established by the Demerara Bauxite Company opened its doors to children of bauxite workers.

However, just before it left office in 1957, the Interim Government tabled a *Memorandum on Secondary Education* to provide financial aid to private secondary schools which achieved certain standards. One of the first tasks of the newly-elected Government was to implement the proposals embodied in the memorandum which aimed at raising academic standards in private secondary schools, broadening their curriculum, improving their physical facilities such as laboratories, etc., and bringing about a more even geographical distribution of secondary school facilities throughout the country. The Government offered to assist these schools by providing recurrent grants towards teachers' salaries, and special grants for the teaching of science, home economics, woodwork, and commercial subjects. Schools had first to qualify for these grants by reaching certain standards set by the Ministry of Education. It was hoped that the overall effect of this financial aid would be an improvement in the quality of the staff, including an increased percentage of graduates, a decrease in pupil/teacher ratio, and a broadening of the curriculum of these schools to include courses in subjects other than those traditionally taught in the academic grammar schools.

The plans for increased Government participation in secondary education found support among most legislators, and the public in general saw it as an acceptance by Government of "the responsibility for the total educational needs of the country" and the first major step in the "creation of a national system of education." Various members of the Legislative Council effusively praised the new measure as a "beacon of light in the field of secondary education," "a charter for the development of the educational programme of the colony," "a new deal for education,"[24] epithets which indicated the increasing importance which Guyanese were now attaching to this level of education.

Of the fifteen schools which applied for aid, nine qualified immediately, and by 1962-63, six more were added to the list. In 1969 the Government completely took over one of them, the Berbice High School, but after this there were no further increases in the number of aided secondary schools because of a change in policy.

[24] See Government of British Guiana, Debate on the 1957 Memorandum on Secondary Education, in *Hansard*, 23 May 1957.

There were many reasons for this de-emphasis on aid to private secondary schools, including the problem which arose because these schools were using the "surplus" funds from their operations for capital improvement of school buildings, which in some cases were private property. The stand taken by the Ministry of Education for basing admissions entirely on students' achievement at the Common Entrance Examination was another issue, one with which the Catholic secondary schools did not fully agree. The result was that the Government proposed, in 1963, to assume responsibility for financing and staffing these aided secondary schools, collecting fees and paying a rental fee for the buildings. The Government's rapid expansion of its own secondary school facilities might be seen partly as an attempt to pressure aided schools to come within the ambit of Government control. However, no agreement was reached between the Government and the aided secondary schools. The Government, instead, continued its efforts to increase the numbers of its own secondary schools. The eventual outcome was that in 1976 the P.N.C. Government nationalized all private schools, including the aided secondary schools.

Equalizing Opportunities for Secondary Education

In their expansion of secondary education facilities in the post-1957 period, the elected Governments were guided by two major considerations. The first was to ensure that whatever secondary educational opportunities existed, they should be equally open to all sections of the population. The second was eventually to provide secondary educational facilities for all Guyanese. Considerations of equity became quite dominant in the period following self-government and independence (equity being interpreted as better representation of all groups, especially the lower socio-economic groups and the rural population in the secondary schools). In September 1962 the Minister of Education, the Hon. C. V. Nunes, in a public statement indicated clearly that this was one of the major objectives of his Government which

> is committed to the policy that in future all sections of the community should have equal chances in life. This means that working class children must be given better opportunities for securing a secondary education. . . . Government has recently made certain decisions with regard to secondary education which are aimed at a progressive implementation of our goal of secondary education for all. . . . It will now be possible for children in most areas of the country to obtain secondary education.[25]

[25] Government of British Guiana, *Statement by the Minister of Education, C. V. Nunes* (Georgetown: Ministry of Education and Social Development, 8 September 1962).

Prior to the 1960s attendance at a secondary school was largely dependent on parents' "ability to pay" for the education. In other words, the demand factor then exerted a strong influence on the expansion of secondary education; this meant that secondary education was largely available to children of higher income groups and those living in the two urban centres. Even though private secondary schools were later opened up in the few rural areas with a heavy population concentration, the children of the lower income groups, especially in these areas, continued to have very limited opportunities for securing secondary education.

But, since 1963 this picture has been changing rapidly. The establishment of a large number of Government secondary schools throughout the country, the abolition of fees in these schools and the virtual freezing of those charged by the aided secondary schools, resulted in the parents' socio-economic background being of less importance in securing a secondary education for their children.

Looked at from another angle, after 1963 the "supply" factor had become the dominant one in accounting for the increased enrolment in Guyanese secondary schools. Seen in terms of investment theory, this substantial reduction in the private cost of education made it a field of investment more within the financial resources of the lower income groups and the resulting increase in the rate of return to the individual made it a more attractive investment to all sections of the population.

It might be argued that since the major part of the private cost of education, especially from this level on, is usually in foregone incomes, then those in the higher socio-economic groups who are financially more able to forego present earnings still have a better chance of obtaining a secondary education. While this is essentially true, students' foregone earnings were becoming less important as an element in the private cost of education in Guyana due to the shrinking population engaged in agriculture and the heavy rate of unemployment among the youths. Over 40% of the entire age groups under 19 years in the labour force was unemployed in 1965; this figure was likely to be higher if only those without a secondary education were being considered.

In such a situation, the actual increase in the supply of secondary education facilities was in itself important in achieving a more egalitarian distribution of educational opportunity at this level. Incidentally, it cannot be assumed, as many Guyanese political leaders have done, that this brought about a more egalitarian social structure. This is a question which in itself needs empirical investigation, although one suspects that with the existing income differentials between those with a secondary education and those without, coupled with the heavy rate of unemployment, there might have been an even less egalitarian

_ | x^2

distribution of incomes between these groups in the country in recent years. O. J. Francis had already indicated that this was beginning to happen when he commented on the Guyanese economic situation in the mid-1960s.[26]

Steps Toward Providing Secondary Education for All

As early as November 1959 the Minister of Education had announced to the Legislature that the Government had plans for "free secondary education for all," since it regarded this level of education as "indispensable to national development."[27] While there is no evidence that any concrete plans for providing "free secondary education for all" existed, one would have thought that, at the time, this declaration was out of touch with the economic realities of the country. But such an observation would have ignored the increasing importance of political factors as against economic ones in influencing educational policy decisions.

In 1963 the Government decided to increase drastically the number of secondary school places available in the country, and buildings originally constructed for primary and all-age schools were opened up instead as secondary schools. The result was that the number of pupils enrolled in the Government-owned and -aided secondary schools increased by about 62% between 1960 and 1964. The new Government, which took office at the end of 1964, continued this policy of secondary school expansion—it was one of the most popular of all Government programmes. The result was that by 1972 about 38% of all Guyanese children between the ages of 12 and 16 years were attending academic secondary schools. If to these 27,069 pupils were added the 36,094 who had completed at least six years of primary schooling and were enrolled in the "secondary divisions" of the all-age schools, we find that just over 80% of Guyanese children between the ages of 12 and 16 were receiving some form of secondary education in 1972.

It will be recalled that the all-age schools offered an academic type of secondary education leading to the College Preceptors Examination, after which successful students could enter an ordinary secondary school. After completing an additional two or three years of study they would take the G.C.E. Examination. So in effect, a very large percentage of Guyanese students over the age of 12 were provided with opportunities to follow an academic secondary school programme which most of them hoped would lead to the G.C.E. "O" Level Examination.

[26] Francis, *Report on Survey of Manpower Requirements*.
[27] Government of British Guiana, Speech by the Minister of Education, in *Hansard*, November 1959.

Another move by the Government was to ensure that secondary education was also avilable in the rural areas. In 1957 when an elected Government took office again, the two Government-owned and all the better private secondary schools were located in the capital city or in New Amsterdam, the only other city in the country. The only rural area which had secondary schools of some acceptable standard was the heavily populated Corentyne Coast, while the remainder of the rural population had no easy access to good secondary schools.

One stated objective of the 1957 *Memorandum on Secondary Education* was to get a more even geographical distribution of secondary educational facilities in the country. But this objective was not being achieved, since rural schools found it difficult to reach the standards required by the Government to qualify for financial assistance and still remain solvent. As a result, political pressures were exerted on the Government to assume direct responsibility for establishing rural secondary schools. In March 1958 a Private Member's Bill was introduced in the Legislature calling for the establishment of secondary schools in those rural areas where no such facilities existed. But while the bill was easily passed no immediate action was taken until 1961, when the first rural Government secondary school was opened up on the Essequibo Coast. After that and specifically between 1963 and 1968, twenty-one new Government secondary schools were established in the rural areas, as compared with only three more in the two urban centres during the same period. By 1969 every educational district was served by one or more Government or Government-aided secondary school.

Table 26 gives the number of primary and all-age schools per Government-aided and Government-owned secondary school in each educational district in 1972, along with the number of secondary school pupils per 1,000 primary and all-age pupils in these districts. It is obvious from these figures that there were still marked inequalities in the distribution of secondary educational facilities, with the more populated areas (which include the two cities and the Corentyne Coast) being the best served, while the more remote areas (Essequibo, North West District and the Interior) were the ones where children had the least opportunities. But as indicated before, this situation represented a considerable improvement over the pre-1957 period, when the rural areas, with the exception of the Corentyne Coast, had virtually no good secondary school. It should be noted that these secondary schools were not specifically regional institutions, but since they had no boarding facilities, it meant that they drew their students mainly from surrounding areas. This practice was later reinforced with the institution of regional scholarships. The only major exceptions were the two elite secondary schools, which, because of their prestige, attracted students from all over the country.

Table 26 *Distribution of Government and
Government-Aided Secondary Schools in
Guyana in 1972 by Educational District*

Name and type of district	Approximate no. of primary and all-age schools per secondary school	Approximate no. of secondary school pupils in district (in Government and Government-aided secondary schools) per 1,000 primary and all-age school pupils
Georgetown (urban)	2.3	317
Corentyne (mainly rural)	4.1	158
New Amsterdam (mainly urban)	14.6	114
West Berbice (rural)	10.3	94
East Coast Demerara (rural)	11.0	84
East Bank Demerara (rural)	11.0	83
West Demerara (rural)	11.0	80
Essequibo (rural)	22.0	53
Interior (remote rural)	26.0	22
North West District (remote rural)	34.0	11

Note: The two elite Government secondary schools were excluded from the above table since they normally drew their population from all over the country and could not strictly be regarded as regional secondary schools.
Source: Calculated from Government of Guyana, *A Digest of Educational Statistics 1971-72* (Georgetown, Guyana: Ministry of Education, 1973).

The Issue of Quality Versus Quantity in Secondary Education

While there were undoubtedly increased opportunities for all Guyanese to attend separate secondary schools, the question which arises was whether the education offered in these new schools was of comparable quality to that provided prior to the 1960s. Were the public pressures for secondary education so great that the Government was in fact providing Guyanese with increased opportunities to secure a lower quality of secondary education? This is not an easy question to answer. The major issue here is how to assess the "quality" of secondary education; this problem is compounded by the lack of agreement among educators as to what is "good quality" education. However, despite this problem, educators are likely to agree that the educational background of the teaching staff gives some indication of the "quality" of education offered by the schools. Beeby, in his book *The Quality of Education in the Developing Countries*,[28] went so far as to argue that the changing level of education and training of teachers was the most useful single index of changes in the quality of education being offered in a country. Therefore, in assessing whether there were qualitative changes in secondary education, the level of qualification of the teachers, and more specifically the percentage of them who were university graduates, will be used. In this exercise, the Government-aided schools will be considered separately from the Government-owned secondary schools.

In 1957-58, when the first secondary schools were granted aid, the percentage of graduates on their staffs was just over 36%; but as can be seen from Table 27, the situation deteriorated over the next decade.

Table 27 *Number and Percentage of Graduates in the Aided Secondary Schools between 1958 and 1972*

School year	Total no. of teachers	Total no. of graduate teachers	Percentage of graduate staff
1957-58	98	36	36.7
1961-62	281	55	19.6
1961-63	279	50	17.9
1963-64	278	52	18.7
1965-66	293	51	17.4
1967-68	317	64	20.2
1969-70	331	69	20.8
1971-72	340	95	27.9

The percentage of graduates in the aided secondary schools dropped from 36.7% in 1957-58, reaching its lowest point of 17.9% in 1962-63, after which it improved moderately. By 1967-68 the figure

[28] Beeby, *The Quality of Education in the Developing Countries*.

stood at 20.2%, and by 1971-72 it had reached 27.9%, which was still below the minimum target of 30% envisaged in the 1957 Memorandum. Part of the reason for the reduced percentage of graduate staff in the aided secondary schools after 1958 was the rate of increase which took place in the student population of these schools, unaccompanied by a corresponding rate of increase in the number of their graduate staff. But between 1963 and 1968, the number of these aided schools did not increase substantially; the increases took place among the Government secondary schools instead, and the supply of graduates began to improve with the output of degree holders from the University of Guyana after 1967. Another factor which affected the number and quality of teachers in these schools was that they were not only paid lower salaries than those in the two established Government secondary schools at the time but their general conditions of service were also poorer; e.g., they had no leave, no pension facilities, and no security of tenure.

Cost was undoubtedly the most important reason why Government was not more generous to these schools from the beginning. An opposition member of the Legislature drew attention to the marked discrepancies in Government expenditure on the aided and the Government-owned secondary schools when, in the Budget Debate of 1963, he noted that "for two Government (secondary) schools with about 1,000 pupils half a million dollars is provided, while for 12,000 children who attend other secondary schools only $86,000 is provided."[29]

With such poor salaries and conditions of service, the aided secondary schools attracted mostly teachers with lower-level qualifications, with the better qualified ones tending to regard their jobs as temporary. The 1962 UNESCO mission, commenting on this situation, reported:

> One school with a total staff of 16 had had 18 changes in the last 18 months, 10 of the staff who had left had gone to the United Kingdom, mostly for higher studies while the other 8 had taken up posts in the civil service since they could command a better salary there than in the school. . . . A school with a staff of 44 had lost 28 of its staff in the course of 1961-62. Half of these had proceeded on higher studies and seven had left for better paid jobs.
>
> Even the older denominational schools which have a stable nucleus of members of their respective religious orders have a high turnover of lay staff. One denominational school has started, most commendably, a scholarship scheme of its own. . . . It is now considering stopping the scheme on finding that the returning graduates soon leave for the Government secondary schools.[30]

[29] Government of British Guiana, Speech by R. Cheeks, in *Hansard*, 23 January 1963.

[30] UNESCO, "Report of the UNESCO Educational Survey Mission," p. 57.

The general conclusion was that the educational standards in these aided secondary schools were falling during the decade from 1958 to 1968.

Looking next at the Government-owned secondary schools, it is necessary to distinguish between the two older, elite schools and the newer ones opened in the post-1960 period. Using every conceivable measurement (percentage of graduate staff, per capita expenditure on pupils, suitability of accommodation, school equipment, success at external examinations, etc.), these elite schools had much better standards than the newly-established Government secondary schools. In fact, there was a tacit acceptance by the various elected Governments that the prestigious position of these elite schools in the secondary system should continue, especially since their prestige was to a large extent related to their pupils' superior academic performance. So, rapid expansion of secondary education had not adversely affected the educational standards in these two elite secondary schools.

But for the newly-established Government secondary schools (those opened after self-government and independence) the situation was quite different. The desire to expand secondary education and at the same time to keep costs down, resulted in the fact that these new schools were in every way of poorer quality than the older Government secondary schools. For many years, in fact until 1967, their teachers were paid at the same rate as teachers in the primary and all-age schools, with small additional allowance for graduate status. This resulted in a poorer quality staff than in the elite schools (judged in terms of academic qualifications), and even when similar salary scales were introduced, the percentage of graduate staff, as can be seen in Table 28, continued to remain much lower than that in the older secondary schools.

The figures in Table 28 show clearly that the new Government secondary schools remained consistently behind the older ones in terms of percentage of graduate teachers on staff. An important point was that, apart from the prestige of the older secondary schools, the newer ones were scattered in the rural areas, some even in the more remote areas of the country. This was partly responsible for their failure to attract more graduate teachers. In addition, on account of their size (about 25% of them had an enrolment of less than 100 in 1968), it was very difficult to envisage them providing the range of educational experiences normally associated with a secondary school.

Further, a study of students' G.C.E. "O" Level Examination results for June 1973 also revealed superior academic performance in every subject area among those attending the older Government secondary schools. This can be seen in Table 29.

While the overall percentage pass was about twice as high for the older Government secondary schools as for the newer Government

Table 28 *Comparison of Staff by Graduate Status in the
Older and Newer Government Secondary
Schools, 1964 to 1972*

	Older, elite Government secondary schools			Newer Government secondary schools		
School year	Total staff	No. of grads	Percentage of grad staff	Total staff	No. of grads	Percentage of grad staff
1963-64	59	40	67.0	117	36	30.0
1965-66	66	56	84.5	126	32	15.0
1966-67	67	48	71.6	305	57	18.7
1967-68	67	53	79.1	321	91	28.3
1968-69	70	48	68.6	379	95	25.1
1969-70	72	52	72.2	465	125	26.9
1970-71	79	57	72.2	569	126	22.1
1971-72	76	57	76.0	654	166	25.4

Source: Government of Guiana, *Annual Reports of the Director of Education or the Ministry of Education* (Georgetown).

Table 29 *Comparison of the Performance of Pupils from
the Two Older as against the Newer
Government Secondary Schools at the G.C.E.
"O" Level Examinations, June 1973*

Subject areas	Percentage of passes in the older Government secondary schools	Percentage of passes in the newer Government secondary schools
English	74.1	22.5
Other Languages	72.5	17.5
Other arts subjects	53.5	37.6
Mathematics	72.5	42.4
Science subjects	69.8	31.2
All subjects	66.4	33.7

secondary schools (66.4% as against 33.7%), the difference in performance in languages (including English) and sciences was even more marked. It was only in the "other arts" subjects—history, geography, etc., and to a lesser extent mathematics—that this sharp difference in performance was somewhat lower.

There were many factors contributing to this difference in levels of students' performance. First, the older secondary schools attracted students with the highest Common Entrance Examination scores. Also, they had better qualified teachers and more facilities, a fact reflected in their higher per capita recurrent cost. Furthermore, the limited enrolment of some of the newer secondary schools affected the quality and range of the educational programme they were able to offer. Up to 1972 15% of these schools had an enrolment of less than 150 pupils; in some the total enrolment was less than fifty. The quality of the teaching staff in these smaller schools was also poorer because of their size and location, making it difficult for them to attract the same quality of teachers as the larger schools in the more populated areas.

Therefore, while the Government was pushing ahead since 1963 with its plans to increase secondary education opportunities, the quality of this education, judged by such indices as the percentage of graduate teachers, per capita expenditure, pupils' success at the G.C.E. "O" Level Examination, etc., was not as high as that previously provided.

However, while this was so, it would be myopic not to look at the indications for the future. In 1963 the Government also established the University of Guyana (U.G.), with the first batch of students obtaining their degrees in January 1968. About half of the students were teachers and have continued as such on graduation. The result was that 186 of the total 365 graduates from U.G. (about 51%) were teaching in the all-age and secondary schools by 1972 and most of the younger teachers in the primary schools who obtained their degree later transferred to these schools. Also in 1966, the University started a diploma in education course for graduate teachers in the secondary schools; 168 graduates had completed this course of professional training by 1973. So, while there was a reduction in the quality of secondary education offered in the newer secondary schools during the decade following the massive expansion of facilities, there were already indications that the situation was improving. The enrolment in degree courses at the University of Guyana had increased by 50% between the academic years 1963-64 and 1972-73, and largely because of the lack of alternative employment opportunities, slightly more than half of these graduates continued on as teachers, mainly in the secondary schools. In addition, in the 1970s the Government agreed to a unified salary scale for all secondary school teachers, resulting in an improvement in the proportion of graduates in the aided and newer secondary schools. Between 1962 and 1972, the percentage of graduates in the aided secondary schools moved up from 17.9% to 27.9%, while in the newer Government secondary schools, the increase was from 15% in 1965-66 to 25% in 1971-72.

Democratizing Entry into the More Prestigious Secondary Schools

The Government, in pursuit of its policy of equalizing educational opportunities, not only provided more secondary school places throughout the country but also began to "democratize" entry into the elite secondary schools. Guyana had developed a stratified secondary school system, and with the expansion of secondary educational facilities of admittedly lower quality, the competition for entry into the better secondary schools became keener.

The classification of these schools by the prestige they enjoyed was as follows:

The Elite Secondary Schools (a) the two Government elite secondary schools—Queen's College (Q.C.) and Bishop's High School (B.H.S.) which prior to 1957 were the only two Government-owned secondary schools in the country, and (b) the three Catholic secondary schools—St. Stanislaus College, St. Rose's and St. Joseph's High Schools. Established in the nineteenth century, they were among the oldest aided secondary schools in the country.

The Non-Elite Secondary Schools comprising (a) the other Government-aided secondary schools, and (b) the newer Government-owned secondary schools.

This stratification among secondary schools was partly a reflection of the relative academic performance of their pupils, with those attending the elite schools doing much better at the external examination than those in the non-elite schools. This difference can be seen in the percentage of passes at the G.C.E. "O" Level Examination in June 1973.

Table 30 *Percentage of Passes at G.C.E. "O" Level Examination among Pupils Attending the Elite and Non-Elite Secondary Schools, June 1973*

Type of schools	Percentage of passes
Elite Government secondary schools	66.4
Elite aided secondary schools	53.9
Other Government secondary schools	33.7
Other aided secondary schools	27.3

Source: G.C.E. "O" Level Examination Results, June 1973.

The superior performance of pupils in the elite secondary schools was further reflected in every subject taken at the "O" Level Examinations. This fact was borne out in an analysis of the June 1972 results, in which the performance of students in the different subject areas in the elite schools was compared with all others who took the examination that year.

Table 31 *Comparison of the Performance of Pupils in the Elite Schools with All Other Candidates Who Wrote the G.C.E. "O" Level Examination, June 1972*

Subject areas	Percentage of passes	
	Pupils in elite schools	Other candidates
English	82.8	18.1
Other languages	60.2	21.3
Other arts subjects	62.5	28.6
Mathematics	67.4	34.6
Science	63.3	22.1

Source: G.C.E. "O" Level Examination Results, June 1972.

In addition, the ethnic groups of lower status (the Africans and the East Indians) were under-represented in the student body of the elite schools. The available empirical evidence to support this point is almost nonexistent and the author can only draw on some figures collected by a doctoral student from Harvard in 1968, which give some information about the ethnic composition of four secondary schools—one from each group. Table 32 is based on this very limited data.

There were many problems in trying to interpret the following data. For example, Herman McKenzie, a Guyanese sociologist at the U.W.I. (Jamaica), pointed out the difficulty in distinguishing between "Mixed" and "Africans" in Guyanese society. Nevertheless, the figures do indicate a degree of under-representation of the lower status groups in the elite secondary schools.

In the days of the colonial administration, little attempt was made to ensure that all students had an equal chance of entering the elite secondary schools. In fact, the upper middle-class groups successfully resisted such efforts and expressed the fear that the "character" of these institutions would be adversely affected if they had too large an entry of scholarship holders. So, between 1945 and 1961, the number of scholarships to these elite secondary schools increased very slowly, from 25 to 70 in sixteen years. When in the mid-1940s the demand for secondary education began to increase, the suggestion was made to abolish the preparatory forms which offered primary education to the children of the higher socio-economic groups and to make use of the vacancies created to provide more secondary education. But in 1949, when an elected representative, D. P. Debiden, proposed to the

Legislature that these preparatory forms be abolished and the size of the secondary school proper increased accordingly, he found only one other member, Dr. C. B. Jagan, willing to support his proposal. When the Government raised the fees of these schools by 25% in 1952, one legislator pointed out that there were "whispered allegations" that this increase was to "prevent the admission of undesirables" into these schools, while another openly expressed the view that the main purpose was to make these institutions more exclusive.

In 1953, when the Minister of Education indicated the need to make the Government elite schools more open to other sections of the society, the *Daily Argosy* took him to task over his announcement, asking "Is he pandering to the whims and feelings of what he calls 'the people'?"[31] Even when the 1957 elected Government decided to abolish the preparatory forms in these schools, one nominated member of the Council, the Hon. Lionel Luckhoo, strongly opposed this step, arguing that "to suggest there is a snob complex at work and that there is discrimination in these schools is a wild statement,"[32] even though the figures at the time indicated that 60% of all entrants to the secondary division of these schools had come through their preparatory forms. One can see from the above remarks how deeply embedded was the elitist and exclusivist nature of these older Government secondary schools in the country's educational history.

From 1957, commencing with the abolition of the preparatory forms, entry to these schools was increasingly democratized. This began with the increases in the number of scholarships available to primary school students. For example, while in 1947 about 70% of the students at Queen's College were paying fees, the figure had fallen to 58% by 1958, and by 1964 all entrants to these schools were holders of "free places," recruited on academic performance at the secondary schools entrance examination. The same principle of admission was extended to all the Government-aided and the newer Government secondary schools. The result was an increasing representation of children from the lower socio-economic groups in the more prestigious secondary schools, a fact which could partially be substantiated by a comparison of the parental background of their free place winners in 1962 and 1963. Vide Table 33.

The information here indicates that, while the largest percentage of free place winners came from lower-middle class parents, nearly one-third of them in 1963 had parents who were manual workers, including farmers, as against a comparable figure of 25% in 1962. A further analysis indicates that between 1961 and 1963 the changes were steadily in the same direction.

[31] *Daily Argosy*, 14 August 1953.
[32] Government of British Guiana, Speech by Lionel A. Luckhoo, in *Hansard*, 3 May 1957.

Table 32 *Ethnic Composition of Pupils in Four Secondary Schools in Guyana, 1968*

Ethnic group	Representation of ethnic group in population (1960 Census) (%)	Representation of ethnic groups in different types of secondary schools			
		Older Government boys' secondary school (%)	Catholic boys' secondary school (%)	Other older aided secondary school (mixed) (%)	Newer Government secondary school (mixed) (%)
Europeans	0.4	3.0	5.0	0.0	0.0
Portuguese	1.0	1.0	21.0	3.0	0.7
Chinese	0.6	7.0	10.0	8.0	0.0
Mixed	11.9	31.0	26.0	6.0	5.5
Total	13.9	42.0	62.0	17.0	6.2
East Indians	50.2	33.0	18.3	41.0	64.0
Africans	31.3	24.0	16.7	42.0	29.1
Total	81.5	57.0	35.0	83.0	93.1
Amer-Indians	4.6	1.0	3.0	0.0	0.7
Total of all groups	100.0	100.0	100.0	100.0	100.0

Table 32 *Continued*

Note: Each school had an enrolment of at least 350 pupils. Also, there was a religious factor involved here because the Catholic schools still gave preference to students of their own religious persuasion. Since the Portuguese in Guyana were mainly Catholics their heavy representation in the Catholic secondary school was a reflection of this admission practice.

Source: Data collected in a survey done by Hon-Chan Chai, a doctoral student at Harvard in 1968.

Table 33   Socio-economic Background of Parents of Free
Place Winners to the Elite Secondary Schools,
1962 and 1963

	Percentage of free place winners in each group	
Socio-economic group	1962	1963
Executive and professional	29.8	19.2
Teachers, clerical, and white-collar workers	33.5	41.4
Small businessmen and shopkeepers	11.0	6.0
Skilled, semi-skilled, and unskilled workers	22.2	29.5
Farmers	3.5	3.8

Source: M. K. Bacchus, "Social Factors in Secondary School Selection in British
Guiana," *Social and Economic Studies*, Vol. 15, No. 1 (March 1966).

Curriculum Changes in Secondary Schools

To understand the nature and reasons for curriculum changes in
Guyanese secondary schools, one must realize that the elite schools,
with their greater prestige, exerted a great influence on the whole
pattern of secondary education in the country.

Also, the Guyana Scholarship, which was awarded annually to the
student with the most outstanding performance at the Higher School
Certificate (later the G.C.E. "A" Level Examination), exerted considerable pressure on the nature of the curriculum offered in the secondary schools. This scholarship crowned the very selective system of
secondary education and allowed the winner to proceed to university
studies in the United Kingdom. It was looked upon by every
Guyanese as the zenith of achievement in secondary education and
competition for it was mainly from the students attending the elite
secondary schools. Between 1882 and 1945 nearly 80% of all Guyana
scholars were students from Queen's College.

Pressure for Curriculum Reform

An examination of the various historical documents which
touched on the question of curriculum reform in the secondary
schools in Guyana revealed that the influential local committees or
individuals who made recommendations on this subject usually
excluded the elite schools from the ambit of their suggested changes.

Even when curriculum reforms were proposed for Queen's College, they were not meant to affect the educational programme of the brighter boys in the more prestigious classical division of the school.

There were a number of "transient foreigners" who had urged that secondary school curriculum reform should start with these elite schools, but such recommendations were generally looked at askance and even with hostility by those living in the country. These locals, who defended the retention of the schools with their heavy emphasis on the arts, especially the classics, were aware of the general unsuitability of this type of curriculum to the Guyanese environment but felt that suggested changes could best be introduced in the non-elite schools.

The 1925 Educational Commission, which consisted mainly of local residents, was "of the opinion that most of these [non-elite secondary] schools adhere too strictly to the secondary [academic] type of education: but to suit the needs of the colony [they] should emphasize the practical side at the expense of the literary, e.g., all [these] schools should teach science, including Hygiene and Physical Training, and the curriculum for girls should include cooking, laundry, needlework, housekeeping and the course for boys, manual training in wood and metal." But these recommendations were not to apply to Queen's College, then the only elite Government secondary school, whose curriculum was to "continue to remain organised as at present."[33]

The only dissenting voice came from the "transient foreigner" on the Commission, Wynn Williams, an H.M.I. (Her Majesty's Inspector) from the United Kingdom, who obviously disagreed with this "hands off" policy towards the Government elite secondary school. In a separate appendix to the Memorandum he wrote:

> The time has come when the object and purpose of this school should be considered in light of modern requirements. The main objective is to train boys for the professions and the university. The course of prescribed studies is severely and exclusively academic and in this respect a little behind the times . . . the inappropriateness of the syllabus for the purposes of the majority at the school may be seen at a glance: they may be suitable for certain types of secondary schools in England but they certainly do appear to be in the highest degree artificial, especially as regards the teaching of science for secondary schools in the tropics. It is almost a scandal that manual work should be entirely neglected in the principal school of the Colony where so much depends on the industrial life of the community, upon the introduction of a highly skilled element in agriculture and upon applied sciences generally.[34]

He also noted that the regulations of the Guyana Scholarship unduly influenced the curriculum of the Queen's College, with the

[33] Government of British Guiana, "Report of the Educational Commission 1925," p. 10.

[34] *Ibid.*, Appendix D, p. ix.

result that "no encouragement is given to the future captains of Industry, Commerce and Scientific Agriculture, notwithstanding the fact that it is in these directions that the colony is in the most pressing need of development."[35] In support of his observations Wynn Williams drew attention to the recommendations of an earlier (1917) committee which urged "the teaching of science to be directed to the Botanical, Agricultural, and Mineral Resources of the Colony." But, as he noted,

> this valuable report was in due course presented to the Governor, but it appears to have been entirely ineffective. The old regime with its venerable adherence to an out-of-date system of examinations is still maintained and no attention appears to have been paid to the recommendations of the distinguished men who laboured in vain to adapt the curriculum to modern requirements.[36]

To reduce the dominating influence of the Guyana Scholarship on the curriculum of the Q.C., he suggested that the examination requirements be "revised in such a way that students who gave promise of being highly proficient in agriculture, geology, sugar technology and some cognate science should be eligible for the scholarship if not given preference over all other types of students."

In conclusion Williams observed that

> no serious attempt is made to arouse and cultivate in the children abiding interests in their surroundings, no effort is made to penetrate the secrets of scientific husbandry and to interest the children in the countless wonders of nature in which the Tropics abound, and the attraction of biology, geology, and entomology, are passed up in favour of the Anarchy of "Stephen's Reign" or the "Religious difficulties of Queen Elizabeth."[37]

He further commented on the reluctance to change among the teachers of the secondary schools, who had "reached the high water mark of conservatism," and defended the existing position "with vigour and single-minded conviction." Even suggestions for reform of less important details were, according to Wynn Williams, "looked upon with deep suspicion and ill-disguised disfavour" while the "tyranny of examinations" were regarded with "feelings amounting to religious fervour."[38] Perceptive though he was, Williams failed to realize how the structure of Guyanese society influenced the curriculum of Queen's College at the time, a point which will be developed later.

In 1933 the Marriot Mayhew Report made a similar criticism of the curriculum of the secondary schools in the West Indies and re-

---

[35] *Ibid.*
[36] *Ibid.*, Appendix D, p. xiii.
[37] *Ibid.*, Appendix D, p. xiv.
[38] *Ibid.*, Appendix D, p. xiii.

commended that "a new and additional type of [secondary] school is needed providing *courses of instruction that are practical in the broadest sense* . . . directed essentially to the stimulation of interest in the *pupils' social and industrial, agricultural and commercial pursuits.*"[39] (Emphasis added.)

Incidentally, the Royal Commission which visited the West Indies after the release of the Marriot Mayhew Report observed that the recommendations for "modern secondary schools" aroused a great deal of opposition in the region.

In 1942 the C.D. & W. Educational Adviser was still urging the Government to review the place and function of secondary schools in the educational system of Guyana as a first step to reforming their curriculum. Influenced by the Spens Report in Britain, Hammond saw a great need for introducing other forms of secondary education besides the academic types, even "perhaps greater in a country where an outstanding need is that young people should be brought up to be constructively minded and apply their minds and wills to the development of the resources of the environment."[40]

Because there was then only one Government-owned secondary school in Guyana (Queen's College), Hammond suggested that the curriculum of this school be widened along the lines suggested in the Spens Report to include a secondary technical and a secondary modern stream in addition to a grammar school stream. Further, in order to secure local support for his proposals, Hammond pointed out that his suggestions were based on the Report of the Consultative Committee in England, "so that those who consider these suggestions may know that what is proposed is not something peculiar in British Guiana but is in line with progressive thought in the British tradition of secondary education."[41] But even these efforts to give respectability to his proposals by indicating that they were "in progressive thought" in the metropole did not result in their acceptance locally.

Efforts to reform the secondary school curriculum were again renewed in 1957, when the Government was preparing its Memorandum on Secondary Education. Staff from the Ministry of Education had discussions with many interested groups about the nature of the secondary education which the Government should provide. Reports from these Ministry officials indicated that many groups, especially the elected members of the various local authorities, demanded that any new secondary school should offer education of the grammar school type.

[39] Government of Great Britain, Colonial Office, *Report of a Commission on Secondary and Primary Education in Trinidad*, prepared by F. C. Marriott and A. Mayhew, Col. 79 (London: H.M.S.O., 1933), p. 86.

[40] Government of Great Britain, Colonial Development and Welfare, *Memorandum on Education in British Guiana 1942*, p. 47.

[41] *Ibid.*, p. 49.

The 1957 Memorandum suggested a diversification of the secondary school curriculum, mainly in the aided schools, through the introduction of a number of "practical," including commercial subjects, which students could offer at the G.C.E. Examination conducted by the Associated Examinations Board in England. What was proposed was the establishment of bilateral schools in which there would be two streams of pupils: those who might later take up more advanced studies at universities or elsewhere and those likely to terminate their studies at the end of their secondary school course.

The Government emphasized that both groups would be studying for G.C.E. Examinations, though one might be doing "a different range" and possibly fewer subjects. In addition, these schools were to plan courses which would be

> better suited to the majority of West Indians who will live their lives in the West Indies and who will need to have the sort of educational background and training which will be rooted in the culture and traditions of this area, which will give a better understanding and knowledge of the territories and which will better prepare children for living in them.[42]

The Government definitely tried to convey the impression to the public that, while the curriculum of the secondary schools would be broadened, their academic orientation would remain. As the Chief Secretary, who introduced the bill in the Legislative Council, explained, "we are not proposing to reduce academic standards but to broaden the basis of them."[43] The general point made to members of the Council during the debate was that "practical subjects" would be less emphasized as compared with the "academic subjects," and this was largely responsible for the tremendous approbation which the bill received in the Legislature. Another factor which contributed to the popularity of these proposals was that they indicated that the elite secondary schools would be left relatively untouched. The Memorandum made this point quite clear when it stated that "it is important that there should be at least one or two schools of high quality to which might be attracted the best brains in the community and the best teachers."[44]

At the time when the private secondary schools applied for aid, the subjects which they offered were, according to the reports made by the officers of the Ministry of Education, mainly in the humanities including English Language and English Literature, Geography, History (usually English History), Mathematics, and Latin. Along with these there was another group of subjects including Religious Knowl-

[42] Government of British Guiana, *Memorandum on Secondary Education 1957* (Georgetown: Daily Chronicle, May 1957), p. 10.

[43] Government of British Guiana, Speech by the Chief Secretary, in *Hansard*, 23 May 1957.

[44] Government of British Guiana, *Memorandum on Secondary Education 1957*, p. 13.

edge or Scripture, Health Science, Economics (mainly a study of the economic structure of the United Kingdom), and British Constitution, all very popular in the private schools. Their popularity rested on the belief that students could more easily secure a pass in these subjects at the G.C.E. "O" Level.

There were, therefore, great hopes that, with the financial assistance that was being provided to these secondary schools after 1957, they would be able to broaden their curriculum and offer a variety of new courses including the sciences, woodwork, home economics, technical drawing and commercial subjects, all of which could be offered at the G.C.E. "O" Level Examination.

The Curriculum Changes which Occurred

Gradually some changes did take place in the curriculum of the secondary schools. As science became more popular in the public and grammar schools in Britain, the subjects assumed more importance in the local elite schools. At Queen's College, the dominance of the classics was gradually reduced and the sciences moved up in importance. This can be seen in the figures in Table 34, which show the average number of classical and science subjects taken by Queen's College students at the School Certificate Examination between 1933 and 1956.

Table 34 *Entries for Classical vs. Science Subjects by Queen's College Students at the School Certificate Examination, 1933 to 1956*

Year	Total no. of students writing School Certificate Examination	Average no. of Classical subjects taken	Average no. of Science subjects taken
1933	36	.83	1.00
1936	47	.76	1.23
1945	55	.40	1.56
1956	138	.49	1.59

Source: Examination Entry Records for Queen's College.

From the 1960s on, the rise in popularity of science and the decline in the classics was even more marked. In 1967 Queen's College had a total of 311 entries in the science subjects—Chemistry (101), Physics (101) and Biology (109)—and only thirty-seven in Latin. In 1971 the entries in Latin had dwindled to seven while the three science subjects had a total of 333 entries. By 1972 Latin had disappeared from the curriculum while the science subjects continued to increase in popularity. At the G.C.E. "O" Level Examinations, the number of entries in the three science subjects from students at Queen's College between 1971 and 1973 was around the same as for the three most popular arts subjects—English Literature, History, and Geography.

In 1957 a course in Technical Drawing was offered by the Government Technical Institute for boys at Queen's College and St. Stanislaus', and while the course was subsequently dropped, it was later reinstated in Queen's College. In 1956 Spanish was introduced at Queen's College, and in 1960 Economics also found a place in the curriculum and was later offered at the G.C.E. "A" Level Examination. In the three elite girls' secondary schools, home economics and commercial subjects were also introduced, even though they were taught mainly to the less able students in these schools.

In addition, many of the newly-aided secondary schools made efforts, though with limited success, to teach some science, especially biology. But apart from these, few other changes were made in the curriculum of the secondary schools, especially in the newly-aided ones. In 1959 the *Daily Argosy* commented that "in this colony one of the problems continues to be the undue influence of bookish and theoretical traditions on the part of our education,"[45] and later, in 1962, the UNESCO team observed that one of the failures of the secondary schools was

> the lack of diversification of curricula to include practical subjects such as commercial studies, woodwork, home economics and even science.... The emphasis on examinations meant the cutting out of "frills" and the inclusion of those subjects likely to give an "easy pass"— scripture and the theoretical subjects, British History, etc. Many schools limit the classroom work to the examination subjects which most readily lend themselves to theoretical teaching and memorization learning. Home economics education and commercial studies were provided in the same two schools that offered these subjects before the introduction of grants-in-aid; woodwork and metal-work and agriculture or science with an agricultural bias in none. The very schools which should provide alternative courses to meet the needs of the wide-spread ability of their pupils are working straight jacketed curricula on outmoded lines.[46]

The above observations were very similar to those made six years previously by the staff of the Ministry of Education, which reported on the programmes offered in those schools before they began receiving aid. It was obvious from these comments that few of the curriculum changes envisaged in the 1957 Memorandum had occurred by 1963. The arts subjects still dominated the curriculum, although

[45] *Daily Argosy*, 23 September 1959.
[46] UNESCO, "Report of the UNESCO Educational Survey Mission," p. 57.

there was more local flavour in some of the subjects, e.g., West Indian history began rivalling English history for popularity with the return of a number of history graduates from the University of the West Indies who went into secondary school teaching. The sciences were becoming more popular because Guyanese were beginning to take up university studies in science-based fields such as agriculture, engineering, and geology, due to the increased availability of jobs in these areas. Yet not much success had been achieved with science teaching in the non-elite schools. The 1962 UNESCO mission noted that rote learning, popular in the aided secondary schools, even extended to the science subjects such as chemistry and physics.

The new Government secondary schools established between 1963 and 1972 also followed the path of the existing aided secondary schools in structuring their curriculum. In this they were partly influenced by such constraints as lack of finances and facilities. But probably more important was the fact that the public was not too concerned with what was taught in these schools as long as they prepared students for the G.C.E. "O" Level Examinations.

Still perturbed by the fact that "secondary education in Guyana has been traditionally academic,"[47] the Government, in the late 1960s, attempted another breakthrough in curriculum reform with the proposed establishment of "multi-lateral" secondary schools, and more recently, community high schools. The main purpose of these schools, some of which came into existence in September 1974, was to reduce emphasis on the "academic" content of secondary education in Guyana by introducing students to such subjects as home economics, agriculture, and commercial studies. It was hoped that this greater orientation towards technical and agricultural fields will produce more "self-reliant" individuals in accordance with the national goals set out for the society by the Government. A $25-million(G) project was launched with loans from the International Bank of Reconstruction and Development and the International Development Association (IBRD/IDA) to establish these schools.

One gets some idea of the subjects which were more heavily emphasized in the secondary schools in Guyana up to 1972 from the subject entries for the G.C.E. "O" Level Examination presented in Table 35. The figures relate to the entries for the G.C.E. "O" Level Examinations in January and June 1972 and show the relatively heavy emphasis which was still placed on the arts subjects. These, along with languages and literature, accounted for nearly 56% of all entries, while the sciences (physics, chemistry, biology, botany, etc.) accounted for only about 22%. The technical subjects (domestic science, handicraft, technical drawing), on which so much emphasis was placed in the

[47] Government of British Guiana, *Nine Year Report 1965-73* (Georgetown: Ministry of Education and Social Development, February 1974), p. 62.

1957 Memorandum, made up less than 1% of the entries. The "popularity" of English language (12,234 of the 14,326 candidates—
85.4%—who entered for the examination took English language as a
subject) could be explained largely by the fact that jobs in the civil
service or teaching nearly always required a pass in this subject. In
addition, little or no attention was devoted to subjects not offered at
the G.C.E. examination.

Table 35 *Total Number of Entries by Subject Groups for
the G.C.E. "O" Level Examinations Held in
Guyana in 1972*

Subject group	No. of entries in group	Entries in groups as percentage of total entries
Languages		
English	12,234	
Other languages	1,721	13,955	23.5
(French, Latin, Spanish, etc.)		
Arts		
History, Literature, Art, Religious Knowledge, Geography, British Constitution	19,181	32.3
Total		55.8
Commerce		
Economics, Commerce, Accountancy	5,150	8.7
Sciences		
Physics, Chemistry, Biology, Food and Nutrition, etc.	917	21.8
Mathematics	7,681	12.9
Technical subjects		
Technical Drawing, Handicraft, Needlework	461	0.8

Source: Government of Guyana, *A Digest of Educational Statistics 1971-72* (Guyana:
Ministry of Education, September 1973).

Factors Responsible for Curriculum Changes

There were many factors responsible for this relative lack of curriculum change, especially in the aided and newer Government secondary schools. These included scarcity of qualified teachers and the

insufficiency of capital for the necessary woodwork shops and facilities needed for teaching some of the subjects which it was suggested that these schools should offer. But the two major functions of the secondary schools were even more important in accounting for the pace and direction of the curriculum changes taking place. These two functions were: (a) the socialization of potential Guyanese elites into the "elite culture" of the society—a role which was performed by the elite secondary schools; and (b) providing students, especially those from the lower socio-economic groups, with an opportunity of obtaining a "passport" to enter into one of the relatively high paying and secure jobs in the modern sector.

While this second function was performed by both types of secondary schools, it was the raison d'etre for the non-elite schools.

The role of the more prestigious secondary schools in socialization of the potential elite became increasingly important as they enrolled more children from the non-white lower-status groups in the society. In addition, because of the rigidity of the stratificatory system, elite status was not "up for grabs" through a process of open competition. It was more carefully regulated and only a few persons were selected for training and subsequent recruitment into elite membership. In other words, while upward social mobility was possible, it was of the type described by Turner as "sponsored mobility."[48]

It was partly because of this that the colonial Government preferred that secondary education be available only to a limited number of Guyanese, and it explains why it never departed from its policy of having very few secondary schools (in fact, only two) which, in nearly every respect, were comparable to the best grammar schools in England. The colonial administration was not concerned with providing equal opportunities for secondary education or even with equal chances for all sections of the population to enter its existing secondary schools.

The elite schools drew their population mainly from children of the higher socio-economic groups, although efforts were always made to admit a few pupils from the lower classes who had, on academic performance, qualified for entry. In the nineteenth century, the pupils at Queen's College were predominantly from the "middle and upper classes" (mainly local Europeans), though interest was shown in attracting children from among the "better class" of the other ethnic groups. In 1877 the Principal of Queen's College, in his Annual Report, specifically mentioned the need to attract "the better class of Portuguese and others" into that school. At the same time, he tried to assure the members of the more elite groups that their children would

[48] R. H. Turner, "Sponsored and Contest Mobility and the School System," in *The Sociology of Education: A Sourcebook*, ed. by Robert R. Bell and Holger R. Stubb (Homewood, Ill.: Dorsey Press, 1968), pp. 219-35.

not be excluded from the school because of its academic standards. While noting that these standards were "high enough for the universities" he pointed out that they were "not too high or too exclusive for the ordinary education of sons of the middle and upper classes, whether they are going into business, the colonial service or any other line of life."[49]

Through a few open scholarships, a small percentage of lower class children were gradually admitted to the elite schools. In defending Queen's College against the attack that there was "too much classicality" and too little "practical learning," the Chief Justice once observed that "one of the inhabitants of this country, a *black man*, had gained sufficient knowledge in this very institution to be sent *home* (i.e., to England), where he was studying theology to be a Minister" and argued that "there were others in the school of equally low degree who ought to be given every help in obtaining this education." The state, as the Chief Justice saw it, ought to encourage "in the poor as well as in the higher orders" the ambition of obtaining an education "that will raise them to the position of judges and legislators."[50]

Despite this expressed liberal attitude to the education of the lower classes, the policy was to keep this group relatively small. Up to 1945 only about 20% of the students in the two elite Government secondary schools were scholarship winners with most of them coming from the middle classes.

Socialization into elite culture, as Turner observed for English society, involved the acquisition of certain attitudes, interests, and special skills which are usually different from those shared by the masses.[51] The English grammar schools became valued for their role in the "cultivation of elite culture" and their programmes

> were built about highly specialized study in fields wholly of intellectual or aesthetic concern and of no "practical" value. Hence ... the protective attitudes towards and interest in classical subjects ... and the great importance of accent and grammatical excellence in the attainment of high status in England.[52]

The elite secondary schools in Guyana also played a similar role in elite preparation, and since the culture of the Guyanese elites was essentially based on the culture of the English elites, the local grammar schools naturally used the same curriculum as their counterpart institutions in England. When Queen's College was first established, the major concern was to "keep up efficiently the full course taught on the classical side of an English Public School or First Grade Gram-

[49] Government of British Guiana, *Report of the Principal of Queen's College 1888* (Georgetown: Queen's College), p. 15.

[50] Quoted in Norman Cameron, *A History of the Queen's College of British Guiana* (Georgetown: F. A. Persick Ltd., 1951), p. 19.

[51] Turner, "Sponsored and Contest Mobility," pp. 225-26.

[52] *Ibid.*, pp. 230-31.

mar School."[53] Latin was compulsory for all new entrants, and over a quarter (28%) of the instructional time in the third, fourth, and fifth forms and 44% in the sixth form was devoted to the teaching of the Classics. In contrast, science was taught only in the fourth, fifth, and sixth forms and was allocated only about 12% of the total instructional time. On the school's speech night in 1872 the audience was entertained with a whole range of very esoteric items, including recitations from "Horace's Ode to Augustus," a translation from Virgil, parts of Achilles and Agamemnon in Homer, Ovid's "Fabiorum Clades," and "Anchisis Umbrea and Aeneas" from Virgil.[54] In 1917 a committee appointed to look into the work of Queen's College urged that Latin should be taught throughout the school with Greek as an optional subject, and recommended that the Principal should always be "a Classical Honours graduate of a residential British University," usually Oxford or Cambridge. Further, the committee made it clear that the proposed introduction of commercial subjects was not to affect the time allocated to the Classics. While the dominant role of the classics changed over time, Latin remained a compulsory subject on the curriculum of Queen's College until about 1955.

As in the training of potential English elites, great emphasis was placed on a good command of the "King's English" as a crucial hallmark of a sound secondary education. For this reason, Guyanese or West Indians, even with honours in English from British universities, were not considered suitable candidates to teach this subject at Queen's College until the 1950s. Teachers of English at this school had to be from Britain.

In general, preference was given to employment of British teachers, since they were thought to be the best persons to introduce these selected Guyanese into the culture of the metropolitan elites. Because of the nature of their role, a lack of knowledge of the local environment was seen as no handicap to their work. Eric Williams, the Prime Minister of Trinidad who was educated in a similar elite school, noted that

> the total disregard of the [West Indian] environment was naturally pronounced in the secondary school, with a staff, English by birth, training, sympathy or all three. The superiority [of such an education] consisted in the public eye, precisely of the British culture and disparagement of the West Indian.[55]

Also, as would be expected of institutions engaged in the training of elites, the behaviour in public of Queen's College boys was a matter on which great emphasis was placed; the standards of decorum used

---

[53] Government of British Guiana, *Report of the Principal of Queen's College of British Guiana 1880*, p. 4.

[54] Cameron, p. 67.

[55] Eric Williams, *Inward Hunger: The Education of a Prime Minister* (London: André Deutsch, 1969), p. 35.

in assessing their behaviour was that of English gentlemen. In one of
its early editions, the school gazette commented on the unsportsman-
like attitude of those boys who booed the umpires' decision, behaviour
which the gazette observed "is an unheard of occurrence on the part
of an English crowd, looking on at a cricket match."[56] Even as late as
the 1960s, Queen's College boys were forbidden to smoke in public,
even away from the school premises, if they were wearing the school
tie or uniform.

The emphasis on what were once considered gentlemanly activities (performance in sports, especially cricket, membership of the
volunteer corps, etc.), also indicates the concern of the staff in preparing these youngsters for elite roles in the society. In the Principal's
report of 1888, he proudly drew attention to the fact that five members of the Georgetown cricket team "in the last important cricket
match" were boys from Queen's College, "*the rest being boys from public
schools at home*," while "in the newly formed 'C' Company of Volunteers *mainly composed of young men from home*, we are represented . . . by
over 25% of the numbers"[57] (emphasis added).

Manual activities were "infra dig" for boys in this school, and, up
to the 1960s, were used as a form of punishment. In the 1950s, when
there was an increase in the number of students coming from the
lower middle and working-class homes, the Principal was very anxious
to stress those extra-curricular activities, such as art, music, drama,
and poetry, which would help prepare these young men to lead a
"cultured" life.[58]

Another point was that general acceptance of the values of the
ruling British group was necessary if these potential Guyanese elites
were later to be relied upon to play a trustworthy role in the colonial
administration. Prithipaul,[59] in a very perceptive study of secondary
education in Mauritius, has shown how the British, after taking possession of the island from the French, attempted to reform the curriculum of the elite secondary school—the Royal College—with a view
to socializing the local French children to accept the general cultural
orientations of the new colonizing power, to learn its language, and in
the long run to transfer their support to it. In Guyana, one sees that
historically, as the different ethnic groups displayed their acceptance
of British and especially English culture, they were progressively allowed to hold senior administrative positions in the country's civil
service.

[56] *The Queen's College Gazette* Vol. 4, New Series, 13 March 1884, De Nostris Rebus.
[57] Government of British Guiana, *Report of the Principal of Queen's College 1888*,
p. 10.
[58] "Address by V. J. Sanger-Davies," Principal of Queen's College, 15 December
1952, p. 1. (Mimeographed.)
[59] D. Prithipaul, *A Comparative Analysis of French and British Colonial Policies of
Education in Mauritius 1735-1889* (Port Louis, Mauritius: Imprimerie Ideal, 1976).

Reasons for Popular Support of the Curriculum of the Elite Secondary Schools

There were many reasons for the strong popular support for the type of curriculum which the elite schools offered and which most educationists considered "irrelevant to the needs of the Guyanese society." First, the role of secondary education as an instrument of elite preparation was one which the upper middle class groups in the society wanted to perpetuate. This is why they were opposed to the proposed changes in the curriculum of these schools to make them "more relevant to the needs of Guyanese society." The training of potential elites could not be reconciled with the teaching of wood-work, agriculture or even the "applied sciences." Further, these subjects did not appear on the curriculum of the English public and grammar schools, which were the reference institutions for the local elite schools.

Secondly, this "irrelevant education" was still functional to the students. For some, the qualification obtained at the end of the secondary school course meant a reasonably rewarding position on the job market. For others, it secured direct entry into a higher education institution in the metropole.

Also, Guyanese, like other colonials, felt it necessary for psychological and economic reasons to compete with their colonizers in the same educational game conducted under the same rules. They, therefore, did not want an education which was different from that being offered in the metropole. Hence, they insisted on having the curriculum of their secondary grammar schools identical with that of the "best schools in England," even if it led to such ridiculous situations as flying biological specimens from England for students in the tropics to do the necessary dissection for the English biology examinations. Shirley Gordon, writing on the development of secondary education in the West Indies, observed that "in most cases they [the West Indians] welcomed a pale replica of English secondary or public school education as a means of showing that they could qualify in the same way as Englishmen for the posts that Englishmen filled in the West Indies."[60]

Eric Williams, commenting on his own educational experience, also noted that while the type of secondary education which was offered at his school was not "the type that was distracted by the West Indian environment" it was nevertheless the type which was "fully endorsed by the community." As an indication of this, he mentioned how, as he walked up and down in his home "reciting the Latin tenses beginning with *amo, amas, amat, amamus, amatis, amant,*" his father "beamed indulgently the while."[61]

[60] Gordon, *A Century of West Indian Education*, p. 224.
[61] Williams, p. 32.

The marked preference by Guyanese for the humanities and the older professions as against scientific subjects continued long after Wynn Williams' observations were made, and is partly reflected in the fields of study taken up by Guyanese scholars between 1939 and 1954. Very few had pursued university courses in those subjects which Wynn Williams and others thought essential for the economic development of the country—fields such as agriculture, sugar technology, geology, engineering, etc. The arts subjects, along with law and medicine, were still the most popular prior to 1954. The sciences and engineering came far behind, as can be seen in Table 36.

Table 36 *Fields of Study Pursued by Guyana Scholars between 1939 and 1954*

Field of study	No. of students	Percentage of total
Arts (including Law)	9	43
Medicine	8	38
Science	3	14
Engineering	1	5
Total	21	100

Source: Government of British Guiana, *Annual Reports of the Director of Education or the Ministry of Education* (Georgetown, 1939 to 1954).

The situation shown in Table 36 was similar to what it was in earlier years. Of the thirty-seven pupils from Queen's College who won the Guyana scholarship between 1882 and 1921, about 50% took up medicine, 37% the arts—including law and divinity—and only one student is known to have pursued a degree outside the traditional fields by studying agriculture.

Curriculum of the Non-Elite Schools

The curriculum of the non-elite secondary schools was strongly influenced by the academic nature of the programmes offered in the elite schools. This is why J. I. Ramphal, a former principal of a private secondary school and later a nominated member of the Legislature, could, in a Council debate on secondary education, say in all sincerity, "True enough we are told that we are trying to provide too much academic [secondary] education, *but there is no other education to provide*"[62] (emphasis added). The author recalls how, as late as 1964 when the Government began to establish its new secondary schools, many parents were still questioning whether their children were getting a

[62] Government of British Guiana, Speech by J. I. Ramphal, in *Hansard*, 19 February 1954.

real secondary education, since they were not doing subjects like Latin and French, traditionally taught in the elite secondary schools. But despite this influence, the non-elite schools faced severe resource constraints in their attempts to copy the curriculum of the elite schools.

Towards an Understanding of the Changes in the Curriculum of Secondary Schools

To understand why the curriculum changes which occurred at the secondary level took place, one has to look not at the recommendations of the various educators or educational commissions, but at some major changes taking place in the society.

With the constitutional changes leading to self-government and independence, there was increasing political pressure on the colonial administration to ensure a shift from ascriptive criteria—such as ethnicity and skin colour, to achievement criteria—mainly educational qualifications, in the selection of candidates for jobs. The pressures were first directed at the public sector and later at the large private companies.

Also, employment opportunities in those occupations which required a secondary education such as the civil service, teaching, etc., were improving rapidly at a time when total unemployment was deteriorating. This meant that secondary education was increasingly seen by parents, especially those of the lower income groups, as a necessary investment in their children's future.

Third, with the wave of egalitarian ideals accompanying political developments, such as the extension of the franchise to the masses and the granting of self-government and independence to the country, the content of "elite culture," which was previously based very much on English culture, was being challenged and was undergoing changes.

The first two changes (greater emphasis on achievement criteria in job selection and the increasing number of white-collar jobs, especially those requiring a secondary education) affected the amount of the demand for secondary schooling while the third (changes in the content of the culture of the "elite") affected the nature of the demand.

Many factors were responsible for the third change, including the fact that this "culture of the elite" did not contain many elements of the original Afro- or Indo-Guyanese culture. In fact the culture of most working class East Indians was probably furthest away from this "elite culture" of Guyanese society. So when the P.P.P. was returned to office in 1957 and 1961, largely with the support of the East Indians, the Government felt it necessary to attempt to de-emphasize the type of "elite culture" which was dominant in colonial Guyanese society. While more Africans tended to accept, either in practice or as an ideal, the "elite culture" of creole society, some of them also began, with the awakening of black consciousness locally, to challenge the traditional conception of Guyanese "elite culture."

An additional reason for this might have been the fact that the social class composition of the parents and of the students attending the elite schools was changing. As this happened the schools became less effective in passing on this elite culture. And further, these parents exerted less pressure on the school and its teachers to maintain the traditional curriculum offerings.

These changes together resulted in a marked shift in the dominant pattern of mobility in the society—from a sponsored to a more open or contest type of mobility. The upshot was that an increasing number of lower middle and working class parents were trying to provide their children with a secondary education essentially as a means of economic self-improvement. The role of the secondary schools, as agencies for the socialization of potential Guyanese into the "elite culture" of the European, therefore began to decline, and while the elite secondary schools still retained their prestigious position in the educational system, this was increasingly a reflection of the superiority of their academic standards.

Before examining the impact of these changes on the curriculum of the secondary schools in Guyana, one needs to separate the two aspects of the role of these schools in promoting upward social mobility. First, secondary education in Guyana helped to reaffirm the social status of the majority of its recipients and conferred higher status on a few upwardly-mobile individuals. Secondly, the holders of the relevant secondary school certificates had the opportunity to obtain better paying, secure jobs in the economy. With political developments towards self-government, independence, and nationhood, this investment aspect of secondary education became in the transition even more crucial than its role in elite preparation.

Effects of the Changes on the Curriculum of Secondary Schools

These changes had an important influence on the curriculum of the secondary schools. As the role of the elite schools in the socialization of a few selected Guyanese into the values and behaviour patterns of the English ruling group was de-emphasized, the popularity of some of the older subjects, formerly considered important for elite preparation, began to decline in relative importance, and greater emphasis was placed on other subjects which were considered more valuable on the job market. For example, science subjects increased in popularity as non-white Guyanese could find jobs in engineering and other science-related fields. At the same time, the classics declined in importance until Latin was eventually dropped from the curriculum of Queen's College in the early 1970s. Spanish began to rival French, which, because of its traditional prestige, was the only living foreign language previously taught in the elite schools. New subjects such as economics and technical drawing were also introduced in the 1960s, and West Indian history began even more strongly to challenge English history for popularity. Home economics and commercial subjects were also introduced into the curriculum of the girls' elite secondary schools.

While the elite schools still continued to set the pattern of curriculum reform considered desirable by the non-elite ones, there were three important factors which adversely affected the ability or the willingness of the latter schools to introduce the same curriculum.

First, there were financial constraints due mainly to the inability of the parents to meet, through higher fees, the additional costs which would have been incurred if some of these curriculum changes had been implemented in the non-elite secondary schools. Later, as the Government took increasing financial responsibility for secondary education, this problem was reduced somewhat, but not eliminated. As late as 1968 the per capita expenditure on pupils in the newer Government secondary schools was still about one-third of that on pupils in the two elite secondary schools.

Secondly, the non-elite private secondary schools, which later became aided were private entrepreneurial enterprises, and as such, the profits or losses incurred in any curriculum change was an important consideration for them. They were not likely to introduce any change which would have either reduced their profits or created a loss.

Thirdly, the risk involved in parental investment in their children's education was greater in the non-elite secondary schools since the likelihood of their students failing the external examination was higher.

An examination will now be made of how these factors influenced the curricula of the non-elite secondary schools and at the same time imposed effective constraints on their reform. It should first be noted that in Guyana it was the acquisition of the Secondary School Certificate itself, and not the number of years of school attendance, which was of importance on the job market. Also, with the exception of English, nearly every subject had equal currency in terms of obtaining a job. For example, candidates seeking entry into the civil service had to secure five passes, including English, at one sitting at the G.C.E. "O" Level Examination. It did not matter what the other four subjects were; the only important factor was the number of subjects passed.

These facts resulted in the introduction into the curriculum of the non-elite secondary schools of those subjects which were less costly to teach and for which the prescribed syllabus could be covered in a minimum period of time. The absence of science teaching in these non-elite schools could largely be explained in these terms, and the recent popularity of biology was partly due to the appearance on the market of a number of good textbooks on tropical biology coupled with the fact that the subject could be and was being taught in many schools without the aid of a laboratory.

The sciences and other subjects, such as technical drawing, home economics, and woodwork, required much more expensive equipment than the arts subjects, and their introduction into the curriculum of the non-elite schools would have meant higher fees in these schools, something the parents could hardly have afforded. Even when the Government began to provide financial assistance for science teaching, the grants were never enough to cover the full additional costs involved, and thus it was more profitable for these secondary schools simply to concentrate on the teaching of the arts subjects. In any case, there was no differential reward for passing science subjects at the G.C.E. examination, even if parents were able to pay the additional fees which would have been required to meet the cost of science teaching in these schools.

Another factor that favoured the teaching of arts subjects and even mathematics was that supplementary inputs in terms of additional students' time devoted to studies at home in the evenings or on weekends, was more possible in these areas, and hence the syllabus could be covered in a shorter time. With subjects requiring laboratories and other expensive equipment, much of the work involved had to be done in school. This was a handicap to students anxious to complete their studies as quickly as possible. It will be recalled that there were a number of subjects in which it was believed students could secure an "easy pass" at the G.C.E. "O" Level Examination and which became very popular in the non-elite secondary schools—subjects like Religious Knowledge or Scripture, Health Science, West Indian History, Economics, British Constitution, and English History. It was very difficult to say whether or not these subjects were inherently easier than others, but they lent themselves more readily to additional inputs of students' time away from the school and this obviously increased a student's chance of passing them at the external examinations.

The main goal of secondary school students was to obtain the Secondary School Certificate, since it was this credential and not the years of secondary schooling which was important for securing a job. The cost of obtaining this final certificate was roughly proportional to the number of years spent in the separate secondary schools. Since many low-income parents could not have afforded the cost of a full five-year course of secondary education, they began to experiment with giving their children different combinations of low-cost, all-age school education and relatively higher cost secondary education in order to obtain a "secondary educational package" that was within their limited financial resources.

So these low-income parents, especially prior to 1962, were letting their children continue their education in the all-age schools until they obtained their primary school certificates at the age of 14 years and then sending them off to separate secondary schools to take the Junior Cambridge Examination after sixteen months, followed by the Cambridge School Certificate a year later. So that after about two and a half years at a separate secondary school, students who were reasonably bright could enter for and secure their Secondary School Certificates. As a result, pressure was increasingly exerted on these non-elite schools to trim their educational programmes and concentrate on the examination requirements so that they could present their students for the external examination in the shortest possible time—in two and a half years instead of the usual five years. In doing this, they succeeded in bringing the required investment in secondary education within the financial resources of the low-income parents and at the same time narrowed considerably their educational programme.

With the Government's expansion of its secondary education facilities after 1962 and the introduction of a common entrance examination at the age of 11, most parents had to keep their children in secondary schools for five years before they could write the G.C.E. "O" Level Examination. However, by then they could afford this education since private costs had fallen considerably with the establishment of non-fee paying Government secondary schools all over the country and the strict regulation of the fees charged by the aided secondary schools. But with the rationing of secondary school places on the basis of ability and the continued high rate of return on secondary education—due partly to the lowering of private costs and the difficulty of adjusting wages downward—there was still a large demand for more secondary education than was met by the new schools. Because of this, many students who failed to obtain secondary school places at the age of 11 stayed on in the senior departments of the all-age schools to take the College of Preceptors Examination. If they were unsuccessful, they could enter the separate secondary schools, where they were allowed to take the G.C.E. "O" Level Examination after another two or three years. The number of students who proceeded along this path to obtain the G.C.E. certificate was great, and in 1968, the total number of entrants from the all-age schools for the C.P. Examination was twice as many as those from the separate secondary schools.

These "short cuts" to the School Certificate and later the G.C.E. Examination adversely affected the range of activities which the non-elite schools could offer to its pupils. In fact, strong pressure was brought on these schools by both parents and students "for examination results in the shortest possible time."[63] They were, therefore, forced to cut out the "frills" from their curriculum. They dropped any activity which did not directly contribute towards the goal of obtaining the prized certificate and concentrated on those aspects of the syllabus which were directly related to the examination. "Straying" into interesting aspects of the subjects but outside the scope of the examination syllabus was a luxury which these students could not afford. In 1963 the UNESCO team, after visiting the non-elite secondary schools, felt it necessary to comment on the parental pressures still exerted on them to complete their five-year secondary school programme in a shorter period. Also, physical education, including organized games and those extra-curricular activities which one often associates with a good secondary school education, was never given much attention in the programmes of these non-elite secondary schools.

An important feature of the instructional activities of these schools was the teaching technique; even those techniques regarded as "educationally unsound" were used if it was felt that they might help the students pass the external examination within the shortest possible time. Hence, the practice by teachers of going through the past examination papers to "spot" questions likely to come up again, preparing or securing model answers to these questions, and having children learn them by heart was a popular instructional technique. The UNESCO Mission commented on the important place attached to rote learning in these schools, noting that "even chemistry and physics are learnt out of textbooks."[64]

Another aspect of the curriculum of these schools was the dominating influence of external examinations, a fact which was understandable in the social context within which these schools operated. First, there was an examination taken midway through the secondary school course, the Junior Cambridge Examination, superseded later by the College of Preceptors. This served a dual purpose. It gave parents an indication of the progress which their children were making and was a valuable clue as to whether further investment in their education was likely to pay off, i.e., whether their children were likely to obtain the necessary School Certificate or a reasonable number of G.C.E. passes if they continued their schooling. The fact that this evaluation was done by an external body gave the parents more confidence in the results as a predictor of their children's future academic performance, especially since the private schools had a financial interest in keeping these children in school as long as possible.

[63] UNESCO, "Report of the UNESCO Educational Survey Mission," p. 56.
[64] *Ibid.*, p. 57.

This examination also provided successful candidates with a certificate that was itself of some value on the job market. If parents could not afford to pay for their children's education beyond this point, their investment so far was still likely to produce a reasonable rate of return. It is true that the number of jobs which could be secured with this level of qualification was becoming increasingly scarce, but its function as an indicator of the risk element involved in any further expenditure on the child's education, still remained. This is why the College of Preceptors Examination was still so popular among the non-elite aided secondary schools. It also explains why, when the Junior Cambridge Examination was abolished, the private secondary schools made every effort to secure a substitute examination and eventually came up with the English College of Preceptors, which itself was then almost unknown in England.

Secondly, there was the "final" examination taken at the end of the secondary school course, the School Certificate or the G.C.E. "O" Level Examination. Passing this examination was quite important for occupational selection into one of the more desired jobs in the labour force. The value of the knowledge which was acquired in the process of obtaining this certificate, or what educators sometimes refer to as "the intrinsic value of the education" either to the individual or to the society, was a relatively minor consideration. The examination was essentially a legitimating device for securing entry into certain types of jobs on the labour market. Using a different analogy, it was a hurdle which had to be successfully overcome for the individual to be eligible for one of those economically and socially more prestigious jobs which the society had to offer.

Great emphasis was, therefore, placed on the outcome of these examinations, and as a result, their requirements continued rigidly to determine the curriculum content, especially of the non-elite secondary schools. In 1950 the Director of Education, writing mainly about these schools, observed that "examinations dictate very largely and in many cases altogether, the curriculum of the secondary schools in the colony. There is, therefore, an overwhelming tendency to look upon examinations as an end in themselves and to subordinate other and more important aims to them."[65]

The same concern for securing passes at examinations, irrespective of the "true nature" of the education obtained, has been observed in many developing countries. For example, Dr. G. B. Jeffreys reported in 1952 that in West Africa, "the passing of examinations has attained such importance in the eyes of the public that the whole field of educational activity is in danger of being determined by the requirements of examination."[66]

[65] Government of British Guiana, *Annual Report of the Director of Education 1950*, p. 29.

[66] Dr. G. B. Jeffreys, quoted in *ibid.*, p. 30.

It is incorrect to think that this "undue concern" for passing examinations is typical of the developing countries only. The same concern also exists among students in the economically more developed countries, but where the two situations differ is in the extent of the concern, which no doubt tends to be greater among students in developing countries. That students in the economically more developed countries are usually somewhat less worried about external examinations is partly due to the fact that their chances of success at such examinations are much better than for their corresponding groups in the less developed countries. Also, failure at external examinations is not usually as catastrophic for the individual's future in an economically more developed country as it is for one in an L.D.C.

On the first point, teachers in the economically more developed countries are usually much better qualified and have superior educational resources available to them as compared with those in the developing countries. As a result, the chances that their students might fail their examinations are much less. This in itself is an important factor in reducing the perpetual concern over examinations. This greater degree of uncertainty about examination success was reflected in the pressures which pupils and parents often exerted on teachers in the non-elite schools as compared with the elite schools.

The second ingredient of this concern was the economic consequence of failure for the parents, who, in view of their incomes, make a proportionately greater sacrifice for their children to obtain a secondary education. In addition, they often find it difficult to afford the cost involved in letting the child return to school for another year to study for the same examination. In many less developed countries there are not many evening classes available to make it possible for students to work and study for that year.

And not only were the prospects of a student re-taking his examination poor, but, as in Guyana, his immediate and long-term job prospects were not good if he failed to secure a certificate. A 1966 study by Sarah Graham[67] examined the influence of examination success on the occupational future of a sample of residents in Georgetown. She found that 60.4% of her respondents who had an even lower level paper qualification than the School Certificate or below, were in her top three (out of five) occupational categories, as compared with only 16.5% who had no paper qualification at all. Incidentally, even those with the low-level qualifications who entered into one of the top three occupational categories tended to be employed in the private sector and possibly even in family enterprises.

[67] Sarah Graham, "Occupational Mobility in Guyana" (unpublished Ph.D. thesis, University of the West Indies, Mona, Kingston, Jamaica, 1973).

Therefore, success at the secondary school final examination usually meant passing into a different way of life, providing students entry into the high wage level sector of the economy where income differentials, job security, and social status were substantially higher than in the low wage or traditional sector. In view of this, it was quite understandable why there were such great pressures, especially on the non-elite secondary schools, to reduce the risk element in getting students through the secondary school examination by cutting out the "frills," concentrating on the core of the examination subjects, and using every device which might help their students achieve success at the external examination. As a result, the constraints imposed by this G.C.E. Examination on the curriculum of these schools was considerable and there was little time devoted to the non-examination subjects or those broader aspects of a subject which might not have been included in the examination syllabus.

Developments in Secondary Education: Summary and Observations

Prior and up to the 1940s, the system of stratification in the country was the key factor in determining access to secondary education. The children of the middle and upper classes were still mainly attending the elite secondary schools, those of the rising lower middle class went to the new private non-elite secondary schools, while the children of the working classes received only a primary school education. There was then only a tenuous link between the primary and the secondary schools provided by a small number of Government scholarships awarded annually—up to 1945 there were only twelve. These allowed some primary school pupils to attend the elite secondary schools.

The demand for more secondary school places began to increase rapidly around the 1940s, resulting in a proliferation of private secondary schools. This was the result of a number of changes, including constitutional ones, which allowed for increasing popular participation in the political decision-making process in the country. This led to a greater demand for Guyanization of the jobs in the public and later in the private sector. In addition, the civil service and the teaching profession were expanding fairly rapidly, providing greater opportunities for secondary school graduates. The relative prosperity of the early 1940s, coupled with the higher incomes of those who began to occupy these expanding lower middle class occupations, made it possible for more parents to pay for secondary education for their children.

Since the colonial administration was reluctant to provide additional facilities to meet this increasing demand for secondary education, there was a mushrooming of private secondary schools, providing a "poor" quality of education but one which these low-income parents could afford. Between 1945 and 1960, the enrolment in private secondary schools increased by about 250%.

There were some pressures on the Government, including those from its own professionals, to regulate standards of these private secondary schools. But when the private schools began opposing the proposed legislation on the grounds that without financial assistance most of them would have to close, the Government withdrew its legislation rather than face the political consequences which were likely to develop following a possible closure of these schools. As a result, they were allowed to continue their operations as "cramming institutions" with their curricula remaining "unsuitable to the needs of Guyanese society." But they nevertheless retained popularity, especially among the lower middle class groups, since they provided the only means by which these parents could afford a secondary education for their children.

With increasing popular participation in the political process since the 1950s, the attitude of the Government towards secondary education changed. One of its major concerns was to equalize educational opportunity, especially at the secondary level. It attacked this problem by first providing more secondary schools throughout the country, especially after 1962, and secondly, by democratizing entry into the Government and Government-aided secondary schools by instituting a common entrance examination. Thirdly, it regulated the fees of the aided secondary schools and increased its assistance to them. Fourthly, it reorganized the all-age schools to provide secondary education up to the third form for students who did not secure entry into a separate secondary school. Those who obtained their College of Preceptors Examination from these schools could later transfer into one of the separate secondary schools and continue their education to the G.C.E. "O" level. The result was a massive increase in the number and proportion of the population attending secondary schools. By 1972 about 80% of the children over 11 years of age in Guyana were receiving some form of secondary education which could eventually lead to the G.C.E. "O" Level Examination.

Curriculum Changes

Many efforts were made, especially prior to 1963, to reform the curriculum of the secondary schools, through authoritative recommendations by educational experts, repeated encouragement by Ministry of Education officials, and even through the introduction of financial incentives by the Government. But none of these had any real influence on curriculum reform, and those curriculum changes which occurred were more the result of two important factors in Guyanese society.

With political development towards self-government and independence, there was a challenge to the traditional content of "elite culture" in the society; as this happened the importance of the traditional secondary school curriculum as a means of elite preparation began to diminish, and its role in preparing individuals for occupational and economic mobility increased.

The second factor was the relatively low income levels of the parents of children attending the non-elite secondary schools. Most of them could not have afforded the costs which suggested curriculum changes would have involved. In addition, the nature of the examination system, the recruiting practice of employers who rewarded the number rather than the type of subjects passed at the G.C.E. "O" Level Examination, and the fact that these schools were private entrepreneurial enterprises, together militated against the introduction of the recommended curriculum changes.

Between 1972 and 1974, the Government was engaged in the establishment of multilateral and community high schools, the rationale being essentially the same theme song played during the days of the colonial administration and based on the assumption that occupational choices can be changed by curriculum manipulation. The lesson that curriculum changes aimed at influencing students' occupational choices will not be effective if the basic reward structure is such that people are not likely to be attracted to these occupations in the first place, has obviously not yet been learned. Given freedom of choice, people are always likely to opt for the type of education, however "irrelevant" it might be from an educator's point-of-view, which will lead them to the economically and/or psychically more rewarding jobs.

The major fillip which can be given to encourage youngsters to enter technical and agricultural fields lies first in the rewards which these fields of activity offer in comparison to others in the economy. Once these fields become attractive in their own right, curriculum changes can play an important supportive role in helping to pass on to those interested in following these occupations, the necessary skills, knowledge, and attitudes which might eventually help them to be more productive.

Economic Implications

Between 1945 and 1972, there has been, as a result of this marked rise in secondary school enrolment, a great rise in the total expenditure and in the percentage of the budget spent on secondary education in Guyana. Expenditure on this level of education has been rising faster than on any other level in the country, excluding university education, and its proportion of the educational budget more than doubled between 1945 and 1972, rising from 7.3% to 15.1%.

While there has undoubtedly been an increasing equality of educational opportunity at the secondary level, it seems that the economic implications of this great increase of expenditure on secondary education and the rapid rise in the enrolment of secondary schools were ignored, or at least not given sufficient consideration. The question which needed to be considered was whether this increase in the expenditure on academic secondary education represented the most efficient way of allocating the country's economic resources. A major problem which has faced Guyanese society, especially since the 1950s, is the failure of the economy to grow fast enough to absorb the increasing numbers who were coming on the job market every year, with the result that the already heavy unemployment rate, estimated at about 25% of the labour force in 1975, has been increasing steadily. The situation would appear even more critical if the unemployment among those under twenty years of age on the labour market were to be considered separately.

The reallocation of the economic resources of the country to pay for this increased expenditure on secondary education has certainly not helped with the problem of what to do with these youngsters now facing the job market armed with their G.C.E. certificates. This raises the issue of the absorptive capacity of the economy for people with this level of qualification. The manpower survey of 1965 indicated that already in that year there were seven times as many persons seeking clerical jobs as there were vacancies. In mid-1974 the author learned from the local secretary of an insurance company that an advertisement by the company for two accounts clerks brought in 144 applicants—nearly all of them with G.C.E. certificates with passes ranging up to ten "O" level subjects.

It is true that the number likely to achieve the level of qualification normally required for entry into the civil service or teaching was being severely reduced by the low level of passes which the secondary school students achieved. But the question which must be considered here is whether the country was securing the best returns possible for its expenditure on this level of education. It has already been seen that in order to achieve a more equitable distribution of secondary educational facilities the Government established a number of secondary schools—some with a pupil population of less than 100—and it was obvious that efficiency in the use of resources was often sacrificed to achieve the goal of a more equitable distribution of secondary school places. If one looked at the failure which students experienced at the different external examinations one would get an idea of the "wastage" of resources.

Between 1963 and 1972 the number of candidates who entered for the P.C.E. Examination rose from 12,157 to 19,659 but the percentage of success varied considerably from year to year. The highest percent of successful candidates yet recorded was 31% in 1972 but this figure was about 4% in 1966 and 1967. At the next level—the C.P. Examination—40.6% of the 4,794 entrants in 1968 and 41.6% of the 4,810 in 1972 were successful. But at the G.C.E. "O" Level Examination the results were much less satisfactory. In 1968 there were 14,194 candidates who entered for an average of 4.03 subjects but the average number of subjects passed was .99. In fact 51% failed outright and the remainder secured an average of 2.4 subjects. An analysis of the June 1972 entries only, from which private candidates were excluded, showed a similarly poor performance. The 9,862 candidates for this examination entered for an average of 4.3 subjects but the average number of passes was only 1.2 with about 47% failing outright.

For the job market in the public sector[68] the minimum number of G.C.E. "O" level passes considered valuable was about four at one sitting. But of the 8,033 candidates in 1968 and 6,422 in June 1972 who entered for four or more subjects only 10.7% and 15.7% respectively, secured passes at this level. Another relevant factor was students' performance in English since the civil service and teaching normally required candidates to have secured a pass in this subject. In 1968 the number of entries for English Language was 12,310 while that for July 1972 was 8,141. Of these, only about 19.6% secured a pass in 1968, and 22.2% in July 1972.

While these high failure rates reduced considerably the numbers competing for the available jobs, the question still remains as to whether this was the most efficient way for a poor country to spend its limited economic resources, that is, by allowing such a large percentage of those between the ages of 12 and 16 to take a three- to five-year academic secondary school course when their chances of passing the final examinations were so low. And even if they could all succeed in successfully completing the secondary programme, the poor job market would soon have frustrated their hopes of finding the type of job which they would have considered appropriate for their new educational status.

Educators might not accept the view that the education of those who go through secondary schools and do not secure a certificate is wasted. But if one looks at the problem from the point of view of the

[68] These requirements were less rigid in the private sector except when personnel were being recruited as trainees and later had to be sent to a higher educational institution overseas to pursue a formal course of study. In other cases the private sector generally used educational attainment partly as a sorting mechanism when there was a large number of applicants for each vacancy and as a test of general intellectual ability and of application to a task.

most efficient use of national resources it certainly represents a misallocation of scarce funds. For, as Graham's study showed, those in Guyana who did not obtain these certificates had very little chance of moving out of the lowest occupational categories—which was their original intention in attempting to secure an education.

There were already signs that educational inflation was occurring and that there was "padding" of the civil service to provide jobs for these certificate holders. The Prime Minister, in addressing a regional conference of the ruling People's National Congress in June 1974, suggested that "the reason why Guyana was able to send stenographers to Zambia every year was because there were too many of these skills chasing after too few jobs in the country." Further, he told his supporters that "too many Government offices were overstaffed, resulting in not enough jobs for these clerks to do."[69]

Demand for secondary education increased with the abolition of school fees in the Government secondary schools and the freezing of those in the aided secondary schools. This, along with the location of new secondary schools all over the country, has considerably reduced the costs of secondary education, raised the private rate of return, and hence increased the demand for this level of education. And the expansion of secondary educational facilities with the establishment of multilateral secondary schools, which began in September 1974, would certainly increase the proportion of youngsters attending secondary schools in Guyana, youngsters who would later arrive on the job market competing for the limited number of white-collar jobs.

The big question facing the policy makers in their laudable attempts to achieve equality of educational opportunity was how far they could continue with the allocation of more resources to secondary education to achieve this goal. But more fundamental is the questionable assumption that this expansion of secondary education has been bringing about greater equality in the society. Even in the U.S.A., where access to educational facilities is quite open, it has been shown that the educational system has not been very effective in achieving greater equality in the society. As Carnoy argues, "the nature of the economic system has a great deal more influence on the distribution of income and occupational status than does the system of schooling."[70] Only when this is fully understood will Governments in the developing countries stop squandering money on inappropriate educational systems in the hope of achieving greater equality in the society.

[69] L. F. S. Burnham, "Address to the Regional Conference of the P.N.C." (Georgetown, June 1974). (Mimeographed.)

[70] M. Carnoy and H. M. Levin, *Limits of Educational Reform* (New York: David McKay Co. Ltd., 1976), p. 5.

6. Post-Secondary and Technical Education

Prior to 1945 there was no educational institution in Guyana for the formal training of lower, middle, or higher level technical personnel. A few of the larger private firms provided some on-the-job training for their skilled craftsmen but brought in expatriate staff for their middle and higher level technical positions. In the public sector, too, jobs requiring higher level training in the technical and applied scientific fields were nearly always filled by Europeans, with the result that very few Guyanese prior to 1945 became interested in pursuing studies in these subjects. So when the C.D. & W. development programmes were started in the 1940s, a major problem in their implementation was the shortage of technical personnel in such fields as engineering, forestry, and geology.

In his address to the Legislative Council in December 1948 the Governor drew attention to the effect of such high level manpower shortage on the progress of various development projects and noted that "The engineering section of our Public Works Department has been 50% under strength for well over a year. . . . Our forestry department is heavily understaffed to meet present and future requirements." He attributed this shortage of technical personnel to the disposition of Guyanese to prefer the legal, medical, and more recently the dental professions. Continuing on this theme, he observed:

> We have 59 qualified Guyanese medical practitioners [then roughly one to every 10,000 of the population] in the colony today and a further 46 in training. We have 33 dental practitioners and no less than 80 said to be training in the U.S.A. and Canada. We have 66 barristers and solicitors and 20 in training. In contrast to these figures we have 5 qualified civil engineers, though 9 are in training. We have only one qualified veterinary officer, though four are said to be in training. We have no Guyanese science master at Queen's College, though two are in training.[1]

In March 1954 the Financial Secretary also expressed concern at the staffing situation in the Government services, especially as this affected the supply of technical personnel needed for the development programme. "We simply have not got the staff," he observed, "which is required to carry out the [development] plan in the way it should . . . this would mean some brake on the speed with which we

[1] Government of British Guiana, Speech by the Governor, President of the Legislative Council, in *Hansard*, 16 December 1948.

can get on with the job."[2] In December 1955 he again noted that the "lack of qualified staff—engineers and foresters—continues to hamper progress."[3] In 1955 the Governor once more observed, "I am particularly worried at the exceptional difficulties and slowness at recruiting the qualified staff which we must have if we are to get ahead, as successfully as we hope, with our very large development programme."[4] The interesting point here is that these shortages existed in a country which for over a century had been providing elementary education for the masses and which for the past seventy years had a compulsory education act.

The original source of the shortage did not rest, as many critics implied, on some innate preference among Guyanese for the professions of law, medicine, and later dentistry. The problem could be more correctly explained by the fact that, prior to 1945, the demand for individuals with these technological skills was very small, and in addition, there was discrimination in the labour market against the employment of Guyanese—especially Indo- and Afro-Guyanese—in senior technical and scientific positions. At that time such posts in the Government services were virtually restricted to whites from the metropole. In the private sector, the situation was even worse and large private companies like Demba and Bookers recruited whites almost exclusively for all their higher level positions. There was little incentive for Guyanese to take up studies in the higher level technical fields, with the result that those who went overseas for professional training pursued studies in areas in which they could establish themselves in private practice without having to depend on Government or private companies for a job. At the time the only fields in which such practice was possible were medicine, law, and later dentistry and this is why Guyanese students at first tended to pursue studies in one of these fields.

Another factor responsible for this shortage of high level technical personnel in Guyana was the lack of students with a good secondary educational background in science subjects. In 1948 the Governor, in discussing the shortage of higher level technical personnel, noted that of the twenty-three students who qualified for entry into a British university, only two or three were students with a good science background.[5] This meant that the gestation period for producing graduates in engineering, geology, and forestry, was not three years, the normal length of an English university honours degree pro-

[2] Government of British Guiana, Speech by E. McDavid, Financial Secretary and Treasurer, in *Hansard*, 26 March 1954.

[3] *Ibid.*, 16 December 1955.

[4] Government of British Guiana, Speech by the Governor, in *Hansard*, 25 April 1956.

[5] *Ibid.*, 16 December 1948.

gramme, but eight years, which included five years of secondary school preparation in the sciences.

The shortage of higher level technical personnel was further exacerbated by the limited number of middle level technicians such as land surveyors, draughtsmen, and laboratory technicians so that the few available professionals had to spend much of their time doing work at a sub-professional level.

Normally when senior technical personnel were needed locally, the Government would intensify recruitment efforts in the United Kingdom to fill these vacant positions. But in the mid-1940s such a solution had become more difficult. First, with the political developments and rising aspirations of the Guyanese public, the legislators and other groups were increasingly putting pressure on the colonial administration to recruit Guyanese for these positions even if it meant training them for the jobs. Second, C.D. & W. development schemes were being launched simultaneously in nearly all the British colonies, making it difficult for Guyana to recruit sufficient senior technical staff from the United Kingdom to fill all its vacancies. The private sector was not yet subjected to such heavy political pressures and continued to recruit its senior staff from overseas, attracting them with higher salaries then those paid in the public sector.

Faced with this new situation, the Government took the following steps to increase the supply of the needed technical personnel:

(1) Granting "conditional" scholarships to qualified Guyanese candidates to pursue professional training overseas in the scientific and technological fields. They were contracted to return to work in the Government services for a specified minimum period on completion of their studies.

(2) Extension of the science facilities at its premier boys' secondary school.

These first two steps were mainly aimed at increasing the supply of technical and scientific personnel at the highest levels.

(3) Establishment of a technical institute in Georgetown in 1951 to provide formal training at the craft and technician levels. Later a Department of Technical Studies was also established at the University of Guyana (1969) and another technical institute in New Amsterdam (1971).

(4) The establishment of a School of Agriculture in 1963 to train agricultural extension workers and future farmers.

In examining the results of these different efforts, attention will be focussed on the success of the public sector in meeting its manpower needs, since the private sector for many reasons had much less difficulty in securing technical staff. Salaries in the private sector tended more often to reflect current market conditions; and large private firms had their own training programmes and were more flexible in selecting trainees, depending much less on formal academic qualifications and more on the candidate's suitability for the job and ability to undertake the training.

Another reason for focussing on the public sector was the relative size of this market for technical skills. In 1965 nearly two-thirds of all senior technical and scientific personnel in architecture, engineering, surveying, chemistry, geology, agriculture, and veterinary medicine were employed in the public sector.

Training of Technologists and Technicians

In order to obtain higher level scientific and technological personnel for the public sector, the Government began awarding "conditional" scholarships. By the mid-1940s Guyanese students overseas were studying agriculture, forestry, engineering, fisheries, and domestic science. In 1948 an additional number of awards were made in engineering, and by 1949 about 80% of all "conditional" scholars, excluding those in medicine, were in the technological and scientific fields.

As Guyanese returned home to fill senior level technical jobs, the interest in these fields among students planning to go abroad to study began to increase, and in his 1954-1957 report, the Director of Education could already note that

> there has been a great awakening towards university training during the period under review. British Guianese have endeavoured to widen the field of their professional qualifications. Formerly students left the colony to take up studies in one of the following—medicine, law, or dentistry, but recently a number of students have been enrolled in various universites for courses in Natural Science, Engineering (Civil and Mechanical), Mining, Geology, Veterinary Science, Economics, Pharmacy, Education, Art, Optics, Radiology, Hospital Administration, Agriculture, Domestic Science.[6]

While the inadequate supply of secondary school students with a good educational background in the sciences was at first restricting the numbers able to pursue higher education in the scientific and technological fields, there was now such interest in these areas that more students in the elite secondary schools were switching from the traditionally prestigious humanities programmes to the sciences.

What was happening was that Guyanese were gradually replacing Europeans in senior technical positions in the civil service and were receiving the same salaries and conditions of service as their predecessors. This meant that they enjoyed better salaries than their non-graduate counterparts in the administrative branch of the civil service, where the senior positions were still held by whites and in some cases by the coloured middle class.

[6] Government of British Guiana, *Triennial Report of the Director of Education 1954-57*, p. 10.

By the 1960s, however, there seemed to have been a relative reduction in the supply of this higher level scientific and technical manpower. Not only were many of these professionals leaving the civil service but the supply of new graduates in these fields suffered a setback. A Government committee[7] investigating the problems of technical education in the secondary schools in 1966, observed that in addition to the existing shortage of technical personnel such as geologists, not enough qualified candidates were available for the Government technical scholarships. The more recent shortage of higher level technical personnel was partly due to the unsettled political situation in Guyana, causing many qualified senior technical staff to emigrate. But there were other contributory factors. As a result of political developments in the country, the private companies were beginning to recruit their senior personnel from among Guyanese, and since their salaries and other conditions were often much better than those in the civil service, they were attracting not only new recruits but those already holding jobs in the civil service.

An even more important factor was the relative decline in the salaries and status enjoyed by the technologists as compared with their non-graduate counterparts in the administrative branch of the civil service. With self-government and independence, new positions with relatively high salaries, including those of Permanent Secretaries—who were now the civil service heads of the various Government Ministries—were thrown open to the administrative staff, most of whom were non-graduates, although some of whom eventually held arts degrees. The senior scientific or technical personnel not only began to receive lower salaries than their top administrative staff, but because of their relative scarcity they were not usually allowed to move across and up into the general administrative branch of the service with the hope of eventually being considered for one of the senior administrative posts. This not only helped to increase their dissatisfaction over salaries but also reduced the incentive for students to pursue studies in these technical fields. William Partin,[8] a technical education expert, writing about the shortage of instructional staff for the Government Technical Institute, commented on the feeling by such staff that they were overlooked when promotions were considered, a feeling he felt was justified. One result of this was that the Government had to continue granting conditional scholarships as a means of recruiting its technical staff. For example, of the fifty-two scholarships awarded by the Government in 1966, forty-three (82.7%) were in science and technology.

[7] Government of Guyana, Ministry of Education, "Report of the Committee on Technical Education 1966" (Georgetown, 1966). (Mimeographed.)

[8] William Partin, *A Report on Vocational Education for the Government of British Guiana* (Georgetown: Government Printer, May 1965), p. 7.

It is also interesting to compare the fields of study which students voluntarily pursued against those which they took up because the Government provided them with a scholarship, either directly or through a bilateral arrangement with another Government. In 1963-64 thirty-two out of the forty-four students (72.7%) studying overseas under some form of Government sponsorship were in technical and scientific fields (engineering, geology, chemistry, architecture, pharmacy, and dietetics), while only eighteen out of seventy-four students (24.3%) who took up further studies under the Government loan scheme, were in these fields. Similarly, in 1968 about 40% of the 168 students studying overseas under Government sponsorship were pursuing scientific and technological studies, while only 21% of the 148 private students on loans were studying in these areas. The private individuals were more likely to pursue arts, social sciences, and commerce—40% in 1968 as compared with 22% of those on Government scholarships.

While it is true that the proportion of students taking up scientific and technological scholarships under Government sponsorship was mainly a reflection of the emphasis placed by Government on these fields, it is interesting to note that even though such graduates were scarce, private students opted more heavily for the non-scientific fields (medicine excepted).

Part of the reason for this was the limited number of students with adequate science backgrounds who were qualified to enter tertiary level educational institutions to pursue technical studies after Government scholars in these areas had been selected. Another likely reason why some students continued to follow the arts stream was the fact that the expected returns on educational investment for science and technology graduates in the civil service were considered low compared with those for the arts graduates, and the latter group still had a better chance of being promoted to the most senior positions in the civil service.

A case can indeed be made on a number of grounds for a continuation of the Government's policy of granting conditional scholarships in science and technology to students who would be contracted to return to work in the Government service for some years. First, the fairly specific nature of the training which some of these fields involved, coupled with the relatively small size of the local market for these skills, might adversely affect the students' desire to pursue such fields unless they had some prior assurance of a job to which they could return when they were qualified. Furthermore, the demand for some of these categories of personnel up to 1965 existed only in the public sector. There was no private sector demand for foresters, and with only one employer in this field, the "risk element" of getting a job when qualified was likely to dampen students' desires to pursue studies in such fields.

There are at least two other reasons which can be advanced for the continuation of the conditional scholarship scheme. Not enough students might have the necessary initial capital to invest in themselves; and since the salary scales in the Government service were low compared with salaries elsewhere, the scholarship scheme helped to reduce the cost of the students' education and made the rate of return on their educational investment better by comparison.

The solution in the first case might, more appropriately, have been to increase the availability of capital through the loan scheme for students wanting to study in these fields. But if the problem was the low rate of return on technical education, either in an absolute sense or compared with other groups such as non-graduates and arts graduates, then the continued granting of conditional scholarships was not going to solve the problem. While the scholarships increased the supply of technical graduates in the country, their retention in the civil service, after their contractual obligations to the Government ended, proved to be a major weakness of the conditional scholarship scheme. Many of these graduates left the Government service soon after or even before their contractual obligations ended. Indeed, if most of these conditional scholars had remained in the civil service until they retired, there would have been no shortage of such personnel today.

This scholarship scheme focussed attention on the *production* of higher level technical and scientific personnel and not on the real source of the problem which was the *retention* of graduates in the civil service and often within the country. It is not being suggested here that the salaries received by senior scientific and technological personnel in developing countries like Guyana are the only factors affecting their retention in the civil service. There are other factors involved. It is true that the Government cannot retain its well-qualified and competent personnel in the civil service if salaries in the private sector are substantially higher. But when differential rates of pay for skills are considered necessary in the civil service there must be legitimate criteria for such differentials. The introduction of what might be considered irrelevant considerations in the distribution of rewards, whether it be political patronage or artifically created opportunities for promotion for some groups, is likely to and did create dissatisfaction and affected the ability of the civil service to keep its more competent personnel. Such losses were greater from among those in the scientific and technological fields who often could easily find jobs elsewhere.

Another point was that private sector employment opportunities for scientific and technical personnel were always so limited that once those trained individuals left the civil service they had to emigrate if they were to remain employed in their specific fields. So, rather than continuing its blind commitment to the conditional scholarship scheme, the Government needed a thorough study of why the civil service has problems in recruiting and retaining higher level technical and scientific personnel. Such a study will certainly involve an examination of, among other things, the general conditions of service and the relative rates of promotion to the higher paying jobs among scientists and technologists in the civil service as compared with arts graduates and non-graduates in the general administrative branch.

In essence, efforts at increasing the supply of high-level manpower in the developing countries cannot be looked at only from the viewpoint of training. The whole socio-political and economic context affecting the retention of such personnel in the civil service or in the country, once they have been trained, is the other side of the problem to which attention needs to be given.

Technician Training

A similar shortage existed among middle-level technical personnel, but instead of attempting to solve this problem by sending students to study overseas, the Government decided to provide such training locally. In 1951 the Government Technical Institute (G.T.I.) was started, and while its original purpose was to provide craft-level training, by 1956 it had moved into the area of training middle level technical personnel. As can be seen from Table 39, between 1961 and 1972, those undergoing technician training e.g., in electrical and civil engineering, telecommunications, and land surveying at the G.T.I. made up between 19% and 32% of the student population. In 1966, the University of Guyana (U.G.) also began training middle-level technical manpower by instituting formal programmes for radiographers and medical technologists and by 1971 its Department of Technical Studies was established. This provided courses for technician training leading to a General Technical and a Higher Technical Diploma in such fields as civil and telecommunications engineering. Courses in other areas leading to diplomas in social work and public administration were also introduced. The ultimate objective was to switch over most of the technician-level courses to the university and let the technical institutes concentrate on craft-level training.

While provisions for the training of middle-level technicians were expanding, very little attention had so far been paid to the recruitment of suitable trainees for these fields, and to their retention as a reasonably satisfied group of "sub-professionals" in the labour force, especially in the civil service.

One of the observations repeatedly made about this level of training was the shortage of students with the necessary educational background interested in careers as technicians. The folklore which still exists as an explanation of this phenomenon is that Guyanese have a traditional preference for "pen-and-ink" or white-collar jobs.

While there is some truth to this, the real explanation lies in the structure of the remuneration and career prospects of individuals who go in for technician-level work in the civil service as against those who select the "pen-and-ink" careers. This point would become clear if a comparison was made of the likely career profiles of two individuals both possessing the required qualifications for entry into the civil service, i.e., at least passes in five subjects including English at the G.C.E. "O" level. For those interested in being trained as technicians, an additional requirement was that some of these passes should be in the sciences (physics, chemistry, biology) and mathematics. If two candidates possessed these qualifications and one entered the administrative and the other the technical branch of the service, for example in drafting, their career patterns and salary scales were, up to 1973, likely to be what is shown in Table 37.

In addition to the career prospects indicated in this Table, there are some other factors to be noted. First, a technician trainee was not eligible for appointment to the technician grade unless he passed the prescribed technician's examination. Second, while a trainee technician would receive his practical training on the job, most of his studies in the theoretical aspects of his work would have to be done in his spare time. The Class II clerk, on the other hand, has no such examination to pass and no extra studies to pursue to secure promotion. Secondly, the salary for the topmost position in the administrative grade was substantially higher than that in the technician grade. Also, while there were no figures available on the rates of promotion within the two branches of the service, there was the belief that these were much better in the administrative section, partly because the administrative branch was much larger and also because it had many more senior positions available. Although chances of promotion to the position of Permanent Secretary were not very great, the fact that it was possible for Class II clerks to rise to such heights was an important motivating factor in attracting people into the administrative rather than the technical branch of the service. A student who selected a career as an air traffice controller, for example, could only hope to rise to one of the two positions of senior air traffice controllers in the country with a maximum salary no higher than that of an administrative assistant. In addition, administrative jobs which place people in authority over others have an inherent attraction to many employees.

As indicated before, the salary structure in the two branches of the civil service bore little relationship to the demand and supply for these skills or to the cost of training. It was part of the legacy of the British colonial administration in which senior administrative posts were held by Europeans while junior administrative and middle-level technical posts were held by Guyanese. As the country moved towards self-government and independence, personnel from what was then

Table 37 *Likely Career Patterns and Salaries of Equally*
Qualified Secondary School Graduates
Entering the Administrative and the Technical
Branch of the Civil Service

Administrative route	Monthly salary 1973	Technician route
	$169	1) *Trainee Technician* e.g., Apprentice Draughtsman
1) Class II Clerk	$221	2) *Technician* e.g. a) Assistant Draughtsman
2) Class I Clerk	$296	b) Senior Assistant Draughtsman
3) Senior Clerk	$352	c) Draughtsman
4) Administrative Assistant	$412	3) Senior Draughtsman
5) Assistant Secretary	$648	
6) Principal Assistant Secretary	$720	
7) Permanent Secretary	$860	

Source: Government of Guyana, *Estimates (Current and Capital) of Guyana for the Year 1973* (Georgetown, 1973).

the lower administrative branch of the services, began to fill senior administrative positions previously held by Europeans and at the same salary scales as their predecessors. This created a severe imbalance in the career prospects of local personnel entering the technical as against the administrative branch of the civil service.

Further, the training required by technicians was continually being upgraded as international standards were raised, and at the same time, civil service salary revisions reinforced the existing salary and promotion differentials between these two groups. Consequently, the administrative staff retained their position of comparative advantage. The result was that the current salary structure and career prospects among technicians in the civil service acted as a deterrent to suitably qualified youngsters wanting to take up careers as technicians.

It is true that there always were many more applicants for trainee technician posts than there were vacancies in the Government service. The unemployment rate in the country was enough to ensure a surfeit of applicants for any position. The problem was their generally poor educational background, especially in the sciences.

In addition to the recruitment of trainees, there were always the problems of retaining the staff once they were trained and the continuous dissatisfaction over salaries among those who, for one reason or another, could not leave the Government service. This problem of shortage of technical personnel was particularly felt at the Government Technical Institute, where most of the staff were expected to have both formal training and on-the-job experience. The Principal continually had to draw attention to the problem of staff shortage in the institution. Partin, in his report to the Government in 1965, observed that one of the perennial problems of the G.T.I. has been the difficulty in recruiting and keeping suitable staff due to the competition for technically competent people, both inside and outside the country. For example, when the new technical institute at New Amsterdam was opened, the Government had difficulty recruiting instructional staff. Seven of the twelve positions were unfilled in 1971, despite the promise of assistance by the Canadian International Development Agency (CIDA) to help the recruits further their education in Canada.

Even when qualified staff became available through the conditional scholarship scheme, it was again not easy to retain the service of these individuals for long, especially after their period of contractual obligation to the Government ended. In addition, it was exceedingly difficult to get persons with the necessary industrial experience to join the staff of the Institute. The candidates who took up the conditional scholarships usually had no industrial experience. By the time they finished their training and returned to work in Guyana, they had very little exposure to industry except what they received as part of their training programme. The jobs as lecturers in the technical institute could not attract suitably qualified persons from industry, where salaries tended to reflect more realistically the market condition for these skills. The salary "straight jacket" in which the G.T.I. found itself was a major reason why a former Principal was always pleading for greater autonomy for the Board of Governors of the Institute so that it could have a more flexible salary scale which would take market conditions into consideration.

Private industry did not have as great a difficulty in recruiting and retaining technicians, and the Government's failure in this direction was due both to the existing salary scales for technical staff and to the imbalance in terms of career prospects which existed between its technical and its administrative personnel.

Craft Training

When the Government started its Technical Institute (G.T.I.) in 1951 the major objective was the training of skilled workmen to meet the needs of the private sector. Prior to this there was no formally organized training scheme for craftsmen. The larger companies conducted apprentice training for their own skilled workers, but in most cases, learning the job came about essentially by "sitting next to Nellie." As late as 1965 Partin observed that "with a few notable exceptions the quality of on-the-job training is poor."[9] For the traditional sector of the economy, the training of "skilled" workers was even less organized. A youngster "apprenticed" himself, for example, to a local carpenter, and, as he showed competence, was given increasing responsibility until he became a journeyman. Later he would set himself up as a carpenter in his own right. Up to 1973 the Board of Industrial Training, which had the legal responsibility to oversee apprentice training, had no standard way of checking on the competence of the apprentices before granting them journeyman status and no effective means to inspect their on-the-job training.

The G.T.I. was established to help with the formal training of apprentices, especially for the smaller companies which did not have all the necessary facilities to provide proper instruction. A major problem faced by the staff of this institute in devising their training programme for craftsmen was that most of the students had no background in the sciences and their education in mathematics left much to be desired. The result was that, up to 1968, about 25% of all students attending were doing "preliminary craft" or "basic technical" courses aimed at giving them some elementary science education and strengthening their mathematics background before they could be allowed to enter into craft training proper. The percentage fell to less than 17% in 1969, and after that, the usual "preliminary craft" courses were dropped. In its place, a one-month introductory course was sometimes provided for those selected for training in one of the skilled trades. But an important point was that many of these students, without any science and a very poor level of mathematics, had at least eight years of prior schooling. The figures in Table 38 show the proportion of the total enrolment of the G.T.I. engaged in such preliminary craft courses.

Commenting on this situation, a report by the International Bank for Reconstruction and Development (IBRD) noted that "the G.T.I. and the School of Agriculture devote much time in teaching basic

[9] *Ibid.*, p. 13.

Table 38 *Number and Percentage of G.T.I.*
Students Undertaking Preliminary
Craft Courses

Year	(a) Total no. of students on preliminary craft courses	(b) Total no. of students enrolled at G.T.I.	(a) as percentage of (b)
1961-62	337	1,401	24.0
1963-64	288	1,071	26.9
1965-66	375	1,361	27.5
1967-68	341	1,305	26.1
1968-69	292	1,723	16.9

Source: Government of Guyana, "Annual Reports of the Principal,
Government Technical Institute." Georgetown, Guyana,
1965-1969. (Mimeographed.)

mathematics and sciences which is the task of general education" and
urged

> the improvement of mathematics and science teaching and industrial
> arts for every student during the first two to three years of secondary
> education which should provide a broader background after which stu-
> dents could be expected to choose between the academic, technical and
> commercial streams.[10]

The point here is that, with the exception of the "elite" schools, a
sound science education was not available to the majority of students
attending secondary schools or the secondary divisions of all-age
schools. The result was that those who wanted to pursue technical
training found themselves at a handicap. To correct this situation,
much of the resources of the G.T.I. had to be devoted to doing work
which students could have done in their previous eight or nine years
of schooling.[11]

This problem had not disappeared, as one might have thought,
with the dropping of the preliminary craft course. Rather it had been
ignored and presented a further problem to the instructional staff of
the technical institutes. Also, when the new technical institute was

[10] IBRD/IDA, "An Appraisal of the Development Program of Guyana," Vol. 4:
Education, 27 February 1967, p. 7. (Mimeographed.)

[11] Professor Ron Dore in his comments on this point argued that when there is a
shortage of science teachers in a country the best course initially might be to concentrate on teaching science to students who will need such knowledge for their job training rather than to confine it to a few secondary schools where pupils will have an unfair
advantage in getting training opportunities. He argues that in this situation there is
nothing to complain about if basic science and mathematics have to be taught to
apprentices attending technical institutes.

opened in New Amsterdam in 1970, a "general education and science" course had to be reintroduced.

The Trade Training programme was the largest one at the G.T.I., and, as can be seen from the figures in Table 39, between 35% and 54% of all students enrolled since 1961 have been taking trade courses.

The trades for which training was offered included carpentry and joinery, electrical, motor vehicle mechanics, agricultural mechanics, radio servicing, fitters and machinery operating, and welding. Most students attended on a day- or block-release basis or in the evenings. However, with time the percentage of full-time students had increased. In 1961 all students at the G.T.I. were attending on a part-time basis, but by 1971 the percentage had fallen to just under 70%.

The formal training of craftsmen was also being undertaken by the two largest private companies in the country, the Booker Group of Companies and the Demerara Bauxite Company, both of which had their own apprenticeship training schools. But it should be noted that the "skilled" craftsmen in the traditional sector were unaffected by the standards of craft training set locally by the G.T.I.

Judging by the nature of the training which craftsmen received, there were, in fact, two groups of them in the country. In the first group were those trained by the larger companies entirely on their own or with the assistance of the G.T.I. The quality of craft training received by these apprentices was undoubtedly very high and compared favourably with similar training offered by the metropolitan centre. In the second group were those craftsmen who learned their jobs without undergoing any formal training. Many of these began working with parents or relatives or with small private contractors or sub-contractors. Skills had to be picked up on the job and the trainees had no exposure to the theoretical basis of their work. One of the major factors responsible for their "poor" training was the relatively low level of education among journeymen and supervising personnel.

In assessing the level of skills among craftsmen in 1965, Partin observed that "the vast majority of the skilled labour force which is now employed, very badly needs additional training. This includes in many cases even those who may be classified as journeymen, masters or foremen." He noted that his observation was supported by "the management of private and Government enterprises and the T.U.C. [which groups] have expressed the view that many tradesmen are not adequately competent."[12]

Here Partin was undoubtedly referring to the situation in the small private ventures operated by individuals working mainly in the traditional, or what Lewis calls the "low wage sector," of the economy.

[12] Partin, p. 13.

Table 39 Distribution of Enrolment at the G.T.I. and N.A.T.I. by Areas of Training between 1961-62 and 1972-73

Year	Total no. of students at G.T.I.	No. and percentage doing preliminary (pre-craft) courses	No. and percentage doing trade (craft) courses	No. and percentage in technician courses	No. and percentage in other business and special courses
1961-62	1,401	337 (24.0)	490 (34.9)	341 (24.3)	233 (16.6)
1962-63	1,056	263 (24.9)	478 (45.2)	231 (21.8)	84 (0.7)
1963-64	1,071	288 (26.9)	534 (49.8)	184 (17.2)	65 (6.1)
1964-65	1,199	310 (25.8)	577 (48.1)	234 (19.5)	78 (6.5)
1965-66	1,361	375 (27.5)	586 (43.1)	257 (18.9)	143 (10.5)
1966-67	1,142	362 (31.7)	416 (36.4)	285 (25.0)	79 (6.9)
1967-68	1,305	341 (26.1)	585 (44.8)	308 (23.6)	71 (5.4)
1968-69	1,723	292 (16.9)	849 (49.3)	437 (25.4)	145 (8.4)
1969-70	1,597	—	850 (53.2)	511 (32.0)	236 (14.8)
1970-71*	1,993	19 (1.0)	1,087 (54.5)	500 (25.1)	387 (19.4)
1971-72	2,126	15 (0.7)	1,187 (53.1)	597 (26.7)	437 (19.5)
1972-73	2,800	19 (0.7)	1,499 (53.5)	729 (26.0)	553 (19.8)

* In 1970 the New Amsterdam Technical Institute (N.A.T.I.) was opened and its enrolment was added to that of the technical institute in Georgetown (G.T.I.).

Source: Government of British Guiana, Annual Reports of the Director of Education or the Ministry of Education (Georgetown, 1962 to 1972).

There was no doubt that the quality of craft training received by the first group of craftsmen working in the larger, mainly expatriate firms was, by overseas standards, very good.

In fact, because of the conditions they offered, the companies in this modern or high-wage level sector had little problem in recruiting trainees. In addition, very few of the craftsmen ever left the firms in this sector, at least not prior to the heavy wave of external migration which was due mainly to political reasons and which acquired momentum in the late 1960s. While their training could not be regarded as "specific training" in Becker's[13] sense—only of value to the firm in which they were trained—these craftsmen tended to remain with the company which trained them because of their higher level of wages as compared with those prevailing in other sectors of the economy, including the Government services.

It was the skilled workmen "trained" in the traditional or low-wage sector who were the main concern of the technical education experts. This was partly because they fell so far short of the experts' conception of the ideal level of education and skill training which workmen in these trades ought to have, and partly because this sector was responsible for producing the larger number of craftsmen. The result was that, as Partin reported, "the problem with technical training at the level of the craftsmen was not the insufficiency of the numbers but the low level of skills acquired." He recommended, therefore, that "the vast majority of the skilled labour force which is now employed very badly needs additional training."[14]

It was in view of this recommendation that the Government, with the support of the IBRD/CIDA and USAID, launched various programmes for improving craft training in the country, especially in the rural areas. The first step was the establishment of a trade training centre, the Guyana Industrial Training Centre, mainly with the financial assistance of USAID. The institution began to enroll students in December 1968, and aimed at providing occupational training "on the lines tried out by USAID in other developing countries." Upon completion, the graduates were expected to be employed initially as helpers to skilled craftsmen before working as skilled craftsmen themselves.

Between 1969 and 1973 the centre graduated 736 students in such fields as carpentry, masonry, plumbing, electrical work, welding and heavy equipment operation, and maintenance, but since no follow-up study has been conducted, it is difficult to know whether they have been satisfactorily absorbed into the labour market.

[13] G. S. Becker, "Investment in On-the-Job Training," in *Economics of Education*, ed. by Mark Blaug (Harmondsworth, Middlesex, England: Penguin Books, 1968), pp. 183-207.

[14] Partin, p. 13.

In September 1971 the New Amsterdam Technical Institute was established with financial assistance from CIDA to accommodate 400 full-time students and 500 evening students at the craft and technician levels with courses broadly similar to those offered at the G.T.I. in Georgetown. By 1972 there were 507 students enrolled in such areas as motor mechanics, electrical installation, welding, plumbing, carpentry, brickwork and masonry, radio servicing, and secretarial training.

In this step towards expanding craft and technician training facilities, the Government was motivated by the increasing number of "unemployed, untrained school leavers," the rationale being that, as the IBRD put it, "the promotion of technical education and training will help to expand production and reduce unemployment."[15]

But there were two major weaknesses in this diagnosis of the educational situation of Guyana. It has already been pointed out that a feature that characterized the Guyanese economy since 1945 was that the total labour force was growing faster than the employed population, with a resulting increase in unemployment. Since educational facilities were becoming more available locally, it meant that the general level of education among the unemployed was also rising. The economy was not characterized by structural unemployment, due to the temporary shortage of trained craftsmen. In 1956, according to the manpower survey, there were 4,266 craftsmen looking for jobs and only 210 vacancies for such personnel. Also, the unemployment rate among "craftsmen and technicians" was 19.2% that year. Further, in the building trades, for which the Guyana Industrial Training Centre was hoping to produce "500 building trades craftsmen annually on a crash program," the percentage of unemployment was 20.8% in 1956 and 25.6% in 1965.

What boggles the imagination is how, in a state of heavy, almost chronic and increasing unemployment due to the failure of the economy to improve, a greater output of trained craftsmen could itself have helped to reduce unemployment as the IBRD report predicted. The administrator of the G.I.T.C. even pointed out that the length of the training period for one of the courses already had to be doubled from six months to one year, not because of any additional skills that had to be taught, but because the labour market for that skill was already saturated. And this was also likely to happen with the other courses which the G.I.T.C. offered.

The second point was an inadequate diagnosis of the nature of the labour market. In fact, there was not a single homogeneous labour market demanding craft skills of the same quality—or at least able to pay roughly the same level of wages to all craftsmen. First, there was the labour market for craftsmen in the modern or high-wage sector

[15] IBRD/IDA, p. 11.

and, secondly, the labour market in the traditional or low-wage sector. As Arthus Lewis pointed out, there is a market difference in the wage levels in these two sectors of the economy in developing countries, with earnings in the high-wage sector seldom being less than 50% more than wages in the low-earning or traditional sector. This effectively makes two job markets for skilled manpower.

But even the modern sector was not homogeneous. First, there were the very modern and larger industrial enterprises—Demba, now Guybau and Bookers—and the smaller, progressive private companies, some of which were expatriate owned. The equipment used by these companies and the expected standards of performance from their craftsmen were almost comparable to those in economically more developed countries. These had relatively little problem in the recruitment, training, and retention of skilled workers.

Second, there were the Government or public corporations which demanded a level of craft training comparable to that of private industries which were also in the modern sector. Like private industry, the Government tended to have modern equipment and expected the performance standards of its craftsmen to be comparable to those in the larger and more progressive companies. But the problem here was that the Government wage schedules were not regulated by the current supply and demand situation but by tradition and by the status which civil service groups were accorded in the past. Craftsmen employed by Government have tended to be at the bottom of the wage ladder, resulting in the general failure of the Government service to recruit skilled craftsmen with the same level of training as those employed in the larger and more progressive private companies.

Up to the 1940s the demand for skilled craftsmen in the public sector was very limited because the colonial government was not very much involved in development activities which required such personnel. Also, the level of skills of these craftsmen was not very high because Government provided no formal training for them. Lastly, since their own investment in their training was minimal, their salaries were low. For example, it was then much more costly to give a youngster secondary education than have him "trained" as a craftsman, and salary scales originally reflected this fact. The difference in salaries between clerical personnel and skilled workmen has continued in the civil service until today, despite the fact that the years of schooling which skilled workmen must now complete have increased, the nature of the training which they are ideally expected to undertake for public service employment has improved, and the cost of the investment in this type of training has risen.

If one compared the 1973 Government salary scales for craftsmen with those of other types of Government personnel whose general education was not much higher and who had no special training (at least nothing comparable to what craftsmen are now expected to undergo), the persistence of this disparity in wages referred to above can be seen.

Table 40 *Maximum Annual Salaries of Craftsmen Compared with Salaries of Lower Level White-Collar Jobs in Government Service, 1973*

Salaries of personnel with skill training	Salaries of lower-level, white-collar jobs
(1) *Maximum salaries under $1,700 per year*	
Cooks ($1,302), Seamstresses ($1,396), Head Laundresses ($1,398), Gardeners ($1,398), Tailors ($1,620), Bakers ($1,620)	Watchmen ($1,398), Messengers ($1,620), Gatekeepers ($1,620), Boathands ($1,620)
(2) *Maximum salaries between $1,700 and $1,900*	
Carpenters, Resident Carpenters, Head Carpenters, Carpenter/Joiners, Assistant Foremen, Mechanics, Cycle Mechanics, Binder/Repairers, Typists, Head Seamstresses, Head Bakers, Coopers, Darkroom Technicians, Coxswains, Captain/Engineers, Assistant Printers, Radio Operators ($1,878)	Checkers ($1,860), Office Assistants ($1,860), Vault Attendants ($1,860) Stores Assistants, Storemen, Rural Postmen, Drivers, Receptionists ($1,878)
(3) *Maximum salaries between $1,900 and $3,000*	
Boatbuilders ($2,020), Engineers, Government Launches ($2,352), Dental Mechanics ($2,352), Foremen Electricians ($2,568), Lumber Graders ($2,640), Librarians ($2,652), Foremen Mechanics ($2,880)	Town Postmen ($2,028), Guards ($2,160), Constables ($2,628), Assistant Storekeepers ($2,652), Class II Clerks ($2,652), Storekeepers ($3,552)

Source: Government of Guyana, *Estimates (Current and Capital) of Guyana for the Year 1973* (Georgetown, 1973).

Persons requiring such skills as tailors, bakers, cooks, etc., were paid no more than gatekeepers, messengers, and general boathands. Also, the majority of the skilled workers were in the salary bracket which had a maximum salary of $1,878 per year—a scale which was almost the beginning one for other types of non-technical personnel with a somewhat similar general educational background.

Promotion was more likely and more rewarding among those who were non-craftsmen—a point which is borne out by the fact that, while a stores assistant receiving a maximum salary of $1,878 per annum (which was the same for most craftsmen) could be promoted to an assistant storekeeper with a maximum salary of $2,652 per annum and then to storekeeper at $3,552 per annum (a salary range beyond the level of all craftsmen), a carpenter moving up to resident carpenter or to head carpenter only moved faster within the same salary scale and towards the same maximum salary of $1,878 per annum. While these are individual examples, they do reflect the relative disparity in incomes between clerical workers and craftsmen in the Government service.

Commenting on the same phenomena, Partin noted that

> particularly in the Government service the salary scales are not encouraging to capable people to engage in skilled technical occupation. Many routine clerical positions have higher salary classifications than some skilled occupations. It is more remunerative to be even a Class III clerk (the lowest level in the clerical service and one which does not even require a secondary education) than a skilled carpenter. The unskilled constable may well receive the same salary as the skilled craftsmen who maintain the force's mechanical and electrical equipment.[16]

Because of the lower salaries which the Government service offered, it was not competing with other industries in the modern sector for skilled craftsmen who had gone through a fairly thorough apprenticeship training which included theoretical instruction but was, in fact, "creaming off" the best "skilled" workmen in the traditional sector whose training and educational levels were much lower. This was why there were constant references to the "poor type of middle supervisory personnel" in the Government services in the craft fields. Many of these craftsmen did not have the necessary education and training to become competent supervisors. And, with its lower wages, it was not surprising that the public sector could not recruit people with the necessary level of education and training capable of taking over supervisory positions. In the Government services, therefore, the problem was not so much a shortage of skilled personnel but the low level of skills of the personnel it attracted with its lower salaries.

The next sector of the labour market was the traditional or low-wage level sector. Incomes here were generally much lower than those in the modern sector. This was reflected both in the lower average

[16] Partin, p. 14.

wage rates of artisans and in their level of formal training. For example, skilled carpenters here could not read blueprints, nor did the motor mechanics have any background knowledge of physics.

Upgrading the quality of training received by artisans in this sector and standardizing it with that in the modern sector would have resulted in a higher rate of private investment in their training, a factor which would have had undesirable consequences. First, if these workmen increased the amount of investment in their training, this would result in a demand for higher wages. Since the traditional sector in which they worked was not economically buoyant and could not afford higher wages for building construction workers, for example, there would have been no demand for such well-trained but high-priced artisans. In such a situation, potential employers in the traditional sector would substitute the lower priced personnel with less formal training to do their jobs and the result would be increased unemployment among these highly trained but expensive artisans. The only way they were likely to avoid increased unemployment was if the modern or high-wage level sector was expanding rapidly enough to absorb them at the wage rate which they were virtually forced to demand because of the higher rate of investment in the acquisition of their skills.

Although there is no research to substantiate the claim, it seems that the heavy unemployment rate among craftsmen and technicians in 1965 (19.2% as compared with an unemployment rate of 6.4% among clerical and sales workers) might have been related to the efforts at upgrading and standardizing the level of skills among all craftsmen. As a result of the additional investment in their training, these craftsmen were naturally demanding higher wages for their skills and were pricing themselves out of the low-wage sector of the economy. Since employment opportunities in the high-wage sector were not increasing fast enough to absorb them, a high percentage remained unemployed. On this point it was probably significant that it was the building and construction trades—which had the greatest number of nonformal "training" arrangements for skilled workers—which reported the highest rate of unemployment in the country.

If we accept the experts' view that the skill level of the practising craftsmen in the low-wage sector of the economy needed upgrading, then the issue was how to achieve this objective without increasing the private cost of training. In the case of Guyana, this might have been attempted by helping the personnel responsible for training and supervising apprentices in the traditional sector improve their own skills and knowledge and also their methods of teaching the apprentices. It should be noted that any new effort at training with substantially increased costs to the individual will result in an increased cost of their services, possibly pricing them out of the low-wage sector of the economy.

The important point which the technical education experts failed to recognize was the dualistic nature of the job market for skilled craftsmen in developing countries like Guyana. Employers in the high-wage sector could afford to pay the wages to compensate for the higher rate of investment which skilled workmen had to make in their training. On the other hand, wages in the traditional sector were often so low that they could not compensate for the additional investment these workmen had to incur in extended formal training pro-grammes. The "better trained" artisans often preferred to wait until "something turned up" in the more remunerative sector of the economy. If this failed they sought employment overseas.

The problem facing developing countries like Guyana is not al-ways the paucity of formal training facilities for skilled craftsmen but rather the failure of the modern sector to expand rapidly enough to absorb these better trained artisans at a wage level which will compen-sate them for the investment in their training.

Agricultural Education

Agriculture continued to be an important sector in the Guyanese economy, employing 46% of the labour force in 1945 and 32% in 1965. Yet despite its importance, little effort was made prior to self-government to establish an agricultural school locally. Most of the Government's energies in this field were directed towards the teach-ing of agriculture in the primary schools.

The legislators, as can be seen from the Legislative Council de-bates, had continuously been urging the Government to establish a school of agriculture to train farmers and "would-be" farmers so that agricultural practices could be improved and crop production diver-sified. Some of their concerns can be seen in the following excerpts from parliamentary reports since 1948.

Nicholson—28 February 1948

"I would like to see the establishment of farm schools. . . . School gardens . . . only tend to play with the situation."

Jagan—3 March 1948

"What should be considered is whether this $36,000 [now being spent on the Social Welfare Department] could be better spent. I think it would be better to start an agricultural school in British Guiana instead of teaching people to make baskets.

Nicholson—3 March 1948

also criticized the Social Welfare Department's budget and suggested that the money be put into cooperative farming and "let us have a farm school."

Gonsalves—3 February 1949
> introduced a bill to establish in Corentyne district a Technical and Agricultural Training School.

Coglan—3 February 1949
> noted that British Guiana had no agricultural college—as compared with Trinidad which was a smaller country.

Collins—12 February 1949
> "An agricultural training scheme should be put into operation to cater to those between 12 and 21 years of age."

Carter—9 February 1954
> pointed out that the sum of $3,000 voted for training agricultural apprentices was inadequate. He saw the lack of knowledge of modern farm production as responsible for the low agricultural yield which farmers get and also for the lack of diversification in agricultural production. He, therefore, suggested the provision of more funds to train agricultural apprentices.

Farnum—19 February 1954
> referred to the need for "a proper system of apprenticeship training in agriculture" to accompany the establishment of a proposed new agricultural station. "The best thing I think would be to establish a farm school along proper lines. The training should be given to the sons of farmers particularly those who would be able to use it on their parents' farm."

Smellie—19 February 1954
> "What the farmers want is instruction in agriculture—practical instruction."

Carter—17 November 1955
> introduced a motion for the establishment of a "pilot agricultural farm school" for youths eighteen to twenty-four years of age, to give them two years of practical training in agriculture with an aim to settling them on a land settlement scheme.

Bobb—24 November 1955
> "I welcome this opportunity to support the plea of the Village Chairman's Conference that Government should consider seriously the establishment of a farm school."

Fraser—30 May 1959
> "I hope the Government would actually do something about the establishment of a farm school."

But these many requests by the legislators to see a farm school established in Guyana went almost unheeded by the colonial administration. In 1955, one member of the Legislative Council finally observed:

> I am well aware that this matter [of establishing a farm school] was discussed on several occasions in the third and fourth Legislative Councils and Council accepted on two occasions the principle of it [i.e. establishing a farm school] and the motion was sent to the Government recommending the establishment of such a school. But it was never implemented.[17]

The Government, in its reply to these suggestions, always raised the issue of cost. In the 1954 budget debate, the Financial Secretary observed that "a farm school is a most expensive undertaking,"[18] and in November 1955 he again spoke of the high cost of such a school and the problem of staffing it. Alternatively, he introduced a motion in the Legislative Council in March 1951 for the country to participate in the establishment of the Eastern Caribbean Farm Institute (E.C.F.I.) in Trinidad which would allow the country to send five students there annually for training. But the legislators rejected the motion, arguing that the number of Guyanese to be trained under this scheme would be insufficient to meet the country's needs and they again urged the Government to establish its own farm school.

This, however, never materialized until after self-government, when the Guyana School of Agriculture (G.S.A.) was established in September 1963. In its desire to put the school into operation immediately, the new Government converted existing houses at Mon Repose belonging to the Department of Agriculture into classrooms, dormitories, and cafeteria. Part of the machinery storage shed was also adapted for laboratories for the teaching of chemistry, biology, and physics, while another building was used for the library and administrative offices. The Ministry of Agriculture supplied the teaching staff on a part-time basis. Two years later, in 1965, the school, with a generous grant of $188,000 from OXFAM, was able to secure better facilities and a full-time staff.

Programme

The school offered the following three types of courses:

(1) Two-year diploma course for students who would become agricultural teachers and possibly even field supervisors or instructors in such agencies as the Agricultural Co-operative Bank, the Guyana Defence Force and even in the sugar industry.

(2) One-year certificate course which was specifically intended to train "would-be" farmers.

[17] Government of British Guiana, Speech by W. Raatgever, in *Hansard*, 24 November 1955.

[18] Government of British Guiana, Speech by E. McDavid, Financial Secretary, in *Hansard*, 12 February 1954.

(3) specialized courses for practising farmers in such areas as livestock and vegetable crop production.

Although the number of graduates produced by the school has so far been limited, the annual output has been increasing fairly rapidly, as is shown in Table 41. Between 1965 and 1973, a total of 318 students graduated from the school at the diploma and certificate levels.

Table 41 *Students Completing Courses at the Guyana School of Agriculture, 1965 to 1973*

Year	Diploma students	Certificate students	Total
1964-65	12	12	24
1965-66	9	6	15
1966-67	5	18	23
1967-68	4	13	17
1968-69	21	31	52
1969-70	20	12	32
1970-71	21	21	42
1971-72	37	12	49
1972-73	44	20	64

Source: Guyana School of Agriculture, "Annual Reports of the Principal, G.S.A." Mon Repos, E.C.D., Guyana, 1965-1973. (Mimeographed.)

The demand for places in the School of Agriculture has always exceeded the supply. The Principal, in his 1967 report, noted that "the number of vacancies compared with the number of applications was roughly 1:16; that is to say that for every 16 applications there was only one vacancy at the school."[19] In 1973 there were still 600 applications for the seventy places available. But the main problem facing the school was the quality of the applicants.

At first the school found it very difficult to attract students with an adequate number of passes at the G.C.E. "O" Level examination, since these, for financial reasons, preferred to enter the administrative branch of the civil service. The starting salary of an agricultural field assistant who completed two years of training at the School of Agriculture was the same as the Class II clerk who entered the civil service directly from high school. Also, the highest position to which an agricultural instructor could have aspired was that of senior agricultural field assistant with a maximum salary of $352 per month in 1973, while a Class II clerk, rising to the level of senior clerk, received the same salary. From here, the senior clerk could move to the posi-

[19] Guyana School of Agriculture, "Report of the Principal 1966-67" (Mon Repos, Guyana, 1967), p. 6. (Mimeographed.)

tion of chief clerk or its equivalent with a maximum monthly salary of $412. Also, the chances of rising further in the civil service were very good and he could conceivably become a Permanent Secretary—a post which in 1973 carried a salary of $860 per month. There was no comparable opportunity for promotion for someone trained in agriculture.

In his 1966-67 report, the Principal observed that the reason for the failure of the school to attract students of academically high quality was that

> there isn't enough monetary incentive in the starting salary of an agricultural field assistant. In fact, the student who enters the G.S.A. with, for example, five G.C.E. ordinary level subjects and does the 2-year diploma course successfully will have lost two increments had he been employed as a clerical assistant in the Civil Service.[20]

In addition to this he would have had to meet the private cost of his two years of agricultural education.

Since 1968 the educational background of students applying for admission to the school has improved and the Principal observed that "interviews for the 1974-75 year revealed that applicants possessed from 4 to 11 G.C.E. "O" level subjects for the diploma course."[21] However, the school has still not yet been able to attract enough students with an adequate science background because of the lack of science teaching in most of the non-elite secondary schools and the better job prospects for those from the elite schools with G.C.E. certificates.

Apart from the increased supply of secondary school graduates, there was another factor partly responsible for this rise in the number of better qualified students applying for entry to the G.S.A. Some of the diploma students were proceeding abroad to do university degrees in the U.S.A. and receiving almost full credit for work done at the school. Two of the better diploma holders of 1968, for example, eventually obtained their Master's degrees in agriculture. This, the Principal noted, has acted as incentive for better qualified applicants to seek admission to the school. Many diploma students were not interested in remaining at the sub-professional level but were anxious to obtain university degrees by combining the less costly course at the G.S.A. with a shortened programme at an overseas university. This reduced the private cost of their professional training and helped to make the course at the G.S.A. more attractive to the better-qualified applicants.

Commenting on the selection of intending farmers for the certificate course, the Principal noted that "experience has shown that it

---

[20] *Ibid.*, p. 3.
[21] Principal, Guyana School of Agriculture, in private correspondence with the author.

is not easy to find students of the 'would be' farmer category." Most of those entering the certificate course were not really interested in working as farmers at all, at least not under the conditions in which most farmers in the country worked. To be a successful farmer in Guyana, one needed a fair amount of capital to purchase enough land, and many of these youngsters were not in any financial position to do so. Recently, there have been some incentives provided by Government to aid agricultural expansion, including duty free imports of such items as agricultural machinery, fertilizers, insecticides, seeds, planting materials, and breeding stock. However, despite these incentives, the rewards to the small farmer remained low as compared with those who enter white-collar employment even in such agriculture-related jobs as extension workers, evaluation officers for the Guyana Agricultural Co-operative Bank, and in other para-statal and private firms.

The student selection panel at the School of Agriculture found that the majority of the students, i.e. those on the Certificate Course are "job oriented."[22] That is to say they were interested in jobs as employees, not as independent farmers. This has been borne out by the types of positions which certificate holders took up on graduation. A follow-up study indicated that not only were they not becoming farmers, but like the diploma students, most of them sought and found jobs in the various departments of Government. On this point, the Principal reported that "although the objective of the certificate course is to train 'would-be' farmers, I understand that a number of them have also filled junior posts in the Ministry of Agriculture and Natural Resources."[23]

The figures in Table 42 show that over 75% of both diploma and certificate holders were employed in the public sector in 1973.

So, while great emphasis was placed on the establishment of a School of Agriculture in Guyana, not enough attention was directed towards reducing the structural constraints in a society which militated against youngsters pursuing agriculture as a career. The theory of an "innate dislike" for manual work, especially agriculture, among Guyanese and West Indians, has resulted in Governments failing to come to grips with the real source of this "dislike" for agriculture. For example, in 1966 it was reported that "there are more than 25,000 persons willing to engage in agriculture but have no land to cultivate."[24] In 1967 Mr. W. A. Davidson, Principal of the G.S.A., pointed out that the motivation of students to enter farming was lacking "be-

[22] Guyana School of Agriculture, "Report of the Principal 1974-75." (Mimeographed.)

[23] Guyana School of Agriculture, "Report of the Principal 1966-67," p. 5.

[24] Government of British Guiana, "British Guiana Development Programme 1962-72" (Georgetown, 1966).

Table 42 *Employment of Certificate and Diploma Holders of the Guyana School of Agriculture, 1965 to 1973*

Type of qualification held	Fields of employment						
	Government departments	Public corporations	Private companies	Own account farmers	Pursuing further studies overseas	Other, e.g., occupation unknown	Total
Certificate in Agriculture	91 (62.8%)	22 (15.2%)	11 (7.6%)	0	2 (1.4%)	19 (13.1%)	145
Diploma in Agriculture	120 (60.4%)	9 (5.2%)	13 (7.5%)	0	26 (15.0%)	5	173

Source: Annual Report of the Principal G.S.A., 1974.

cause of the subsistence farming for the most part practised by their parents and/or relatives. They see farming as a hard, back-breaking affair, with little or no attraction in life. Herein lies a problem for the agents of change."[25]

It will be recalled that arable land was in short supply in Guyana and the capital costs for drainage and irrigation were usually very high. So, the most productive work of the G.S.A. was its effort to improve farming techniques among practising farmers and the proper training of agricultural extension workers. But the problem with those trained as agricultural field assistants was their lack of practical agricultural experience under the farming conditions as they existed among the subsistence farmers in the country. As late as 1971 a UNESCO report noted that "extension staff" do not appear to enjoy credibility in the farming community as a whole. In fact, this is one of the problems found in most agricultural departments in third world countries. While the staff, including the lecturers in the Colleges of Agriculture, might have a sound theoretical knowledge of their subject, they often lack practical agricultural experience and thus enjoy little credibility in the eyes of the local farming community.

The training of "would-be" farmers would be successful only if accompanied by measures to improve the system of land distribution. Some West Indian economists have agreed that the most important factor retarding the economic development of Guyana and the West Indies in general is the institutional legacy of a system in which most of the better agricultural land is used or controlled by the plantations. This has stagnated the development of an economically vibrant peasant sector. For example, it has been estimated that "throughout the West Indies, 79% of the total number of farms account for only 13% of the total acreage in farms, and all these farms are under five acres. By contrast, 0.6% of the total number of farms account for 55% of the total acreage, and all these farms are over 100 acres."[26]

The plantations also control the most fertile, well-drained and well-irrigated lands. It has been argued that efforts to improve the standards of living of the independent peasantry in Guyana and the West Indies by making more land available to them have not been very successful, resulting in the suggestion by some economists that the birth of an independent peasantry can only be achieved by the destruction of the plantation system.[27]

Lloyd Best, in writing about the possibilities of social and economic reconstruction for Guyana, has urged that "all publicly

[25] Guyana School of Agriculture, "Report of the Principal 1966-67," p. 3.
[26] Clive Y. Thomas, "The Political Economy of Exploitation in the Caribbean," *Black Lines* Vols. 2 and 3, Nos. 2 and 3, Special Double Issue (Winter 1971 and Spring 1972), p. 43.
[27] Beckford, see chapter 8.

owned land, Crown lands or otherwise, be ceded to the Local Authorities"[28] as a first step towards diversification and improvement of agricultural production. This would mean taking back from the sugar estates those lands which had been leased to them by the Government, whether or not these were cultivated.

Whatever steps are taken in this direction, the point is that unless the peasant sector has well-drained and well-irrigated lands available as a first step towards improving the farmers' standard of living beyond the subsistence levels, any large-scale effort at agricultural education will be futile.

University Education

The development of higher education in the region has been documented elsewhere and will not be dealt with here, except in passing. As part of the post-1945 efforts of the United Kingdom Government to establish universities in the British Colonial empire, the University College of the West Indies (U.C.W.I.) came into being in 1948. This new institution, like its counterparts at Ibadan, Makerere, and elsewhere, was until 1962 a college of the University of London.

U.C.W.I. was originally located in Jamaica and each of the participating territories, which included Guyana, contributed financially to its support. The faculty of medicine was the first to be established in 1948 and eventually other faculties followed—arts, sciences, social sciences, education, and even later, engineering and agriculture.

It is difficult to assess the impact of this university on Guyana, especially since only a small percentage of Guyanese students studying overseas were enrolled at the University of the West Indies (U.W.I.). In 1952 only 17.5% (31 out of a total of 177) of Guyanese students in different countries overseas (excluding the U.S.A., for which the figures were unknown) were registered at the U.W.I. However, as the university expanded and diversified its programme, Guyanese students began attending in greater numbers, with the highest proportion registered in medicine. As can be seen from Table 43, their numbers began to fall only after Guyana withdrew its financial support from the university in 1963.

From its very inception there was some dissatisfaction with the U.C.W.I. among middle-class Guyanese. A source of criticism was the location of the institution and the cost of attending it. As one member of the Legislature indicated in 1948, "it will be equally expensive to send a boy to the West Indian University in Jamaica as to send him to a university in England."[29] This was, in fact, the case.

[28] Lloyd Best, "Working Notes towards the Unification of Guyana," *New World Quarterly* (March 1963), p. 32.

[29] Government of British Guiana, D. P. Debidin, in *Hansard*, 20 February 1948.

Table 43   *Guyanese Students Enrolled at the University of the West Indies, 1948 to 1965*

Year beginning October	Medi-cine	Science	Arts	Social Science & S.W.	Engin-eering	Edu-cation	Agri-culture	Total
1948-50	13	9	5	—	—	—	—	27
1951-53	48	25	22	—	—	3	—	98
1954-56	93	24	46	—	—	10	—	173
1957-59	122	53	111	—	—	8	—	294
1960-62	146	100	113	45	10	10	18	442
1963-65	134	53	57	40	7	3	5	297

Source: University of the West Indies, *Annual Report of the Principal* (Mona, Jamaica, 1950-1965).

Also, the middles classes were still worried about the standards and prestige of the new University College. D. P. Debidin, a legislator, expressed the view of quite a large percentage of this group when he said in the Legislative Council that "even if it cost a little more I would send my son to a better university if I had the opportunity to do so and let him have the best."[30]

This prejudice against the new University College persisted for quite some time, and in 1952 there were six Guyanese studying for arts degrees at the U.W.I. as compared with sixteen in the United Kingdom. However, by the 1960s this prejudice was, to a large extent, overcome; in 1963, the last year of Guyana's full participation in U.W.I., there were fifty-four Guyanese students doing arts subjects overseas (the U.S.A. excluded); of these, thirty-five (64.8%) were enrolled at the U.W.I.

Upon the achievement of self-government in 1960, the Government of Guyana decided to establish its own university and started phasing out its contribution to the University of the West Indies. There were many factors responsible for this decision. Among them was the fact that U.W.I. represented a "high cost institution," especially when the cost per returning graduate was considered. For example, a Ministry of Education paper (undated) prepared in 1964 estimated that, excluding capital grants

the total contribution made [by Guyana] to the operating cost of the U.W.I. between 1948 and 1961 was about (G) $3.3 m [about $1.65 millions U.S.]. During that time, only 41 graduates returned to offer their services to the country. This meant that the real cost to the country of training a Guyanese graduate at U.W.I. during these years was (G) $80,000 [or $40,000 U.S.].[31]

[30] *Ibid.*

[31] Government of British Guiana, Ministry of Education, "An Economic Justification for the University of Guyana" (Georgetown, ca. 1962). (Mimeographed.)

At the time, the Government envisaged that the comparable cost for an arts of science graduate at its proposed university would be under $G8,500.

The other reason advanced by the Government was the need to increase the number of middle-range technical cadres, to train an "adequate number of high-level professionals to exercise intellectual leadership in Guyana and man positions of highest responsibility," and "to undertake active research."[32] The argument here was that the forty-one Guyanese graduates returning from U.W.I. between 1948 and 1961 was not enough to meet the needs of a country soon to acquire its independence.

In view of the latter criticism, the U.W.I. offered to establish a college of arts and science in Guyana. This would have allowed students to pursue a general degree locally and those who wanted to do professional training in medicine, engineering, and agriculture would still have had the facilities of the U.W.I. open to them at the campuses providing such training.

But the Government's decision not to take up this offer indicates that there were other reasons for the establishment of the University of Guyana. First, many of the leaders in the Guyanese Government had a basically different conception of a university education from that which was typified by the U.W.I., and they were very dissatisfied with the elitist nature of that institution. In fact, the Premier of Guyana ·strongly felt that the country needed a more populist-oriented institution which would have a greater impact among all sections of the community, especially the working classes. The Government originally envisioned an institution along the lines of the U.S. land grant colleges which would be actively working with various community groups, helping them to solve their problems.

Secondly, and possibly as important as the first consideration, was the dissatisfaction of Government with what it considered to be the over-riding political orientation of the U.W.I., which it felt was dominated by a politically conservative approach to social and economic problems. The Government was, therefore, hopeful that the proposed University of Guyana would create an educated nucleus which would develop a socialist perspective in the analysis and solutions of Guyanese problems. Although this was never clearly stated, it was implicit in the first objective of the new university mentioned in the Government's booklet, *Year of Education 1963.* The objective was:

> to create an intellectual nucleus in Guyana, partly as a centre around which some systematic definition of the national purpose can take place and partly as a defence against the persistent battering from external

[32] Government of British Guiana, Ministry of Education, *Year of Education, 1963* (Georgetown, 1963), p. 19.

colonist and reactionary ideas (against which colonial and backward societies are so helpless.)[33]

Developments at the University of Guyana

The University of Guyana started in 1963 in a rather non-traditional manner, and was, from its inception, an independent university. It began as an evening college and remained so until September 1973, when full-time students were admitted.

There were many criticisms of the university by local middle-class groups and individuals who disapproved of an independent university for the country. They were worried about whether the degrees awarded by "Jagan's or Nunes' night school" would be accepted by other institutions of similar rank in other countries. Many urged the Government to seek for the fledgling university some form of attachment with a well-known, established, and internationally acceptable centre of learning. McGill University in Canada was suggested and at one time considered as a possible sponsor for the proposed new university. But the Government was itself hesitant about any form of tutelage which might have interfered with the flexibility of the young university and eventually decided against such an approach.

Instead, it sought to win recognition for the University of Guyana by the appointment of an internationally distinguished academician, Dr. Lancelot Hogben, D. Sc., LL. D., F.R.S., as its Principal and Vice-Chancellor. The Principal set up a system of external examinership to ensure that standards were maintained, while at the same time giving the university the flexibility it needed to be innovative.

A distinguishing feature of the new university was its proposal for involvement in a major way with the study of local problems. The plans were for all Government-sponsored research units to become the nuclei of various institutes of the university which would still maintain close contact with the relevant government departments. Institutes were proposed in the areas of "Agriculture, Forestry, Fisheries, Geology, Education, and Social Technology."[34]

The idea behind this proposed transfer of all Government-sponsored research to these various institutes of the university was not only to update the quality of the research currently being undertaken in the country but also to increase the relevance of the instructional programme. In addition, it was expected that, since the institutes were part of a university, they would be in a better position than Government departments to attract assistance from overseas educational foundations for their research. It was further envisaged that Government field personnel, who found important problems on which

[33] *Ibid.*

[34] University of Guyana, "Report of the Principal on Research and Research Institutes in the University" (Georgetown, 1962). (Mimeographed.)

they wanted to do research, would be able to withdraw temporarily from their jobs and pursue their investigation under the auspices of one of the appropriate institutes. This would have helped to ensure that research attention at the university was being focussed on the more immediate problems faced by practitioners in the field.

However, with the change of Government in 1965 and the resignation of the first Principal soon after, many of these original ideas were not pursued and the University of Guyana became a somewhat more conventional university. The overriding preoccupation became one of attaining "respectable" academic standards which would have acceptance throughout the academic world. The result was that the original proposal for the establishment of institutes working closely with Government departments on the research problems faced by practitioners in the various fields never really materialized. In addition, the idea of the University of Guyana working with community groups to help them cope with their own local problems was never really implemented.

Enrolment

Between 1963 and 1972 the number of students entering the University of Guyana increased by 114%. Interestingly, the percentage of students enrolled in the natural sciences has remained fairly constant and the enrolment as a whole was fairly evenly distributed among the arts, natural sciences, and the social sciences, as illustrated in Table 44.

But despite the efforts by the university to maintain a more balanced production of graduates in these three faculties, we find that of the 365 students graduating from the university by 1972 only 17% were holders of natural science degrees. This was due to the high percentage of dropouts among the natural science students (see Table 45).

The high dropout rate among second-year social science students could largely be explained by the fact that many of them were teachers, and the Ministry of Education refused at first to grant social science graduates the same salaries as arts and natural sciences graduates. So, many of those who originally enrolled in the social sciences switched over to the Faculty of Arts.

But as far as the natural science students were concerned, the heavier dropout rate was due to the greater difficulty these students experienced in obtaining their degrees. Also, even among those who graduated it was observed that natural science students took a longer time to secure their qualifications. About 41% of the arts graduates had completed their degrees after four years while only 18% of the natural science graduates had obtained their degrees by this time.

Table 44 *Enrolment of Degree Students at the University of Guyana, 1963 to 1972*

Year of entry	Arts	Natural Science		Social Science	Total
		No.	Percentage		
1963-64	60	42	25.6	62	164
1964-65	60	44	28.6	50	154
1965-66	41	34	38.3	45	120
1966-67	70	53	27.5	70	193
1967-68	50	49	33.1	49	148
1968-69	72	82	37.4	65	219
1969-70	84	109	42.2	65	258
1970-71	104	65	26.7	74	243
1971-72	100	62	26.3	74	236
1972-73	94	69	27.5	88	251
Total	735	609		642	1,986
Percentage of total	37.0	30.7		32.3	100

Source: A. Baksh, "Education and Economic Development: The Relevance to Guyana" (Turkeyen: University of Guyana, Department of Sociology, February 1973). (Mimeographed.)

Table 45 *Dropout Rate by Percentage of Degree Level Students from the University of Guyana, 1963-64 to 1970-71*

Year of dropout from faculty	Arts	Natural Sciences	Social Sciences
2nd year	16.9	30.8	30.5
3rd year	14.8	30.3	13.2
4th year	3.9	21.8	10.7
Total dropout 2nd to 4th year	35.6	82.9	54.4

Source: A. Baksh, "The Pattern of Higher Education at the University of Guyana, 1963/64-1971/72." Turkeyen, E.C.D., Guyana, 1973. (Mimeographed.)

This underrepresentation in the output of natural science graduates led Baksh[35] to raise the issue about the importance of this phenomenon for the country's economic development needs, at a time when increasing stress was being placed on the teaching of sciences in schools.

Employment of Graduates

In Baksh's study of U.G. graduates, it was found that the majority, at least up to 1973, have been employed in the public sector—mainly in teaching. In 1972 nearly 51% were employed as teachers and another 12.6% were in the civil service. Only 4.7% found jobs in the private sector and another 2.2% were employed in public corporations. Of the other graduates, 7.4% were employed by the university (2.7% in lecturing and the others in administration) while 19.2% had gone overseas permanently or for postgraduate studies. This pattern of employment was not changing very much and the public service was employing even more of these graduates. For example, among those who graduated more recently (between 1969 and 1972), about 66% went into or remained in teaching and about 24% went into the civil service.

One factor undoubtedly responsible for this was that immediately on graduation those in teaching or in the civil service were given graduate status and placed on a special salary scale for graduates. In fact, Baksh's findings revealed that the salary improvements which graduates received were quite substantial. For example, while 77% of students during their final year at U.G. were receiving salaries of less than $300(G) per month, within an average span of about two years after graduation, 54% were receiving over $500(G) per month. While some of this was due to annual increments and promotions, most was a result of the new status which graduates automatically received on securing their degrees.

A more recent development has been the post-1966 introduction of certificate and diploma courses in such fields as education, public administration, and medical technology and the establishment of the Department of Technical Studies, which aims at producing middle level technical manpower mainly for the private sectors and for public corporations. So far, the university graduates have not found jobs in the private sector. It will be interesting to see if the situation will change when the holders of technical diplomas begin appearing on the job market.

[35] Ahamad Baksh, "Education and Economic Development: The Relevance to Guyana" (Turkeyen: University of Guyana, Department of Sociology, February 1973). (Mimeographed.)

7. Expenditure on Education

The rapid expansion of Guyanese education services since 1945 obviously exerted great pressures on the financial resources of the country, especially since its per capita real income was increasing very slowly, if at all, during the period under review. This chapter will examine what percentage of the total Government expenditure and the overall wealth of the country was being spent on education, and whether a new pattern of educational expenditure was emerging during this time.

There were obviously sources of expenditure on formal education other than the Government; for example, voluntary agencies, industrial enterprises, and private individuals; but in this study, attention will be devoted entirely to Government expenditure, which, in Guyana, accounted for over 90% of all local expenditure on education. The recurrent and the capital or development budgets will be reviewed separately.

The Recurrent Budget

During the last three years of World War II, Guyana had experienced an "unprecedentedly high level of prosperity,"[1] with the result that the annual recurrent budget nearly doubled itself, at current prices, between 1941 and 1946. Expenditure on education during this period rose faster than on most other Government services, and the Education Department increased its share of the recurrent budget from 9.9% in 1942 to 12.2% in 1946.

In the post-1946 period this increase continued but before making an analysis of the changing pattern of such expenditure, it will be useful to list and categorize those items in the recurrent budget being included here as "recurrent expenditure on education." It will be misleading to take the total budget of the Ministry of Education, since some of these funds were not spent on educational projects at all. In addition, there were certain items of educational expenditure appearing in the budgets of other Government departments. These had to be pulled together.

The following categories of expenditure on education were finally selected:

[1] Government of British Guiana, Budget Speech by the Colonial Treasurer, in *Hansard*, 1946.

Administration of Education Salaries and allowances for the administrative and professional staff of the Department or Ministry of Education and the expenditure on local examinations. During the period when the Ministry of Education was part of a larger unit (the Ministry of Education and Social Development) an estimate was made of the administrative costs of the education services alone;

Primary Education All expenditure on primary schools including such items as teachers' salaries, school feeding, school broadcasts, and "other charges";

Secondary Education Expenditure on Government-owned and Government-aided secondary grammar schools and the additional cost of Government scholarships tenable at these schools. An estimate of the current expenditure on the new Government secondary schools established after 1963 had to be made since the operational expenses of these schools were still being met from the general vote "Primary, Multilateral and Secondary Schools";

Teacher Education Expenditure on the Government Training College for Teachers, the cost of overseas and vacation courses for teachers, the In-Service Teacher Training Programme, and the College of Education preparing teachers for the multilateral schools;

Vocational and Technical Education The operational costs of the Government Technical Institute, the Guyana Industrial Trade Centre, the New Amsterdam Technical Institute, the Carnegie School of Home Economics, and an annual grant to the Fredericks School of Home Economics;

Higher Education Grants to universities or institutions of similar rank, including the University of Guyana, and general scholarships to universities through non-"conditional" scholarships to civil servants.

In examining the pattern of recurrent educational expenditure, the following questions and issues will be highlighted: (a) Whether educational expenditure was keeping pace with or out-stripping increases in the total recurrent budget of the Government; (b) Whether the nation was devoting a smaller or larger proportion of its national economic resources to education; and (c) Whether the pattern of recurrent expenditure on education was changing over the period.

Recurrent Expenditure on Education as Compared with Total Government Recurrent Expenditure

An answer to the first question, i.e., whether educational expenditure was keeping pace with total Government expenditure, can be gleaned from the figures in Table 46. A comparison was also made between the rates of increase in the total Government expenditure (recurrent) and that on education and this was also graphically illustrated in Chart 3.

There are two points which emerge quite clearly from Table 46 and Chart 3. First, recurrent expenditure on education moved closely

Table 46 *Educational Expenditure in Guyana as a
Percentage of the Total Government Recurrent
Budget, 1945 to 1972, in $(G)*

Year	(a) Total recurrent budget		(b) Recurrent budget for education		(b) as a percentage of (a)
	$ Millions	Rate of increase	$ Millions	Rate of increase	
1945	12.2	100	1.5	100	12.3
1950	20.6	169	2.6	173	12.6
1955	36.3	298	4.5	300	12.4
1960	50.5	414	7.6	507	15.0
1964	69.4	569	11.3	753	16.3
1968	98.2	805	15.7	1,047	16.0
1972	153.0	1,254	24.2*	1,607	15.8
1974**	222.0	1,819	38.9	2,593	17.5

* It was impossible to identify any expenditure on school feeding from 1972.
** All figures represent actual expenditures except those for 1974 which were estimates of expenditure as approved by the Legislature.
Source: Government of Guyana, *Annual Estimates 1945 to 1974*.

along with total Government recurrent expenditure until around 1955 (to be more precise, until 1957), when the former began to increase at a faster rate. Incidentally, this was the year when responsibility for education was finally taken over by an elected minister. Second, almost throughout the period, education was taking an increasing share of the recurrent budget. While in 1942 it accounted for 9.9% of Guyana's total recurrent expenditure, by 1945 this figure had moved up to 12.2%, and by 1974 had reached 17.5%.

Educational Expenditure as Percentage of National Income
The second question raised was whether the nation was spending a larger or smaller part of its total wealth on education. An increase in educational expenditure or in the percentage of the budget allocated to education does not give a definite answer to this question. To throw further light on it, an estimate was made of the proportion of the national income spent by Government on educaton.

Unfortunately, it was impossible to find a continuous series of national income figures extending over the whole of the period, so the 1948-1960 figures prepared by Kundu[2] were used instead as the basis for the estimates which are presented in Table 47. The figures

[2] Kundu, p. 309, Table 2.1.

Chart 3 *Rise in Educational Expenditure by Government Compared with Rise in Total Government Recurrent Budget, Guyana, 1945 to 1974*

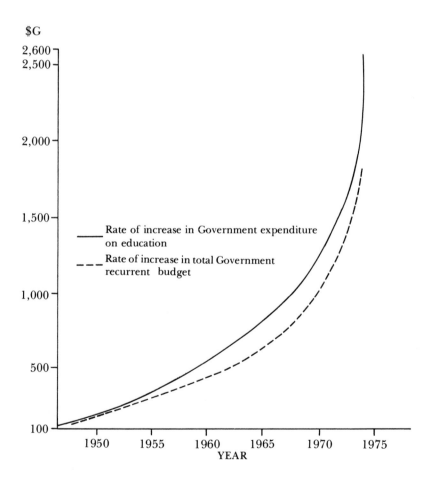

Table 47 *Recurrent Budget for Education*
(Excluding University Education)
as a Percentage of National
Income, 1948 to 1960

Year	Percentage of national income spent on education
1948	1.8
1950	2.3
1952	2.2
1954	2.2
1956	3.1
1958	3.0
1960	3.1
1963 (UNESCO estimates)	4.3

Source: Government of Guyana, *Annual Estimates 1945 to 1974*
(Georgetown, Guyana).

for 1948 to 1960 exclude expenditure on university education, which was relatively small prior to the 1960s.

An independent study done by a UNESCO team in 1962 produced almost identical figures. It estimated that in 1952 Government expenditure on education represented about 2.2% of the national income and that this figure rose to about 3.1% in 1960 and to 4.3% in 1963. The Planning Division of the Ministry of Education also calculated the percentage of the G.D.P. spent on all levels of education including university education in both the capital and recurrent budgets for the years between 1965 and 1972 (see Table 48).

The figures in Table 48 indicate that during the period of the study, the nation was allocating a greater proportion of its resources to education, or, in other words, expenditure on education was increasing more rapidly than increases in national wealth. Between 1952 and 1963, per capita incomes had risen only about 17% while educational expenditure per head of population had more than doubled. The result was that by 1965 Guyana was already spending a greater part of its national income on education than most developing countries—allocating 4.5% for the purpose as compared with an overall figure of 3.8% for developing countries for that year. Further, while the expenditure on education in developing countries represented on the average about 15.5% of their national budgets in 1965, the Guyanese figure that year was 16.7%

Table 48 *Expenditure (Capital and Recurrent) on Education as a Percentage of G.D.P., 1965 to 1972*

Year	Expenditure on education as a percentage of G.D.P.
1965	4.56
1966	4.34
1967	4.74
1968	4.58
1969	4.91
1970	4.48
1971	4.41
1972*	5.36*
1973	7.71*

* The percentage for 1972 was recalculated on the basis of the actual expenditure given in the Nine Year Report 1965-73 of the Ministry of Education. That for 1973 used the revised estimates given in the same document.

Source: Government of Guyana, Ministry of Education Planning Division, *A Digest of Educational Statistics 1971-72* (Georgetown, Guyana, September 1973).

The Changing Structure of Recurrent Expenditure on Education

An examination of the structure of the recurrent budget for education (see Table 49) shows a noticeable shift in financial allocation to the different levels of education between 1945 and 1974. The most striking change in the structure of the budget was the marked and steady drop in the percentage of education funds spent at the primary level. In 1945 about 85% of all Government recurrent expenditure on education was at the primary level, but by 1972 this figure had fallen to 64%. On the other hand, financial allocation to education at other levels, especially secondary and higher education, was increasing. While the former had taken 7% of the educational budget in 1945, this figure slightly more than doubled by 1972, reaching 15% by that year. The rate of increase in expenditure on higher education was even greater, rising from 1.1% in 1945 to 11.7% in 1972. But this rate of increase was due largely to the fact that expenditure on higher education in the 1940s was minimal.

Table 49 *Percentage Distribution of the Recurrent Budget for Education, 1945 to 1979*

Educational level or activity	Percentage of budget allocated in the following years								
	1945	1950	1955	1960	1964	1968	1972	1974*
Administration	3.7	3.5	3.0	3.1	3.5	4.4	3.3	3.3
Primary education	84.3	80.5	75.8	73.4	71.9	69.0	64.4	64.8
Secondary education	7.3	7.6	8.2	9.6	11.6	12.6	15.1	15.2
Teacher education	1.3	1.5	1.6	2.4	2.1	1.8	1.4	3.7
Vocational and technical education	2.3	4.2	4.9	3.7	3.2	3.1	4.1	3.7
Higher education	1.1	2.8	6.5	7.7	7.7	9.0	11.7	9.4
Total	100.0	100.1	100.0	99.9	100.0	99.9	100.0	100.1
Actual expenditure ($G 000s)	$1,495	$2,591	$4,446	$7,652	$11,308	$15,682	$24,077	$38,917

* Figures for 1974 represent the estimated expenditure as approved by the Legislature.
Source: Government of Guyana, *Annual Estimates 1945 to 1974.*

The Capital Budget

Nearly all major capital expenditure on education prior to 1965 was financed under various C.D. & W. schemes, and the development programmes which were approved by the C.D. & W. authorities for Guyana formed the main source of the information used in this part of the study.

The development programmes were fairly flexible and actual expenditure often differed greatly from the original allocations. So, it became necessary to look at both the official allocation and the actual expenditure of these funds. The former will probably throw some light on what the policymakers saw as important educational needs at the time, while the latter will represent the compromises which had to be made, considering the existing financial realities, on one hand, and the increasing political pressures for more educational services on the other. These figures are presented in Table 50.

Allocations and Expenditure up to 1948

While there was no long-term development plan prior to 1947, it was possible to gather information on the different separate C.D. & W. projects approved during this period. The 1947 Annual Report on British Guiana showed that the estimated total cost of all C.D. & W. projects which had been approved by December of that year was about £2.18 millions, and of this amount, about £85,000 or 4% was allocated to education.

The allocation and expenditure of capital funds at different educational levels during this period can be seen in section A of Table 50. These figures show that, up to December 1948, over 80% of capital allocations for education was at the primary level, mainly for primary school buildings (43%) and houses for primary school teachers (30%).

While the allocation for primary school buildings was quite inadequate to meet the needs of the rapidly increasing school population, a relatively large sum was allocated for teachers' houses, something that might have been considered a much less important need. However, this was part of a deliberate policy at the time to reduce teachers' demands for salary increases. The C.D. & W. Educational Adviser had, in fact, suggested that "less will be heard of the need for increased salaries of teachers if the teachers can be provided near the schools, with satisfactory and comfortable housing."[3]

There were many reasons why only 60% of the funds allocated for education had been spent by 1948. Among these were the difficulty of obtaining supplies and trained personnel, the issue of ownership and control of the new school buildings, and the sanitation demands of the Central Board of Health. But it should be noted that the

[3] Government of Great Britain, Colonial Development and Welfare in the West Indies, *The Future Cost of Education*, p. 5.

Table 50 *Percentage Distribution of Allocation for and Expenditure on Capital Projects in Education*

Education levels	(A) Period up to December 1948		(B) 1949-53		(C) 1954-55		(D) 1956-60		(E) 1960-64			(F) 1965-72	
	Allocation to 1948	Expenditure	Allocation	Expenditure	Allocation	Expenditure	Allocation	Expenditure	Allocation	Expenditure 60-62	Expenditure 63-64	Allocation	Expenditure
Primary School buildings, teachers' houses, etc.	80.1	77.4	52.7	57.0	100.0	94.0	62.3	86.8	70.7	86.4	61.4	39.4	40.0
Senior primary Senior schools, home economics and handicraft centres, etc.	2.7	2.4	18.5	0.0	—	—	34.5	1.8	19.5	9.8	2.9	46.6	49.2
Secondary	12.4	19.6	24.2	27.7	—	—		9.2	9.8	3.2	—	2.3	0.0
Teacher education	—	—	—	—	—	—	—	—	—	—	—	—	—
Vocational and technical education	4.8	1.0	4.6	15.3	—	6.0	3.2	2.2	—	—	—	5.8	—
Higher education	—	—	—	—	—	—			0.7	—	35.7	5.8	10.7
Total	100.0	100.0	100.0	100.0	100.0	100.0	100.0	100.0	100.0	100.0	100.0	99.9	99.9
Total amounts ($G 000s)	$416.7	$254.9	$1,737.0	$1,625.0	$975.0	$529.1	$2,650.0	$1,257.5	$4,100.0	$2,558.7	$644.2	$1,715.0	$744.9

dominant position of primary education in the recurrent budget in the post-1945 period was also reflected in the actual capital expenditures. Up to 1948, 77.4% of all C.D. & W. funds expended on educations were for primary educational facilities.

Capital Allocations and Expenditure, 1949-53

In 1947 a Ten-Year Development Programme, representing the first major attempt at long-term economic planning, was produced. It envisaged a total development budget of up to $G20 millions; of this sum, $G1.7 millions or 8.5% was allocated to education. This was the highest percentage of any development budget ever allocated to education during the entire period covered by this study, indicating the great hopes which most Guyanese shared in the immediate post-war years about the role of education in the country's social and economic reconstruction.

It will be observed from section B, Table 50, that in this Development Programme, the implementation of which actively began in 1949, the allocations to education were much more balanced than in the previous period. Primary education, which was allocated about 80% of the previous budget, was now given only about 53%. Instead, greater emphasis was put on education at other levels, especially post-primary education, which was being offered to the senior pupils in the "primary" schools. This tendency towards a more balanced allocation of funds for all levels of education continued and was reflected in most subsequent capital budgets.

Educators and economic planners were becoming increasingly concerned about students' job prospects when they left school and were highly critical of the strong academic emphasis in the curriculum of most secondary schools. They saw the need for stronger pre-vocational bias in their education and were supportive of senior schools in which such subjects as agriculture, woodwork, handicraft and home economics were to figure prominently. In view of this generous amount, 18.5% of the capital budget was allocated for "senior" schools.

Major Darlington, invited by the Government to advise on the establishment of a junior technical school, argued that the country's more immediate need was for craft training for young people who were already in jobs and were trying to become skilled craftsmen. He, therefore, recommended the establishment of a technical institute, which was to be the first institution in the country to provide formal training for craftsmen. The development planners, now seeking economic justification for education expenditure, readily accepted the new proposal. As a result, funds previously earmarked for senior schools and pre-vocational training in primary schools were spent instead on the new institute. This was the second occasion on which efforts to reorganize the post-primary sections of the "primary" schools by providing a more practical education were frustrated.

While expenditure on secondary education of the grammar school type again figured prominently in the capital budget (27.7% of the 1949-1953 budget and about 20% of the previous one, was spent on this level of education) it did not really reflect the interest of the colonial Government in providing this type of education. Rather, it was the result of public pressure to have the Government's two elite secondary schools modernized and extended. After these projects were completed, the capital allocation for secondary education never reached these proportions again until after self-government was achieved.

Allocations and Expenditure, 1954-55

In 1953, a World Bank Mission which assisted with the preparation of a new five-year development programme, criticized as "over-generous" the amount of funds allocated to the social services—including education—under previous development budgets, and pointed out that the pressing need for the development of the economic sectors will "leave little scope for years to come for the capital expenditure which will permit educational expenditures on a broad front."[4] As a result, it recommended capital expenditure for education at the primary level only, and even here its concern was to maintain existing services rather than to improve them. Of the recommended development budget of $G66 millions, less than 1.5% was for education. This drop in the percentage of the capital budget allocated to education was very sharp (from 8.5% in the previous programme to 1.5% in the World Bank Programme) and was viewed by educationists as a great blow to their growing hopes for educational reform, especially at the post-primary level.

After the political crisis of 1953 which led to a suspension of the constitution, the Government introduced a "stop-gap" Two-Year Development Budget of $G44 millions, of which about 25% was earmarked for social services as compared with 11.3% in the programme recommended by the World Bank. But despite this fact, the percentage spent on education was quite small. It had been suggested that the political problems of 1953 might have arisen from the relatively advanced educational level of the population, coupled with lack of other opportunities; and the provision of housing facilities was meant to appease the lower-income groups and convert their support to a more "responsible" political party. This is why about 90% of all expenditure on social services in the 1954-55 capital budget was in the field of housing.

[4] International Bank for Reconstruction and Development, *The Economic Development of British Guiana* (Baltimore: Johns Hopkins University Press, 1953), p. 75.

Allocations and Expenditure 1956-1960

During this period education was still being treated as a social service and continued to have a low priority in the development budget. Capital funds were once again allocated mainly for primary schools, since this was the only level of education for which the Government had a legal responsibility. Another reason was that expenditure on primary schools was least likely to be accompanied by large increases in the recurrent budget. Most of the age group six to fourteen years was already in school—admittedly under crowded conditions—and even the teacher/pupil ratio was legally fixed. While additional primary school accommodation was going to ease overcrowding and possibly increase the effectiveness of teachers, it was not going to impose too heavy an additional burden on the recurrent budget.

However, in the actual expenditure of funds, there were some changes. While less than half the allocations were spent by 1960, secondary education nevertheless came in for a slightly more favourable treatment than was originally intended. In 1957 the Government began implementing a policy of aiding some of the better private secondary schools, spending 9% of the capital budget on assisting them to improve their facilities. Incidentally, it is interesting to note that this was the third occasion on which the "practical training programmes" planned for post-primary education were side-stepped in favour of other educational programmes more in public demand. While about 35% of capital funds were originally allocated for "home economics and handicraft centres," only 1.8% of the actual expenditures went into such projects.

Allocations and Expenditure, 1960-1964

Although self-government was achieved in 1961, the development plan was formulated prior to the time the new Government took office. However, the popularly elected representatives did have some voice in financial matters even before 1961, and while the 1960-64 Development Programme was drawn up mainly by colonial civil servants, there were some inputs from the elected elements in the legislature.

Again, those projects which it was thought would contribute directly to economic growth were given priority, even though the allocation for education (3.6% of the new capital budget) was a marked increase over the 1.5% in the 1954-55 development budget. This was another indication of the growing influence which the elected representatives, and through them the masses, were having on decisions about programme priorities.

It was decided to identify the expenditure before and after 1962, in order to examine whether there were any marked policy changes after the newly-elected Government had settled into office.

It can again be seen that while the percentage of funds spent on education at the primary level, including expenditure on home economics and handicraft centres, was about 95% in the 1960-62 period this figure dropped substantially to 64.3% during 1963-64 after the new, popularly-elected Government had been in office for about a year. In reality, the percentage of the funds for education spent at the primary level was even less, since many new buildings earmarked for primary schools were later converted into secondary schools. If this adjustment is made, the actual percentage spent on primary school facilities was only 46%, not 64.3%.

A major trend in educational expenditure in the period after self-government was that the proportion of funds spent on educational facilities above the primary level began to increase; in addition, there was greater diversification of the educational services. This is reflected in the capital budget. Technical education and the multilateralization of secondary education to provide industrial arts and home economics programmes were increasingly stressed and so was higher education. At the primary and secondary levels, efforts at diversifying the educational facilities were apparent in capital expenditure on libraries, audio-visual aids, curriculum material, and in the provision of some facilities for handicapped children. This can be seen in Table 51, which gives the actual capital expenditure on education between 1966 and 1972.

Observations

Over the period 1945-1974, there were marked changes in the attitude of the Guyanese Government to expenditure on education; the most obvious fact suggested by the preceding data was that, as the influence of the elected representatives increased, the proportion of Government funds spent on education also rose. Under the colonial administration, the civil servants, who then wielded power over resource allocation, were reluctant to spend money on providing more education for the masses, despite soaring popular demand for these services. Their preference was for "money-bearing" projects, and they continuously expressed concern about whether the country could afford the additional costs being incurred by the social services, including education. They were prepared to endorse only new projects which they thought might produce direct economic returns. This is why, between 1945 and 1957, the only new educational projects introduced were an experimental senior school (which was to serve as a model institution for the introduction of a more practical curriculum in the all-age schools) and a technical institute for the training of skilled craftsmen, mainly for the private sector. Later, when the operational costs of the first senior school were found to be much higher than for the "primary" schools and its contribution towards

Table 51   *Capital Expenditure on Education, 1966 to 1972*

Projects	Actual expenditure ($G 000s)	Percentage of total expenditure
School buildings: Primary and secondary	3,202	15.60
Furniture for schools	584	2.80
Teachers' houses	113	.50
Equipment: Audio-visual aids, school libraries, etc.	1,121	5.50
Home economics and industrial arts centres and equipment	380	1.80
Special education for handicapped children	26	0.10
Technical education	3,281	16.00
Higher education	6,433	31.30
Special IBRD Project: Teachers' college multi-lateral schools	3,805	18.50
Loans to students	1,607	7.80
Research	5	.02
Total	20,557	99.92

Source: Government of Guyana, *Development Budget 1966-72* (Georgetown, Guyana, 1966).

producing "practical-minded" youngsters who would choose a farming career was in doubt, further expenditure on the project ceased and only one senior school, the experimental one, was ever established.

The only time that this narrower interpretation of education was not strongly emphasized by the colonial civil servants was during the period just before the end of World War II. The postwar euphoria of building "new societies" and the primary role of education in this task of social reconstruction—which pervaded the air in most metropolitan centres—spilled over to the colonies. Locally, there were two points then advanced for providing more education for the masses. First, it was felt that education was going to be, in some kind of undefined way, an important instrument in helping Guyana's overall social, political, and economic reconstruction. The West Indian Royal Commission, which investigated the causes of social and political unrest in these colonies during the late 1930s, had placed great faith in the role of education in ameliorating social and economic conditions. "We would like to emphasize," the Commission wrote,

> that educational advancement is a matter in which it is unwise to carefully count the cost. Failure to provide educational facilities on the right lines must inevitably bring retribution in numberless ways, not the least among which would be loss on property and financial stability far outweighing any temporary savings achieved.[5]

The second point was that education was a fundamental right of mankind and it was the duty of the state to provide it. The Education Sub-committee unquestioningly accepted this view in drawing up its education plans for the postwar years. In their report, the members remarked that they were

> confident that the days are long past when education is to be regarded as a matter of public welfare.... It is no longer a mere missionary service; it is a public responsibility which should be accepted and borne as a duty second to none in importance and consequence to the welfare of the country.[6]

These views were widespread during the period, and as Brian Holmes noted, "post-war educational policies were based more on concepts of social justice than on realistic assessment of allocation problems."[7] These postwar attitudes were reflected in the fact that between 1942 and 1950, the proportion of the recurrent budget allocated to education rose from 9.9% to 12.6%, and in the capital budget for the 1947 Ten-Year Development Programme, the educational allocation was proportionately higher than in any subsequent development budget.

After the postwar euphoria about social and economic reconstruction had died down and the immediate realities of a colonial economy were faced, there was a marked change in attitude towards expenditure on education. The colonial administrators now had a more restricted view of development; they saw it mainly in economic terms, and were largely concerned with projects likely to increase the G.D.P. immediately. In this context, education was perceived more as a consumption and not so much as an investment item, and like other welfare services, was accorded a low budgetary priority. Colonel Spenser, the newly-appointed Economic Adviser to the Government, and the Financial Secretary were the two strongest and most influential exponents of this view. In 1947 the former, writing on the choice of projects for the development programme, observed that

---

[5] Government of Great Britain, *West Indian Royal Commission Report*, p. 133.

[6] Government of British Guiana, *Papers Relating to Development Planning 1947* (Georgetown, 1947), p. 20.

[7] Brian Holmes, *Problems of Education* (London: Routledge and Kegan Paul, 1965), p. 143.

> it cannot be too strongly emphasized that both the taxable capacity of the Colony and its ability to maintain Social Services depends entirely upon National Income and Output. . . . Concentration of expenditure mainly upon Social Services is no solution to this problem of development, which can only come from an increase in National Income itself. Funds spent on properly conceived economic development can raise the National Income and gradually relieve the cause of poverty, while money spent on Social Services can only constitute a beneficial redistribution of National Income and a drastically limited one at that.

Further, in criticizing the first Ten-Year Development Plan, Spenser argued that "it is regrettable that welfare schemes, i.e., hospitals, schools, nutritional needs, etc., are far more conspicuous and clamant than the economic and productive schemes which are required to pay for them."[8] The Financial Secretary, who held essentially similar views, also spared no opportunity to point out, especially in the Legislature, that "as an under-developed country, we are devoting far too much of our revenue to Social Services . . . we should want every penny we can secure from revenue to sponsor economic schemes."[9]

But while these key civil servants wanted to restrict rigidly almost all educational expenditures, there were certain legal and political constraints which had an almost independent influence on the amount of funds allocated for this service, especially in the recurrent budget. First, education was compulsory for children between the ages of 6 and 14, and optional between 5 and 6 and between 14 and 16. In addition, the pupil/teacher ratio was legally fixed. Also, while these legal constraints could have been removed, the political atmosphere at the time was such that it would have been extremely difficult for the Government to make any obvious reduction in the quantity or quality of existing services. For example, Hammond's plan to get West Indian Governments further to dilute the teaching staff in the primary schools met with strong popular opposition throughout the West Indies and had to be scrapped. And a similar fate befell J. Nicole's recommendation for the introduction of the double shift system aimed at containing Guyana's rapidly increasing primary school budget.

Civil servants, including the Governor, used every opportunity to inform legislators and the population of the problems created by rising educational expenditures, and in these efforts, they were strongly supported by the press. In 1950, for example, it was reported that "the Financial Secretary had informed the Director of Education that there would not be enough funds for primary education for the next ten years with the increasing child population, if the present

[8] Col. D. A. Spenser, *The Financial Position of British Guiana 1920-46* (Georgetown, Government of British Guyana, n.d.), p. 8.

[9] Government of British Guiana, E. M. McDavid, Financial Secretary and Treasurer, in *Hansard*, 16 November 1951.

structure of primary education was to continue,"[10] and in the following year, he announced to the Legislature that "it seems tolerably certain that revenue, without impinging on other essential services, will not be able to finance the large number of children seeking admission to the schools on the basis provided by the Education Code."[11] Also, in 1952 the Nicole Committee had reported that "the educational needs of the rapidly growing school population had far outstripped the financial resources which can be made available for meeting them."[12]

The *Daily Argosy*, which accepted the official view that the rapid increases in educational expenditure were deflecting funds needed for economic projects, as early as 1945 argued that the sum spent locally on education was "*comparatively colossal*" and later indicated that "the annual expenditure which the taxpayers of the colony will be called on to face can fittingly be described as staggering."[13] In 1947 the editor, recommending an increase in fees at the girls' Government secondary school, noted with approval that the Colonial Secretary "quite correctly pointed out that the Government must have reached the limits of its expenditure on education."[14] Even the Director of Education accepted the view, almost unquestioningly, that education was imposing too heavy a financial burden on the country and pointed out that the cost of additional teachers "cannot be faced with equanimity."[15]

But the masses remained unimpressed by these arguments; not only did they resist almost every effort by Government to reduce the quality of education, but continued to demand, through their elected representatives, an increase in educational services. With more opportunities for upward social mobility opening up after the 1940s, the masses saw education as the only means by which their children could share in these opportunities for social and economic advancement. And no homilies from the Governor, the Financial Secretary, the Economic Adviser, the Director of Education, or even newspaper editors, were going to deter them from attempting to give their children "a good education" as a passport to what they perceived as a new way of life.

So when the constitution was changed in 1953, allowing elected representatives a greater voice in the executive and legislative processes, the influence of these popular pressures on Government policy

[10] *Daily Argosy*, 19 September 1950.

[11] Government of British Guiana, E. M. McDavid, Financial Secretary and Treasurer, in *Hansard*, 28 November 1951.

[12] Government of British Guiana, Department of Education, *Report of the Primary Education Policy Committee 1952*, p. 6.

[13] *Daily Argosy*, 8 July 1945.

[14] *Ibid.*, 2 August 1947.

[15] *Ibid.*, 17 September 1951.

became increasingly manifest. There was a gradual shift from a somewhat conservative to a more liberal attitude towards expenditure on education. For example, in 1953 the Legislature approved a proportionately large, though numerically still small, increase both in the number of students admitted to the Teachers' Training College and those awarded scholarships to secondary schools. These decisions were obviously not in line with the views of key civil servants. The Financial Secretary warned the elected members of the Legislature that the colony has "reached its peak" regarding expenditure on education and that they "should go slow on expenditure on these social services and concentrate more on economic development."[16]

But these first faltering steps towards increasing the provision of educational services were soon halted with the suspension of the constitution and the removal of elected members from the Legislative and the Executive councils. While the new Government, comprised of nominated members and a few senior civil servants, did not noticeably cut back on any existing educational services, it did not encourage any change in the existing system which might have required additional funds. So, between 1950 and 1955, the percentage of the recurrent budget for education declined slightly, from 12.6% to 12.4%. This trend continued until about 1957. However, just before the Legislative Council was prorogued, the interim Government introduced a bill which accepted the principle of aid to private secondary schools and the next Government was left to implement the measure.

The return of an elected element in the Legislature, with some executive responsibility for education, marks a watershed in Government expenditure on education. Between 1945 and 1957, such expenditure only kept pace with increase in total Government expenditure, but after that, it began to rise considerably faster, especially after the country achieved self-government. Yet the period between 1957 and 1960 could essentially be seen as one of transition, especially since a colonial civil servant, the Financial Secretary, was still responsible for over-all budgeting of the colony's funds. Between these years, while expenditure on education was rising, the Government was still not providing many of the facilities which the populace was demanding. As a result, it came in for steady criticisms from the Opposition, which expressed strong disagreement with the then-dominant view "that a welfare service or a social service like education should not have too much money expended on it."[17] In speaking at a budget debate in January 1960, the Leader of the Opposition, Mr. Burnham, observed "that this Government adopts a wrong attitude to the spend-

[16] Government of British Guiana, E. M. McDavid, Financial Secretary and Treasurer, in *Hansard*, 1 July 1953.

[17] Government of British Guiana, L. F. S. Burnham, in *Hansard*, 15 February 1959.

ing of money on education" and went on to "accuse the Government of propagating the fallacy that education is not productive." After noting the discrepancy between expenditure on education and that on other projects such as drainage and irrigation, Mr. Burnham asked:

> In an underdeveloped country like this, a country which at the moment is seeking constitutional advance . . . , in a country that needs to impress the world about the fact of its nationhood, a country, the leaders of which are clamouring for independence, are we going to neglect education?[18]

These views, as put forward by the Leader of the Opposition, had tremendous popular appeal. The Minister of Education, on the other hand, tried to express the current view, which was still strongly influenced by key civil servants, that the expansion of educational services should follow only in the wake of economic development. He attempted to articulate this point both to the legislators and to the public in general. Speaking in the Legislative Council in January 1960, he tried to "assure members that the Government will only be justified in spending more money on education *as the needs of the community demand it. . . .* This is a poor country . . . we cannot go on producing graduates for whose services there is no demand."[19] Earlier, at a public meeting in November 1959, he tried to

> plead for an understanding of the vast economic and other social problems facing the people and the Government of this country that make it incumbent upon us all, in assessing priorities with our limited resources, to have *first* regard to our physical and economic problems, thus laying a secure base on which the education and cultural superstructure of the state can be firmly built.[20]

However, despite these speeches, the people remained unimpressed, especially since many did not fully understand the economics of the development policy suggested by the Minister of Education. Economic development to them meant an increase in the opportunities which existed for their children to obtain one of the economically more rewarding and socially more prestigious jobs in the society. Since education was seen as a major means by which their children could secure these jobs, it was believed that any Government interested in their welfare would give top priority to education.

Hence, when self-government was achieved in 1961, and the elected members had full control over the country's financial affairs, the Government, largely due to increasing popular pressures, began adopting a more liberal attitude in providing educational facilities.

[18] *Ibid.*, 7 January 1960.
[19] Government of British Guiana, B. S. Rai, Minister of Education, in *Hansard*, 20 January 1950.
[20] *Ibid.*

This approach was explained in the 1961 *White Paper on Education Policy*, which stated that education should be

> available on an equal basis to all sectors of the population, whatever their economic and social position. . . . An educated citizen is our best investment in progress and development and education is recognized by this Government as one of the liberating forces in our struggle against ignorance, reaction, bigotry, superstition and political and economic exploitation.[21]

The result of this new attitude was an increase in budgetary allocations for education. Even the Leader of the Opposition, who, since 1958, criticized, at every budget debate, the Government's outlook on education, admitted that

> there seems to have been a change of attitude on the Government's part. If I interpret pages one and two [of the White Paper] correctly, the Government is accepting the important position which education holds and should hold in our community and no longer subscribes to the view put forward by a previous Minister of Education in 1959 that education is a non-productive service and therefore should yield priority at all times to other services which are alleged to be productive.[22]

The massive expansion of educational services after self-government in 1961 meant that educational expenditure continued climbing at a much faster rate than total recurrent expenditure, rising from 15% of the annual recurrent budget in 1960 to 16.3% in 1964. This percentage declined somewhat after independence, partly because of the rapid rise in other expenditures—such as establishing diplomatic missions abroad and funding of the armed forces—which accompanied independence. Nevertheless, the total sum allocated to education still rose rapidly during this period. By 1974 the expenditure on education was again following its post-1957 trend, i.e., increasing proportionately faster than the recurrent budget, and absorbing 17.5% of the annual recurrent budget. The rate of these increases is illustrated in Chart 4. The same general trend was also observed in the capital budget, with education being allocated an increasing percentage of the funds, especially since self-government and independence.

[21] Government of British Guiana, *Memorandum by the Minister of Education and Social Development on Educational Policy 1963* (Georgetown, 1963).

[22] Government of British Guiana, L. F. S. Burnham, in *Hansard*, 2 April 1963.

Chart 4   *Increase in Percentage of Government Recurrent Budget Spent on Education, 1945 to 1974*

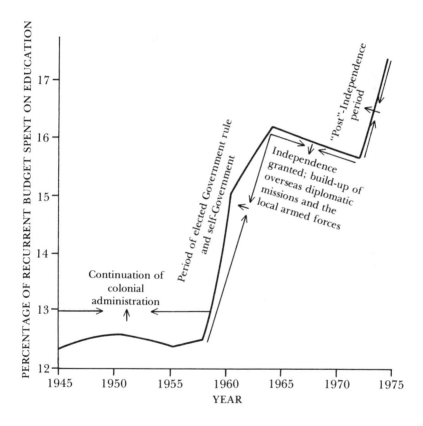

8. Conclusion

Many aspects to the development of Guyanese education emerged from this study. Possibly the two most outstanding features were the rapid increase in the demand and supply of education since 1945; and the relative failure of efforts to reform the curriculum of the primary and secondary schools to produce a greater congruence between the skills and attitudes which the schools tried to develop in their students and that which the economic system needed for its further development.

Increases in Demand and Supply of Education Since 1945

During the period 1950-1970 alone, first and second level enrolments in Guyanese schools rose by 120% and 315% respectively. While these figures were lower than the average increase (211% and 465%)[1] for third world countries during the same period, the Guyanese situation has to be seen against the fact that in 1945 about 90% of all children of primary school age in that country were already attending school. Further, if all the students enrolled in the separate secondary schools were added to those in the secondary divisions of all-age schools, about 70% of Guyanese youths of secondary school age were, in 1972, receiving a secondary education which could eventually lead them to the G.C.E. "O" level examination. The same rapid increase in enrolment was also noted in all post-secondary educational institutions which offered training courses for teachers, craftsmen, technicians, and workers in agriculture and in university programmes. One effect of these increases was that the percentage of trained teachers in the primary schools almost doubled between 1945 and 1975, increasing from 20% to 45%, even though enrolments had risen sharply and the average class size had fallen from 44.8 pupils in 1948 to 27.7 in 1971.

This rapid expansion of education was reflected in an increase in budgetary allocations. The Government's recurrent expenditure in this field moved up from 9.9% of the total recurrent budget in 1942 to 17.5% in 1974. Also, the percentage of the national income spent on education rose from 2% in 1948 to over 7.7% in 1973, by which time the Guyanese figure was almost twice the average (3.91%) for developing countries.

[1] World Bank, *Education: Sector Working Paper, December 1974* (Washington, D.C.: The World Bank, 1975), p. 13, Table 1.

Furthermore, there were no signs that this increasing demand for education was abating. Rather, it continued to grow, with the population seeking further quantitative and qualitative improvements—such as a higher percentage of trained teachers in the primary schools and of graduate teachers in the secondary schools—in the existing educational services. The Government, on the other hand, has continued to make every effort to provide new educational services and to upgrade existing ones, and has recently even accepted financial responsibility for providing nursery and kindergarten education.

Factors Responsible for Expansion of Educational Services

The marked inrease in enrolment in the different educational institutions resulted from certain pressures which, to an extent independently influenced both the supply of and demand for more educational services—though these factors operated with different force at different periods of time. In Guyana, as in many other developing countries, and as Myint[2] observed specifically in the case of South East Asia, demand factors were mainly responsible for the rapid increase in student enrolment in the 1940s, especially at the post-primary level. After that, continuing increases had been largely due to forces on the supply side, especially as the state began to assume greater responsibility for the provision of education.

Social unrest in Guyana and the West Indies, which triggered the appointment of the West Indian Royal Commission in 1939, gave some indication that the masses in this region were becoming increasingly dissatisfied with their social and economic conditions and were prepared to assert themselves more forcibly in order to have their voices heard. An almost immediate result of those disturbances was the introduction of constitutional reforms which allowed greater popular input into the political decision-making process, reforms such as the granting of universal adult suffrage, and later the shifting of executive responsibility for the administration of the country into the hands of elected representatives. This resulted in a greater responsiveness by policymakers to popular political pressures, and brought about the enactment of measures by the Government which directly increased the demand for education. For example, largely through the efforts of elected legislators, employment practice in the public and later in the private sector became less discriminatory against the two major ethnic groups in the country—the Africans and the East Indians. This resulted in an opening up of job opportunities

[2] H. U. Myint, "The Universities of Southeast Asia and Economic Development," in *Economic Theory and the Underdeveloped Countries* (New York: Oxford University Press, 1971), p. 226.

at the higher levels to these groups, and eventually led to increased popular pressures on the Government to provide more education, especially at the secondary and *post-secondary levels*, enabling local staff to qualify themselves for these posts.

While the senior civil servants, in whose hands the ultimate responsibility for policy making still rested before self-government was granted, attempted to put a curb on educational expenditure in order to divert resources to "revenue yielding projects," they could not entirely ignore the increasing political pressures for more and better educational services. For example, it was the strong opposition by the Guyanese public to Hammond's plan for the further dilution of the primary school teaching staff and to Nicole's recommendation for the experimental introduction of the "shift system," which they saw as "part of a scheme for the oppression of the people by our Imperial masters,"[3] that prevented the implementation of these recommendations.

The Government's involvement in the provision of more educational services was even more evident after the achievement of self-government and independence. There was a marked difference in the attitude between colonial civil servants and elected representatives towards the Government's assuming greater responsibility for the provision of more and higher levels of education for the masses. The major reason was that a Government which held office by election rather than by appointment had to be more responsive to popular pressures. Even after 1966, from which time it was reported that elections were heavily rigged and thus dependence on the popular vote reduced, the Government still needed some degree of popular support if it was not to convert the country entirely into a police state. This meant that some of the more popular demands continued to be met; one of the most important of these was the provision of more educational services, especially at the post-primary level.

One factor contributing to the increased supply of educational services by the Government was a belief in the role of education in bringing about greater social equality.

Traditionally, education, especially at the primary level, was used by the ruling groups in Guyana as a instrument of social control rather than to provide opportunities for upward mobility of working-class children. This was why, when it became obvious that the abolition of slavery was inevitable, the plantocracy eventually agreed to let the churches, especially the Established Churches, provide, within the context of Christianity, primary education for the masses. It was suggested by these religious authorities and accepted by the planters that this was the best means of producing a pliant, willing, and submissive work force from the children of ex-slaves; this was largely

[3] Government of British Guiana, J. A. Nicholson, in *Hansard*, 18 July 1952.

why a Compulsory Education Act was introduced in Guyana as early as 1876.

By the 1940s, while the composition of the social and political elite had changed somewhat, the ruling group still shared the view that education was a valuable instrument of social control. They, therefore, argued that the franchise should be extended only to those who were literate in English. For the working-class groups in Guyana, this meant that only those who had attended the local primary schools would have been able to use their votes "sensibly" and to elect "responsible" representatives—individuals who would prove no threat to the dominant elite—to the legislature. This indicated that they still had faith in the role of the educational system in "properly socializing" young Guyanese to accept the view of the dominant groups in the society.

But when the popularly-elected representatives came to office, they saw education in a different light—essentially as a means of providing upward mobility for all sections of the society thus reducing the inequality in educational opportunity which existed between the different socio-economic groups and between different geographical regions in the country. This was one of the goals of nearly all the popular political figures; they wanted to ensure that potentially able students were not denied an education because of their parents' inability to pay. The P.P.P. Memorandum on Education of 1963 stated that it was the Government's policy

> to ensure that educational opportunities are available on an equal basis to all sections of the population whatever their economic and social position. In fact, a student who has the ability to profit from a certain type of education should not be debarred from enjoying such an education because of his parents' inability to pay for it.[4]

In 1968 the P.N.C. Government expressed the same sentiments when, in its policy statement, it mentioned the need for a "real equality of opportunity in all fields of endeavour in the country." As a result, it proposed still further increases in secondary education facilities so that "adequate and free secondary education will eventually be brought within the reach of every [Guyanese] child qualified to receive it."[5]

In addition to trying to provide equal opportunities through education, the Government of Guyana, like those in other LDCs, held the view that education in some unclear, unstated, and even miraculous way would by itself produce economic and social development. This was clearly expressed in the 1963 Government *Memorandum on Education Policy* which stated that:

[4] Government of British Guiana, *Memorandum by the Minister of Education and Social Development on Educational Policy 1963*, p. 1.

[5] Government of British Guiana, *Memorandum on Educational Policy 1968* (Georgetown, 1968).

In devising a national system of education and in drawing up an educational programme for British Guiana, the Government is fully cognisant of the fact that *education plays a vital role in the economic and social advancement of the country*. An educated citizenry is *our best investment in progress and development....* Our children and youths are among the most precious of our assets and we hope that through *our educational system we would be able to enhance tremendously the value of these assets to our economy*.[6] (Emphasis added.)

Similarly, in the 1965 Speech from the Throne, which was prepared by the P.N.C./U.F. Government, the Governor observed: "My Government is deeply conscious of the fact that the *success of any proposals or plans for social and economic reconstruction or rehabilitation is largely dependent on the re-organization of our educational system*."[7] (Emphasis added.) And later, in its *Memorandum on Education Policy*, submitted to the Legislature in 1968, the P.N.C. Government indicated that, despite the additional costs involved, it was proceeding with a programme of educational reform which included more secondary school places, changes in the school curriculum, etc., because: "The Government *firmly believes that education is the chief means of democratizing and developing the society. It is the surest means of carefully mobilizing the diverse talents of the population to contribute effectively to the development of a truly independent nation*."[8] (Emphasis added.)

These sentiments, shared not only by the various Guyanese Governments but by most others in developing countries, tend to overemphasize the role of education in social and economic transformation by ignoring the fact that education is only one cooperant factor in the production process and can only be effective when other factors are present. Nevertheless, such views were and still are strongly held and continue to influence the provisions of schools and other formal educational institutions in these countries.

Factors Responsible for Increasing Popular Demand for Education

While the increased supply of education as a free or highly-subsidized commodity helped to stimulate further demand for it, there were additional factors on the demand side which contributed to the increased enrolment noted in nearly all educational institutions.

Population Pressure

The high rate of natural increase in the population (about 3.5% between 1945 and 1960 and 2.5% after that), coupled with a general

---

[6] Government of British Guiana, *Memorandum by the Minister of Education and Social Development on Educational Policy, 1963*, p. 1.

[7] Government of British Guiana, Speech from the Throne by His Excellency the Governor, in *Hansard*, March 1965.

[8] Government of British Guiana, Ministry of Education, *Memorandum on Education Policy 1968*.

improvement in the health of school children was largely responsible for the increased enrolment in the schools and in the greater regularity of school attendance observed during the period.

Changing Attitudes to Education

Another factor contributing to the higher school enrolment was the emergence of a more favourable popular attitude to education, brought about largely by a gradual shift from ascriptive to achievement criteria in the selection of individuals for jobs. Prior to the 1940s Guyanese society was quite rigidly stratified, and colour and ethnicity were very important factors in occupational selection. Higher-level jobs were virtually reserved for expatriate whites and local Portuguese, and to some extent the coloured population, while Africans and East Indians, who formed the majority of the population, were virtually excluded from these positions.

At first representation by these two major non-white groups in certain white-collar occupations was in favour of the Africans. For example, in 1931 East Indians comprised less than 7% of the primary school teaching force; the other positions were held mainly by Africans. Also, in 1941 the representation of this latter group in the civil service was three times as great as the former. Despite these differences, both ethnic groups, who together then formed about 80% of the population, experienced great difficulty in securing jobs which normally required the successful completion of a secondary school course; this was responsible for the fact that their demand for this level of education was limited. Prior to the 1950s the country produced relatively few secondary school graduates and these were immediately able to find jobs that traditionally required recruits with this level of education. In other words, there was then a close correspondence between the supply and demand for secondary school graduates.

The only opportunity for the non-white groups to rise substantially up the social ladder was through one of the independent professions, but not many of them had the economic resources to obtain the necessary training. Law and medicine, which at first were the two most popular fields, required qualifications that had to be obtained mainly in the United Kingdom, where it was very difficult for students to help defray the cost of their education by doing part-time work. This meant that the first group of non-white Guyanese who became doctors and lawyers were from the small group of economically more affluent families. However, later, when professional qualifications in dentistry obtained in the U.S.A. were locally recognized, children from the less well-to-do families were able to enter this profession, since they could help finance their education by working. This also began to happen in the field of medicine, as U.S. trained medical doctors were given limited recognition locally, and in the field of law, as students registered at the Inns of Court in England began to work while studying for their bar examinations. These opportunities for students to contribute to the cost of their education helped to increase the desire of the less affluent families to give their children a secondary education which would enable them to proceed overseas at some later date to obtain professional qualifications.

Another factor contributing to the increasing demand for secondary education was the relatively rapid rate of expansion of the civil service, especially after the 1940s. Since there were not enough candidates of a lighter complexion who had the necessary educational qualifications for these jobs, other ethnic groups were gradually recruited to fill them.

Lastly, the political pressures which the masses began to exert through their elected representatives resulted in the steady opening of neary all jobs in the public sector, on an equal basis, to the various ethnic groups in the society. The private sector followed the same direction. Already in the 1950s the largest private employer in the country, the Booker Group of Companies, which previously employed Europeans in nearly all senior positions, began to throw open not only their topmost positions to Guyanese but, like the Government, began to grant scholarships to eligible Guyanese to pursue professional and technical training overseas which would qualify them for these positions. This gradual shift in the criteria used for recruitment, especially to senior jobs, from ascription to "attainment"[9] and then mainly to achievement, resulted in an increase in occupational aspirations among those groups previously discriminated against and a corresponding rise in their educational aspirations.

Further, the resulting increase in demand for education soon produced an excess supply of qualified candidates beyond the demands of the job market, gradually raising the level of education required for entry into certain jobs. Primary school teaching was one of the more outstanding examples. In the 1940s one could become a primary school teacher with only a primary education, but by the 1970s this had become virtually impossible and a secondary school education was increasingly required. In addition, while entry qualification for certain jobs did not change, it was clear that competition for them was becoming keener. In such a tight job market, candidates whose educational levels were above the required minimum had a better chance of securing these jobs. These factors, the rising level of education required for entry into certain jobs, and the increasing competition for the limited number of jobs available, also contributed

[9] F. W. Riggs, *Administration in Developing Countries: The Theory of Prismatic Society* (Boston: Houghton, Mifflin, 1964). Riggs uses the term "attainment" to refer to a combination of both ascriptive and achievement criteria.

further to the growing demand for higher levels of education in the country.

Increasing Ability of Parents to Afford Education for their Children

The increased financial ability of many parents to pay for their children to attend secondary school, especially following the relatively substantial economic growth during and immediately after World War II, was another factor which contributed to rising school enrolment. Rice production had increased and Guyana gradually became the main supplier of rice to the West Indian markets. Air and naval bases established by the U.S. during the war years also provided some local employment. And, with wartime restrictions on the importation of food, some areas of peasant agriculture were given an economic boost. The result was an increase in disposable incomes in many households, especially among the middle and lower-income families; since this money could not be spent on traditionally imported items, more families began to invest in their children's education.

Evidence of this was seen in the number of private secondary schools which mushroomed in the country during these years. While the academic standards of these schools were low and many were what the *Daily Argosy* dubbed "cramming institutions" which "tried to squeeze their pupils through" the examinations that would produce the longed for certificates,[10] they continued to be attractive because their fees were low and within the financial resources of the parents—most of whom could not have afforded a more expensive type of secondary schooling.

As graduates from these schools began to find niches for themselves in teaching or in the civil service, this stimulated the desire of the yet-lower-income groups for this level of education. They, therefore, began to exert more political pressure for the extension of such education facilities, with the result that the various elected Governments had to provide more non-fee-paying secondary schools. This increased availability of "free" or low-cost secondary education reduced considerably the amount of investment which parents had to make in their children's education at this level and put the cost within the financial resources of many more.

The Effect of Increasing Unemployment on Demand for Education

Growing unemployment, especially among the young, was another factor influencing the demand for more educaton. This deteriorating situation was due partly to the failure of the modern sector to grow as fast as the population seeking to enter it and partly to the increasing mechanization in some industries, notably sugar and rice. By 1965 it was estimated that about 53% of the fourteen to nineteen age group in the Guyanese labour force was unemployed.

[10] *Daily Argosy*, 6 November 1949.

Such high and increasing unemployment is now a characteristic feature of most developing countries. Singer, using a "moderate definition" of unemployment from which he excluded "low productivity employment," estimated that about 25% of the labour force of the LDCs were unemployed. He also noted that, according to Turner, unemployment in those countries was increasing at the rate of 8.5% per annum. Using these two figures, he indicated that "a projection into the future would yield frightening percentage of unemployment—43% by 1980 and 73% by 1990."[11]

This increase in unemployment among young school leavers meant that the opportunity cost of their remaining in schools was falling rapidly. Since one of the major elements in the cost of education of this older school-age group was incomes foregone, this high rate of unemployment in Guyana resulted in a further reduction in the private cost of education and in an increase in the private rate of return on such investment. Unemployment was increasingly becoming the alternative to continuing one's schooling beyond the compulsory attendance age. This increased the demand for schooling by making it an economically and socially more rewarding investment. In addition, unemployment, as some economists now agree, increases the demand for more schooling in other ways. The unemployed are likely to be those with less schooling and this in itself proves to be an incentive for people to get as much education as possible to put them in a better competitive position for jobs.

Ronald Dore observed that "The paradox of the situation is that the worse the unemployment situation gets . . . the more useless educational certificates become [and] the stronger grows the pressure of an expansion of educational facilities."[12]

Another feature of Guyana and other developing countries is that if an individual fails to secure a paid job he usually experiences great difficulty in trying to create employment for himself outside peasant farming. Such enterprises require not only ingenuity but also a certain amount of capital, which is often beyond the resources of most school leavers and small potential entrepreneurs. Even the cost of a bicycle might prove a big stumbling block to someone without financial resources who wants to start an activity which demands this means of transportation. In such a situation, it is no wonder that these youngsters opt for more schooling.

As Carnoy pointed out, schooling is even more important to people who do not have physical capital. "The fact that the school

[11] H. W. Singer, "Dualism Revisited: A New Approach to the Problems of the Dual Society in Developing Countries," *Journal of Development Studies* Vol. 7, No. 1 (1970), p. 67.
[12] Ronald Dore, *The Diploma Disease* (London: George Allen and Unwin, 1976), p. 4.

selects people for higher income streams makes it attractive for people without physical capital who want to improve their economic position."[13]

This is not to deny the fact that many small-scale entrepreneurs in developing countries are able to eke out an existence with little capital resources. But those who have had, say, a secondary education, usually expect a standard of living much beyond the mere margin of existence. Therefore, with very limited alternative opportunities for securing a comparable standard of living, many youngsters prefer to go to school and reach the level of academic attainment which would increase their chances of securing a reasonably "good job," i.e., one likely to provide them with a "reasonable" standard of living.

The Dualistic Structure of Wages

By far the most important single factor which was responsible for further stimulating the demand for education, even though supply of educated personnel was already outstripping the demand of the labour market, was the structure of wages in the country. The Guyanese economy was characterized by a fairly marked dualism in its economic structure, a feature which can be observed in most LDCs.

Boeke[14] was one of the first social scientists to draw attention in a systematic way to the existence of "two clashing social systems" within the social and economic structures of colonial societies. While he exaggerated the nature and degree of this dualism, there are undoubtedly certain marked differences between the two economic sectors of most developing countries. As Higgins observed, "the basis of this dualism [observed by Boeke] is not essentially social but economic and technical."[15] Ranis and Fei also noted that the LDCs are characterized by the coexistence of two economic sectors, a "relatively large and overwhelming stagnant subsistence agricultural sector," which they referred to as the "traditional or indigenous" sector, and a "relatively small . . . commercialized industrial sector," which they called the "modern or enclave sector,"[16] while Jalée describes these foreign economic enterprises which largely make up the modern sector as a "modern oasis in the middle of a primitive desert."[17] Focussing on the wage differentials between these two sectors, Johnson comments on

[13] Martin Carnoy, "The Political Consequences of Manpower Formation," *Comparative Education Review* Vol. 19, No. 1 (February 1975), pp. 115-128.

[14] J. H. Boeke, *Economics and Economic Policy of Dual Societies* (New York: Institute of Pacific Relations, 1953).

[15] B. Higgins, "The Dualistic Theory of Underdeveloped Areas," *Economic Development and Cultural Change* Vol. 4 (January 1956), p. 114.

[16] G. Ranis and J. C. H. Fei, *Development of the Labour Surplus Economy: Theory and Policy* (Homewood, Ill.: R. D. Irwin, Inc., 1964), p. 3.

[17] Pierre Jalée, *The Pillage of the Third World*, translated from the French by Mary Klopper (New York: Monthly Review Press, 1968), p. 77.

the marked disparity of incomes in the "centre" and the "periphery"[18] of most LDCs, while Lewis,[19] using the same criteria of income differences, noted that the economies of the developing countries are usually characterized by a "high wage" and a "low wage" sector.

Myint defines dualism as the "continuing existence of a 'modern sector' and a 'traditional sector' within the domestic economic framework of an underdeveloped country." The modern sector, he notes, is often identified within an exchange economy as the sector "consisting of large-scale economic units employing capital-intensive methods of production" while the traditional sector is identified with the "subsistence economy . . . employing labour intensive method of production."[20] Singer, while using the concept of dualism more broadly to include international dualism, i.e., the gap between the rich and the poor countries, identifies its following four key elements: the coexistence of "superior" and "inferior" conditions in a given space at the same time, the chronic rather than the assumed transitional nature of this division, worsening of the "inferior" versus the "superior" conditions with the "superior" sector not only being unable to pull up the "inferior" one but possibly even serving to pull it down. Further, he sees internal dualism in the LDCs increasingly manifesting itself in the division between the employed and the unemployed.[21]

The modern or high wage sector in the economies of the developing countries comprises those industries or commercial enterprises which are usually owned by foreign and, to a more limited extent, by "progressive" local investors. In Guyana, the sugar and bauxite industries would fall into this "modern" or "high wage" sector and so would all the Government services and state-run enterprises. Both wages and the prestige enjoyed by workers in this sector tend to be high as compared with those in the traditional sector. It was not uncommon for the daughters of relatively wealthy but low status merchants to accept jobs with the more prestigious firms in the modern sector of the Guyanese economy rather than work in the family business, even if it meant—as it often did—that their incomes were just enough to meet the additional expenses involved. However, it was the prestige of these firms, for example, the chartered banks or even the Government service, which was the major attraction.

Firms in this sector usually employed the more educated individuals, those who had at least a secondary education, especially for

[18] H. Johnson, *Economic Policies towards Less Developed Countries* (New York: Brookings Institute, 1967).

[19] W. A. Lewis, "Economic Development with Unlimited Supplies of Labour," *Manchester School of Economic and Social Studies* (May 1954).

[20] H. U. Myint, "Dualism and the Internal Integration of Underdeveloped Economies," in *Economic Theory and the Underdeveloped Countries* (New York: Oxford University Press, 1971), Part 4, chapter 14.

[21] Singer, p. 60.

their white-collar positions. Even their skilled workmen were expected to have had a fairly high level of schooling and to have undergone some formal apprenticeship training. This was partly because the equipment and methods of industrial production which these firms used were relatively "up-to-date" and not markedly dissimilar from those used in the economically more developed countries, even though in some cases there was a time gap in the type of equipment used. The relative modernity of production methods used by firms in this sector was, to some extent, due to the fact that they were producing commodities for an export market or were closely involved with firms engaged in such production. As a result, they "needed" the technological and commercial sophistication which was considered up-to-date or necessary for effective international competition. It is true that in the public service, which formed the largest employer in this sector, the technology used was often far from modern, but its major qualification for inclusion in this sector was the relatively high income levels of its workers.

The traditional or low wage sector was dominated by peasant farmers who were merely ekeing out a minimal existence from the soil; but in addition, there were the local entrepreneurs—small shop-keepers, hucksters, independent artisans in the building trades, such as carpenters, and painters, and others who serviced the needs of those in this sector. Their methods of production were often "primitive," but with the poor or limited market for the commodities or services, the difficulties and cost of transportation and the limited supply of capital available to them, such a situation was not unexpected. Even in cases where local entrepreneurs had more up-to-date equipment, the wages paid were usually very low and job security often non-existent.

In addition, the "skilled" workers had not received any kind of formal training but learned their jobs by working alongside other "skilled" workmen. As a result, they had no knowledge of the scientific principles on which their practice might have been based. In short, the knowledge base of the skills which they had acquired was traditional and one's reputation as a workman rested not on any prior academic attainment or ability to understand the principles behind a practice, but on success in solving specific problems. Productivity in this sector, judged by average output per individual, was no doubt lower than in the modern sector, largely because of the differences in the technology used.

But even in cases where output or profits were high, the entrepreneurs were able to exploit their workers by paying them low wages because of the presence of what Lewis refers to as "unlimited supplies" of labour. The only reason why more of these workmen did not move into the "high wage level" sector was that their skills were not easily saleable in that sector, and in addition, the number of jobs there was not only very limited but was increasing very slowly—much more slowly than the rate of increase in the total labour force.

But what was most striking was not only the fact that there was a difference in the income levels of workers in these two sectors—this was to be expected from the fact that one sector was demanding "higher" levels of education and skill training than the other—but also the *degree of difference* in their incomes. The large income differences between jobs in the traditional and those in the modern sector of the economy were the starting-off point for Lewis' two-sector theory of economic development in the LDCs.

The basis of this dualistic economic and wage structure was laid in the colonial days but has continued to exist to the present. For example, using the Government salary scales for 1973,[22] one found that the salaries of the lowest grade clerks in the Guyanese civil service, positions requiring only a secondary education, were up to about 400% higher than the average per capita income for the country as a whole. And one has to remember that virtually no clerical civil servant in Guyana ever remained in this lowest grade all through his working life. In other job categories, the income differences were even greater. The incomes of non-graduate and graduate teachers in secondary schools rose to about 630% and 1150%, respectively, of the per capita G.D.P.

But even then it was not only the existing salaries which were important but also the income levels which people eventually expected to achieve once they entered the civil service. And it was still possible for the holder of only a secondary school qualification eventually to rise to the highest administrative post in the civil service—that of Permanent Secretary, which in 1973 carried a salary of about 1500% higher than the per capita G.D.P.

In addition to the size of these income differences, there were additional perquisites which made the civil service so attractive—job security, pensions, extended vacation and sick leave with pay, and up until recently, leave passages for the civil servant and his wife to go abroad, in some cases as far as the United Kingdom. And the same kind of favourable job conditions, sometimes even more favourable, existed in the Government-owned corporations and in the large companies in the modern sector.

The persistence of the income differentials between the two sectors of the economy has had a very important influence in raising the level of educational aspiration of the population. This became even more marked as access to these high-paying and high-status jobs in the modern sector were increasingly thrown open to all, and was to a

[22] See Government of Guyana, *Estimates (Current and Capital) of Guyana for the Year 1973* (Georgetown, 1973).

large extent dependent on the candidate's formal education. It was also a major reason for the increasing level of education among the unemployed, who tried to acquire as much education as possible in the hope of obtaining a job in the very rewarding but slowly expanding modern sector.

Education, therefore, provided for the children of the masses the only real opportunity for economic self-improvement, by giving them a chance at obtaining the necessary academic credentials for entry into the high wage sector of the economy. In most cases, it did even more than that; it gave children of the working class possibly the only chance to transform their life styles from that of their parents who eked out a marginal existence in the low wage sector. Further, because of the extended nature of most families, the improved economic and social position of someone working in the modern sector had spill-over economic and psychic effects on his parents and even on other members of his extended family,

This factor was to a large extent responsible for the continuing popular pressures on the Government to provide more post-primary education. From their past experiences, parents believed that if their children could get a "good" secondary education, their economic and social futures would be guaranteed. So, even when job opportunities were no longer as rosy as they had been in the past, the demand for this level of education continued to grow rapidly since the prizes, if one secured a job, were extremely attractive and the alternative relatively dismal. It is true that the element of chance in terms of finding a suitable job with a secondary education had increased, but extending the lottery analogy, parents and pupils were both aware of the fact that unless one had a ticket, i.e., a secondary school qualification, one did not have a chance.

Michelson, in explaining people's economic behaviour in situations of uncertainty, noted the following comments by Marshall, written over five decades ago: "If an occupation offers a few extremely large prizes [as do jobs in the modern sector of the LDCs as compared with those in the traditional sectors] its attractiveness is increased out of all proportion to their aggregate values and the prospect of success becomes greater than the deterrent of failure, resulting in larger numbers wanting to enter those occupations."[23]

In addition to the size of the prizes, the consequences of the alternative, i.e., working in the traditional sector, in itself had a negative motivating influence by pushing individuals to obtain an education. In other words, the situation seemed to be one in which there was no other choice for the individual but to try and get more education. A somewhat similar problem often faced the black population of

[23] Stephen Michelson, "Rational Income Decisions of Blacks and Everybody Else," in *Schooling in a Corporate Society*, ed. by Martin Carnoy (New York: McKay, 1972).

the U.S.A., where it was observed: "It may be rational for a black to acquire an education although the expected return is negative. It may be rational to aspire to high education although the chances of accomplishment are slim. It may simply be the best strategy available to them."[24]

Another important point was that often there was no fixed educational qualification for entry into jobs. Therefore, the educational level expected of recruits for certain jobs rose as the market became saturated with students possessing lower-level educational qualifications which were once acceptable entry qualification for these jobs. In other words, the value of lower-level qualifications became deflated as candidates with higher qualifications began to compete for the same jobs; this inflation in job qualifications also resulted in increased demand for yet higher levels of education. Such a tendency has been most noticeable in the teaching profession, the police force, and other branches of the unclassified civil service where secondary education was increasingly being demanded for jobs which previously only required the completion of about eight years of primary schooling.

Lastly, the complementary or interlocking nature of the demand for education meant that as the educational qualification for a job increased, it created for those aspiring to enter that occupation a complementary demand for education at all supporting levels below that. In addition, successful completion of one level of education was a strong motivating factor for students to go on to yet a higher level.

When all the above-mentioned factors found in the Guyanese situation are put together, and these are factors which are also present in most other developing countries, the rapid expansion of education services and the decision which parents made to give their children more education, even when unemployment rates were rising, becomes increasingly understandable.

Economist Martin Carnoy thus summarized the education/unemployment dilemma increasingly being faced by most LDCs:

> As schooling expands unemployment moves up to influence the more highly educated graduates. The rapid expansion of primary schooling greatly increases the supply of primary school graduates, also increasing their unemployment rate. This lowers the income foregone and increases the economic pay-off of attending secondary school. If the government responds to demands for more secondary places, eventually the increased supply of secondary school graduates combined with downward inflexible wages, creates unemployment among secondary graduates. This increases the demand for university expansion, and results in university unemployed. Thus while the average schooling of the labour force is increasing the average schooling of the unemployed is increasing as well. The tendency over time to lower social rates of return that this expansion produces does *not* eliminate the demand for more schooling by individuals. Quite the contrary, unemployment in-

[24] *Ibid.*

creases the difference between private rates and social rates, tending to raise private rates to "infinity" and the private cost of attending school falls to zero.[25]

Failure of Efforts at Curriculum Reform

The second important observation on Guyanese educational developments was the continued "irrelevance" of the school curriculum to the objective social and economic needs of the country and the great difficulties experienced by the Ministry of Education officials in trying to reform the curriculum along the lines desired by the Government.

The major reason for this was the size of the income and the resulting status differentials between jobs, especially those in the modern as against those in the traditional sector of the economy. This played an important role in influencing the career aspiration of students, and consequently, the subjects they wanted to study in school. Such wide income differences—and they are wide indeed in most developing countries—make it difficult to attract students away from educational programmes which they think would increase their chances of obtaining one of the high-paying, prestigious jobs, even when these fields of employment become over-crowded, to programmes which are likely to lead to jobs considered necessary for national development, e.g., farming, but in which the income and status returns are low.

What was most noticeable in this study was the perspicacity which the population revealed about the subjects and programmes which had the greatest "pay off" on the job market. It was this, rather than the perceived "relevance" or "irrelevance" of any course by the curriculum planners which influenced students' choice of what to study. This was the reason for parents encouraging their children to pursue the "academic" rather than the "practical" courses, and it was also why, when the value of the Primary School Certificate fell on the job market, students' interest in obtaining this qualification declined. The certificate only began to interest students again when its value increased and it virtually became a prerequisite for those wanting to pursue the College Preceptors course, following which they could enter into the G.C.E. programme. Further, when the Government in 1962 decided to allow the "primary" schools to offer programmes leading to the College of Preceptors Examination, large numbers of older students stayed on in these schools, even beyond the compulsory attendance age, to avail themselves of this new opportunity. This happened despite the fact that curriculum experts considered the English-based C.P. syllabus even more irrelevant to the needs of

[25] Carnoy, "The Political Consequences of Manpower Formation," pp. 122-23.

Guyanese society. Also, as the higher level technical jobs were increasingly thrown open to Guyanese, science subjects became more popular. This was reflected in the growing preference for the science over the arts subjects by students in the elite secondary schools, which had the resources to provide facilities needed for teaching these subjects.

The main objective of the ruling groups in providing universal primary education was to help working-class children develop a greater liking for and efficiency in the various types of manual occupation which it was presumed they would inevitably follow after completing their schooling. This is why the Government, through its Department of Education, placed such stress on the teaching of practical—including agricultural—skills and the development of a wholesome attitude to manual work.

But the masses were not prepared to accept their lowly social and economic position forever, seeing education, even primary education, as their children's first step out of the low status agricultural and manual work in which they were engaged and up the occupational economic and social ladder. Pupils were quite prepared, obviously with parental encouragement, to follow virtually any course of study which they perceived was likely to lead to better job opportunities. They did not want to be farmers in a situation in which the job was not only a "hard back breaking affair," as the Principal of the School of Agriculture noted, but also one in which income levels were low and uncertain, when they saw better possibilities—such as the chance of entering a relatively well paid white-collar job in the public service—opening to them.

This explains why the attempts by the Ministry of Education to influence curriculum changes along the direction that would lead students to jobs necessary for the economy, for example, farming, but in which the economic and status returns were low, were not very successful, at least not up until 1972. Since then, additional efforts have been made to broaden the programme of secondary education through the establishment of multilateral and community high schools. The multilateral school project, which was financed through a loan from the International Bank for Reconstruction and Development, will represent another attempt at diversifying the curriculum offered at the secondary level by providing "technical, commercial and agricultural" courses in addition to the present academic ones, while the Community High Schools are expected to "take on a more vocational orientation."

These newly-proposed attempts at curriculum reform are obviously not very dissimilar from earlier efforts in this direction. For example, the 1957 *Memorandum on Secondary Education* stressed the need for secondary school curricula which would strike a balance between academic courses for those likely to enter universities and courses with a "prevocational or a technical bias" for those who had abilities of "a different but not inferior kind." It was naviely assumed that once the pronouncement that "a first rate painter should not be considered superior or inferior to a skilled surgeon"[26] was officially made, and curriculum programmes which were considered valuable to the overall economic needs of the country were provided, pupils would, without much reluctance, opt for them, probably irrespective of the income levels of the jobs to which they were likely to lead. These assumptions have proved incorrect and it is unlikely that the present efforts at curricula reform will be more successful unless they are accompanied by a marked reduction in income differences between white-collar and manual workers.

In summary, one can see that the two major problems, the rapid rate of expansion in education and the resistance to changes in the curriculum of schools to make it more geared to the objective economic and social realities of the society, stemmed from essentially the same cause, i.e., the dualistic nature of the wage structure, to which could be added the wide income differentials even among those in the high wage sector of the economy.

Understanding the Origins of the Problems

Historical and Structural Factors

Before examining possible ways and means of overcoming these two major educational problems which Guyana and most other third world countries face, it will be useful to look at the historical influences which gave rise to them and the structural features of these societies that have helped to perpetuate these problems. This will help us to understand why, despite the fact that most of these countries have now achieved independence, and why, in spite of their efforts and reforming zeal, they have not been able to change substantially the traditional colonial educational systems which they inherited.

In the days of colonial rule, there was in Guyana, as in other colonial societies, a great degree of congruence between the educational system and the dominant social, economic, and political institutions. The educational system, as part of the superstructure of the society, was essentially compatible with the economic substructure of plantation society and helped to reinforce and reproduce the economic and social relationships which characterized that society. This point has been amply documented in the earlier chapters of this study. The failure of the many efforts at radically reforming the inherited colonial educational system points to the fact that, while there might have been some changes in these societies over time, the basic features of their social and economic structure have essentially

[26] Government of British Guiana, *Memorandum on Secondary Education 1957*, p. 10.

remained intact, a point which has been made repeatedly by social scientists writing about West Indian societies.

But back to the colonial experience. The major motivating factor of the colonizers was the economic exploitation of the resources of the colonies. The colonial powers were not interested primarily in the social and economic development of the colonized nations, except in-so-far as such efforts were likely to increase the resources available for their own exploitation. This is not to deny the goodwill and devoted efforts of many individuals to help the colonized, but we are concerned here with the dominant ethos of the system of colonialism. To carry out this exploitation successfully and efficiently, a certain amount of social order and social stability was necessary. And, although physical force was often used as an instrument of social control, it was highly inefficient and always precarious. Efforts were, therefore directed at building voluntaristic support for the colonial system among the local population. The aim was to produce people who were loyal, cooperative, relatively docile, and believing in the superiority of the colonizers. The school system had, as one of its main goals, the effective socialization of the population along these lines, and its efforts were reflected in nearly every aspect of the curriculum offered in the schools. This explained in part why in the schools of Guyana, English history, covering such topics as the "Anarchy of Stephen's Reign" and the "Religious Difficulties of Elizabeth" was taught at the secondary level and local history ignored.

Another prerequisite for efficient exploitation was the ready availability of manpower with the basic skills needed by the European-dominated sector of the economy, which either produced the raw materials and agricultural products needed by the colonizers or was responsible for the distribution of manufactured products, mainly from the metropole. Trained and trustworthy personnel were also needed to assist in the overall administration of the country and in providing such basic services as education and health care.

It was obvious that a commitment to the existing society with its marked inequalities in income and status distribution could not depend solely on the teaching of values supportive of the system. To be effective, values had to be reinforced by a reward structure which would ensure that those selected to help operate or administer the system would have a vested economic interest in its maintenance. This marked the origins of the dualistic wage structure which is characteristic of Guyanese and other third world countries and which lies at the root of the two major educational problems identified by this study, i.e., educational inflation and continued irrelevance of the curriculum of schools to their objective social and economic realities. During the colonial era, great importance was, therefore, attached not only to technical competence and job skills but also to loyalty towards the colonial system, especially among those in higher level jobs in the society. This was reflected in the level of salaries paid in the modern sector. In fact, looking at the remuneration received by expatriates, one finds that there were the following three main elements in their salaries:

A *scarcity element* for persons with higher level education or special skills which were not readily available in Guyana. Europeans, therefore, had to be brought from overseas to fill such vacancies, and as a result, their salaries were higher, reflecting the relative scarcity of such personnel on the local market;

A *"rent" element* for being white. It was felt by most recruiting agencies that even if a local person had the same level of qualifications as the European, the latter, by the mere fact of his ethnicity, had a much greater ability to get things done within a colonial context, and for this "superior quality" firms were willing to pay them more than the locals. While this "rent" element in income also existed in the civil service, it was not as obvious in Guyana as it was in some African countries, where salary differentials for certain higher level positions—such as secondary school teaching—were based on ethnicity. The rent element in Guyana was manifest in the level at which Europeans were appointed in the civil service and the rate at which they were promoted.

A *"loyalty" element*. This applied especially to those working for the British colonial administration. The metropolitan power was conscious of the fact that one way to ensure the loyalty of its civil servants, especially those in positions of responsibility, was to pay them relatively well. This made it easier for civil servants, even the local ones, to identify themselves with the interests of the ruling group, and it gave them a feeling of superiority over the masses.

Because this loyalty to the British crown, especially among the civil servants, was of paramount importance, and further, because it was assumed by the ruling groups that they could most readily depend on the loyalty of Europeans from the metropole, all senior positions in the civil service, especially "key" posts such as that of Governor, Chief Secretary, Commissioner of Police, Superintendent of Prisons, Chief Justice, etc., were virtually reserved for them. This pattern of recruitment continued almost until the country was granted self-government, although a few Guyanese of proven loyalty and competence were sometimes promoted to senior posts. Even senior secretarial positions, such as personal secretaries to the heads of Government departments, were, for a long time, reserved for European or coloured girls, who, because of their ethnicity, were assumed to be more loyal to the colonial authorities. At the turn of the century, we find, for example, that while the Principal of Queen's College, then the only Government boys' secondary school in the country, was anxious to see "some of these [civil service posts] . . . open to general competition," he, at the same time, reminded his readers that "a certain proportion of these posts will have to be confined to candidates of British origin, for it is best to admit frankly that in an English colony it is not only desirable but necessary that the higher Executive Departments should be mainly officered by men of British birth."[27]

The three elements in the salaries of expatriates, especially those in the public service (scarcity, rent, and loyalty payments), were also found, obviously in different proportions, in the remuneration of personnel throughout the public sector. In fact, all those employees in Government and semi-Government jobs, even those who held positions as messengers, were relatively well rewarded as compared with those in the traditional sector of the economy such as peasant farmers.

The life style of these Government employees, especially those in the middle and higher level posts, which was made possible by their higher incomes, not only distinguished them as a "class" apart from the rest of the society but also added legitimacy to their positions of superiority and their role of governors and administrators. Even among those in the lower level positions, their incomes allowed them to live a somewhat different life style from the masses, with, in some cases, quite different consumption patterns. The psychological investment in this new life style helped to strengthen further the loyalty of this group to the metropole. To be "booted out" of a job was always a hideous prospect to contemplate, largely because of the tremendous drop in standard of living which had to be faced when a civil service position was lost.

The recruitment policy and reward structure of the private sector was akin to and had similar effects to that in the civil service. For the senior and sometimes not-so-senior positions, the private companies recruited expatriates from the metropole who were given quite high salaries and generous fringe benefits. British personnel were brought out by such firms as Bookers, Barclays Bank, and Sandback Parker, while Canadian personnel were recruited to work in Canadian-owned companies like the Demerara Bauxite Company, the Demerara Electric Company, and the Royal Bank of Canada. While local personnel filling lower level jobs were relatively poorly paid by comparison, their incomes were usually higher than those earning their livelihood in the traditional sector.

There were many reasons why the private firms in the modern sector could afford to pay better wages than could be earned in the traditional sector, but these shall not be examined here. Suffice it to note that the result of this wage policy was that workers in the modern

[27] Government of British Guiana, *Report of the Principal of Queen's College 1888*, p. 13.

sector had both relatively high status and high incomes vis-a-vis their counterparts in the traditional sector of the economy, a factor which reinforced their support for the existing economic system and helped to bring about fairly effectively the bourgeoisifcation of this element of the proletariat. Efforts at instituting a fairer wage policy, which threatened the relatively entrenched position and economic superiority of this more affluent group of workers vis-a-vis the masses, have tended to be strongly opposed by them.

In fact, not only has this marked dualism in the wage structure continued, but there has been a steadily worsening of the income differential between these two sections of the work force. This growing difference can be seen partly in the results of a study done by Brewster[28] on wage levels in Guyana. His research findings indicate that while real wages in the export or modern sector of the economy increased by 49% between 1948 and 1962, the corresponding increase in the domestic sector was only 17%. He further compared the increases in real wages of unskilled workers in various sectors of the economy and found that while those for the bauxite and sugar workers had increased by 300% and 155% respectively, between 1948 and 1962, wages for similar workers in the domestic sector had increased by only 96%. Also, while the ratio of wages in the highly capitalized and mechanized bauxite industry to that in the rice industry, which is largely small farmer owned and operated, was ten to six in 1948, this had fallen considerably by 1962, when it was 10 to 3.2.

Another important factor accounting for the continuation and further polarization of income levels in the society was the fact that the traditional sector has benefitted very little from the economic developments in the modern sector. The two major industries, bauxite and sugar, which dominated the modern sector, had developed strong linkages with the metropolitan centres and very weak ones with the remainder of the economy. This, as Beckford[29] convincingly argues, is a specially marked feature of plantations, but it was also characteristic of the other major economic enclave, the local bauxite industry. The result was that the masses benefitted relatively very little from the presence of these industries in the country. Even in their consumption patterns, those who were employed in the modern sector often spent much of their incomes buying commodities which were imported from the metropole. And these commodities not only consisted of bicycles, cars, refrigerators, etc., but also foodstuffs including packages and canned foods.

In fact, instead of a positive economic spill-over from the modern to the traditional sector, there was a negative one, since the technological improvements and increasing mechanization taking place in the

[28] Brewster, "Some Features of Guyanese Economic Development."
[29] Beckford, pp. 18-29.

modern sector added considerably to the already deteriorating unemployment situation. This was most strikingly revealed in the sugar industry. As socialist commentators observe, the capitalist economies under which most LDCs operate are not essentially concerned with the social problems which accompany the substitution of machinery for labour. Their primary focus is usually on maximizing profits for their shareholders. This concern for maximizing returns to capital rather than labour, has, as Carnoy pointed out, produced increasing unemployment "because capitalists prefer capital intensive technology and such technology tends to reduce the growth of demand for labour and put a downward pressure on wages."[30] So, as the trade unions in developing countries like Guyana became better organized and more effective in bargaining for higher wages, the companies became more anxious to increase their pace of mechanization. This resulted in both the reduction of their work force and the creation of an even smaller elite corps of workers in the modern sector with a wage differential widening in their favour in comparison with those in the traditional sector.

These differences in incomes between workers in the two sectors of the economy contributed to the development and/or strengthening of a vested interest—even by the workers who were employed in the modern sector—in the maintenance of the existing social and economic structure. Many of them increasingly saw their interests as being closely linked with those of the colonizing power or the exploiting companies. The only reason why these groups were sometimes supportive of local independence movements was their belief that they would be even better off economically by being promoted into jobs which Europeans would have been forced to leave. They did not clamour for the type of independence which would result in sharing with the mass of the population the economic and social privileges which they had acquired over time.

The trade unions in these countries, especially in more recent times, have been mainly concerned with ensuring that the relative incomes and standards of living of their members, who were usually employed in the modern sector, were safeguarded. They tended to oppose any measure aimed at raising the standards of living among the peasants and the unemployed if this meant that their own economic position, both in relative and absolute terms, would be adversely affected. Further, they have been very influential in getting Governments to introduce measures such as minimum wage legislation which protected the interest mainly of their members but did nothing positive for the masses labouring in the traditional sector. In fact, by virtue of the strength stemming from their organization, they have been fairly

[30] Carnoy, "The Political Consequences of Manpower Formation," p. 115.

successful at maintaining the economic position of their members even though this meant, as it often did, a deterioration in the economic position of other groups—usually the less organized ones—in the society.

As Robert Theobald observed, the organized workers in the developing countries are those "with the greatest power to obtain the largest increase in wages leaving the less well organized workers behind."[31] For example, in his study of the Jamaican economy, Ahiram[32] presented empirical evidence which supports this statement, at least as far as Jamaica was concerned. At the higher echelons of the occupational structure, the civil service and the teachers' associations were also nearly always successful in their salary negotiations with the Government, since their loyalty and support were crucial to the colonial powers.

All these factors were responsible for the creation and the continuation of a dualistic wage structure with substantial differences in incomes among workers in these two sectors. By the time the colonial rulers were ready to give over political control of the Government to the elected representatives of the masses, the stratificatory system, with its dualistic wage structure, was not only formed but had taken deep roots. Therefore, when foreign companies like Demerara Electric and Demerara Bauxite were nationalized, the new local administrative and technical elite which filled the resulting vacancies, demanded and received the same salaries as their expatriate predecessors. This, it was argued, was necessary to emphasize the fact that the local holders of these positions were in no way inferior to the expatriates who previously held these posts. It was, however, largely a result of the pressures exerted by the already privileged groups to ensure that their relative social and economic position in the society would not only be maintained but improved.

Theoretical Support

So far it has been pointed out that the dualistic structure of Guyanese society, which influenced both the amount and the type of education demanded by the public, had its roots in the history and structure of a colonial society. But another factor which influenced the willingness of the Government to continue providing more formal education was Arthur Lewis'[33] two-sector theory of economic de-

---

[31] Robert Theobald, *The Rich and the Poor: A Study of the Economics of Rising Expectations* (New York: New American Library, 1961), p. 95.

[32] E. Ahiram, "Income Distribution in Jamaica, 1958," *Social and Economic Studies* Vol. 13, No. 3 (September 1964), and "Distribution of Income in Trinidad, Tobago and Comparison with Distribution of Income in Jamaica," *Social and Economic Studies* Vol. 15, No. 2 (June 1966).

[33] W. A. Lewis, "Economic Development"; also "Unlimited Labour: Further Notes," *Manchester School of Economic and Social Studies* (January 1958).

velopment, or some extension or modification of the theory. In fact, Lewis' theory, as Beckford[34] notes "is the foundation of much of the existing formulation of the development problem," including agricultural development in the third world.

While the type of education offered in Guyanese schools was basically determined long before the formulation of Lewis' theory, it did much to legitimize the educational planning efforts in the country since the 1960s. Lewis argued that the dynamics of development in the LDCs inhered in the modern sector, which, according to him, will gradually expand and eventually envelop the traditional sector. This was because these counries, with their "unlimited supplies of labour," were in a position of comparative advantage vis-a-vis the economically more developed countries especially in areas of production in which a high labour component was necessary. On the assumption that wages in these countries would remain constant, due to the "unlimited supply" of labour which was available, Lewis argued that as technical progress took place, profits would increase and this would favour capital formation and the amount of reinvestment in the economy. The ultimate result would be an increasing demand for labour and an exhaustion of the surplus labour due to its absorption in the expanding modern or industrial sector. By the time this happened, a country would have reached its stage of economic take-off. As Ranis and Fei, who essentially subscribed to Lewis' theory of development, put it, "in such economies [i.e., the LDCs] the centre of gravity must continuously shift toward industry through continuous reallocation of labour from the agricultural to the industrial sector."[35] This pull which the modern sector will increasingly exert on labour supply will largely be for manpower with various levels of formal education or training; this will mean that schools and other educational institutions will gradually but steadily need to increase their output of such personnel.

Another point was that since the products from the LDCs would have to be competitive on the international market, not only in price but also in quality, the production processes used and the output of skilled persons from the schools and other educational institutions to work in these industries would have to be quite similar in standards to those in the economically more developed countries. As Beckford explains,

> the implicit assumption of the [two-sector] model of development is that because the so-called "modern sector" utilizes production techniques that are similar to those found in the more advanced countries in the world it offers development possibilities akin to the development patterns of these countries.[36]

[34] Beckford, p. 49, n. 26.
[35] Ranis, p. 3.
[36] Beckford, p. 49.

The popularity of the manpower approach to educational planning in the LDCs was to some extent due to the fact that it was congruent with this theory of development. The projection of the manpower needs of the economically less developed countries was based on the occupational structure of industries in countries at a somewhat higher stage of economic development. From these figures were calculated the numbers of personnel with different levels of education and training likely to be required by the developing economies. Or as Myint observed, education was looked upon as "the chief" missing component of economic development and educational planning was "based on the assumption that it is possible to estimate how many people with what type of specific training and qualification will be required to sustain a *given* pattern of economic development"[37] (emphasis added).

So, much of the education and training offered formally in the LDCs was focussed on the assumed needs of the emergent modern sector, with the added underlying assumption that factor inputs in the production process were fixed. The content of the training was taken for granted because the nature of the technology to be used was taken as given. Since factor inputs were conceived as fixed, it was almost impossible to develop a more flexible production process which would have allowed substitution between the two major factors of production—technology and educated manpower—in order to ensure that maximum use was being made of the scarce capital resources and available manpower in the LDCs.

The general acceptance of the inherent superiority of Western technology for the needs of the developing countries has limited the possibility of factor substitutability and to a large extent determined the content of the training offered by schools and other educational institutions in these countries. As a result, their educational programmes were essentially copied from those in the metropolitan centres and not usually geared towards producing skills, knowledge, and attitudes which would have been useful to those employed in the traditional sector where production was characterized by low capital inputs and "primitive" technology. And as has been noted, even when the less prestigious schools attempted to correct this deficiency, parents, pupils, and even teachers resisted the introduction of programmes which were geared to preparing individuals to work more productively in the low-wage sector of the economy. Little or no attention was paid to the possibility of upgrading traditional skills or skills acquired in the traditional way which might have ensured a better utilization of resources already available in the LDCs.

[37] Myint, "Education and Economic Development," in *Economic Theory and the Underdeveloped Countries*, p. 213.

This is not to deny that some efforts were made at introducing middle-level technology in these countries. But these have so far not been very successful, largely because of the lack of interest by the multinational corporations which find it easier, and probably cheaper, to try and sell to the LDCs their equipment originally produced for the economically more developed countries rather than to engage in further research to develop others more suited to the economic realities of the poorer countries. For example, Simmons, in his study *Education, Poverty and Development*, cites the case of Central American fishermen who, a few years ago, had little trouble repairing their outboard motors because of the simplicity of the machines. Then "tolerances became fine, parts more fragile, and the mechanisms more complex thus making local repair impossible, lengthy or expensive."[38] This example can be multiplied many times to illustrate the point that when introducing or developing new production methods, the companies which operate in the modern sector are not essentially concerned about the "needs" or problems of the developing countries. There are many business reasons for this, and Singer, in commenting on this situaton, notes:

> A foreign firm (and especially a large transnational company) is not likely to show any great interest in developing labour intensive technologies—the handling of large masses of local labour is notoriously a difficult, politically touchy and unrewarding job for such foreign firms. In any case, the foreign firm is expected to pay "decent wages"—the standard of decency being set with some reference to the firm's wages to its staff in its home base in the richer country or to the firm's size and profits—usually resulting in wages at a considerable multiple of average incomes (and certainly of rural incomes) in the under-developed country. This higher wage would in any case reduce much of the incentive for using local labour and for spending a lot of research and development money on production functions directed towards that end even if the managerial and political reluctance to encouraging use of local labour did not exist. Moreover in so far as the higher wage standards of foreign enterprise tend to spread to indigenous enterprise in the modern sector as well, the discouragement of indigenous labour saving technologies becomes more general.[39]

The Inadequacy of the Two-Sector Theory of Development

It is now obvious that the nature of the development envisaged by Lewis for the LDCs has not taken place and is not likely to take place because of the many structural constraints which exist both internally and externally, for example, in the relationship between the modern enclave and the traditional sector and between the developing and the economically more developed metropolitan countries. It is generally accepted that in spite of the "unlimited supplies of labour" in the

[38] John Simmons, *Education, Poverty and Development*, Bank Staff Working Paper No. 188 (Washington: IBRD, 1974), p. 48, n. 1.

[39] Singer, p. 65.

LDCs, wage rates in the modern sectors have not remained constant, as Lewis predicted they would, but have, in fact, been rising steadily to the relative disadvantage of those earning their living in the traditional sectors.

Beckford, Carnoy, Frank, Singer, *et al.*, have all attempted to draw attention to some of the constraints which retard the development of these countries. Beckford has pointed out that in plantation economies (and this point can in many ways be extended to other modern sector enclaves of the LDCs), the focus of production is on meeting the demands of the metropolitan markets and that this tends to reinforce local underdevelopment by increasing the dependency of the local economy on that of the metropole. For example, local resources such as land and infra-structural development, including research, tend, in this context, to be disproportionately allocated to the plantations at the expense of the peasant sector, while the economic linkage and the economic spillover between the plantations and the rest of the economy is minimal. Therefore, the continued presence of the modern plantations sector in these economies is, according to Beckford, one of the major causes of the underdevelopment of the peasant sector and of the economy as a whole.

Singer points out that the "dualistic fission" stemming from the use of inappropriate technology has contributed to third world underdevelopment and that its effects are increasingly seen in the rising proportion of unemployed in these countries. Part of the root cause of this phenomenon is, according to Singer, the disproportionate allocation of research and development funds spent in the world, with 98% spent in the developed countries—usually on projects tied in with their own needs—and only 2% in the developing countries.

Frank and Carnoy, on the other hand, see that the underdevelopment of third world countries has resulted essentially from the spread of the international capitalist system, which increases their dependency on the economically richer countries and interferes with the possibility of any creative effort by these countries to solve their own development problem by utilizing to the full the factors of production which they have most readily available. Carnoy further argues that the very nature of the capitalist system, with its major interest in the maximization of profits for its shareholders, makes this an unsuitable economic system for third world development, in fact, for development in any country. This is because the overriding concern for profit maximization makes it unlikely that the capitalists will take any major step which might eventually aid the development of the countries in which they invest their capital—if such step is likely to reduce the amount of profits they expect to make. Implicit in this argument is the view that concern for profit maximization—especially in the short run, which is the focal interest of capitalists operating in the third world—can be and usually is antagonistic to the long-term development of a country, especially a poor country. Incidentally, the term "development" is used here to include much more than just increases in the per capita G.N.P. of a country.

However, despite the different foci by these writers, their common theme is that past emphasis on the development of the modern sector has been one of the major sources of the under-development of the traditional sector—in which the great majority of the population in these countries live and work—of the economy of the LDCs. Further, even with such emphasis and the preferential treatment given to the modern sector in the economic policies of most of these Governments, one finds that, for some of the reasons previously stated, it has not only failed to influence to any marked degree the development of the traditional sector but has been unable to provide jobs for the increasing numbers who are seeking to enter it. And as Singer notes, this growing unemployment, which is largely due to the technological dualism, has many "frightening consequences" for third world development because if the present trend continues, unemployment in these countries would reach 43% by 1980 and 73% by 1990[40] if every potential employee began to offer his or her services on the job market. In Guyana, where the same pattern of development has been pursued, one sees that the modern sector has been expanding very slowly indeed. Therefore, with the fairly rapid population growth that has taken place and the increasing mechanization of industries, it is estimated that the rate of unemployment and underemployment has been rising steadily during the entire period covered by this study, the former reaching about 25% in 1975.

Only a few third world countries, have the resources of the oil-rich OPEC countries, the political connections of Puerto Rico, Korea, Taiwan, or other "favourable" factors which would help bring about a fairly rapid development of their modern sectors. These few countries with resources, such as oil, can afford to use education as a consumption item, and since capital is not, at the moment, in short supply, they can also attempt to build up their modern sectors, as some OPEC nations seem to be doing. This development in the long run might provide increasing employment opportunities for the nationals. But for most developing countries with their serious resource limitations, both in physical resources and capital, the modernization of their economies is much more problematic than was envisaged by Lewis.

Also, as was pointed out earlier, the economic and status rewards received by those employed in the small, modern sectors of the LDCs are so high when compared with those working in the large traditional sector that the former become the reference sector in terms of

[40] *Ibid.*, p. 67.

the occupational aspirations of the population. This is why it has been suggested that unless the number of jobs created annually in the modern sector is extremely large a gradual improvement might, in itself, increase rather than diminish unemployment.[41] Each new job in the modern sector attracts a large number of rural workers, who are usually willing to seek every opportunity of exchanging their present marginal employment in agriculture or in other self-employed, traditional occupations, in the hope of securing one of these relatively high-paying, modern-sector jobs.

Coping With the Problem

The increased output from the educational system, which was occurring faster than the ability of the economy to absorb such manpower in productive employment, has resulted in a high and increasing rate of unemployment among the educated in Guyana. In fact, this study has revealed that while there might have been some structural unemployment in the Guyanese economy due to the unavailability of persons with certain types of skills or experiences, the amount of such personnel shortage was relatively small. In almost every occupational category, the number of unemployed greatly outstripped the number of vacancies which existed.

But this gap between "educated" personnel available and the demands of the economy for such personnel would have been even more noticeable had it not been for certain mechanisms which developed locally and played an important role in helping to "cope" with this problem.

First, while secondary education was being provided in most parts of the country, the academic standards of the new schools were considerably lower than those of the older secondary schools. The latter had a higher per capita pupil expenditure, a higher percentage of graduate teachers, and more up-to-date facilities such as laboratories and libraries. As a result, their students did better at the external examinations. In the new secondary schools, a very high percentage of students was failing to obtain the number of G.C.E. "O" level passes required for entry into many jobs in the modern sector; this was reflected in the overall examination results. For example, it was shown that in June 1972 about 47% of all the candidates who entered for the G.C.E. "O" level examination failed outright. Also, while they entered on an average for 4.3 subjects, the average number of subjects passed was about 1.2. In addition, only 22.2% of the 8,141 candidates who entered for the English Language examination were successful.

These efforts at securing a "good" G.C.E. "O" level certificate were repeated two or more times and still many candidates failed to

[41] *Ibid.*, p. 70.

obtain the level of pass which was normally required for the better, white-collar jobs. The latent funtion of this experience was to "cool off" many youngsters, since it helped to get them to lower their level of occupational aspiration. When these candidates failed to obtain the necessary number of passes, they tended to blame themselves rather than the system for their failures. The system at least provided them with an opportunity to obtain the necessary credentials for access to the better jobs.

Another mechanism which has helped to cope with this problem is the increase and even padding of the public services. The civil service has expanded rapidly and so have the teaching profession, the police force, and the armed services. In 1972 the service sector, which was heavily made up of Government services, accounted for about 43% of the country's G.N.P. In fact, in that year alone, while there was a zero rate of growth in real production and a drop in the G.N.P. per capita from the previous year, the service sector was the only one to expand. And it did so at a rate which was about 50% greater than its average rate of increase over the previous five years.

With increasing output from the secondary schools and a very slow rate of increase in job opportunities in the private sector, competition for public service employment obviously became keener. As this happened, recruitment was again becoming very particularistic, with Government supporters and their children more likely than non-supporters to find employment in the public sector. Though inexcusable, the phenomenon is understandable largely because of the fact that supporters of the Government were more likely to have direct or indirect access to those who occupied the corridors of power and so had their pleas for jobs more easily heard. The deciding factor here might not be only the ethnicity of the candidate but because non-supporters tended to be of one ethnic group, it manifested itself and is interpreted as racial discrimination against one major group in the society—the East Indians. In a "plural" society like Guyana, such practices can only exacerbate the relationships between the ethnic groups; one is increasingly seen as the "exploiter" and the other as the "exploited." But it helps to satisfy the supporters of the Government and probably to increase the loyalty to the political party in power by those selected for public service positions.

Another coping mechanism for dealing with this "over supply" of educated manpower has been the increase in the brain drain which the country has recently been experiencing. This problem was a more complex one since there were many additional factors in Guyana, as in other developing countries, which contributed to their loss of trained personnel to the developed countries. But the greater output of "educated" or "trained" manpower on the job market in a situation in which the economy was unable to absorb them, has been an important factor in the increased desire of many youngsters to emigrate; this helped to push the "departure index" in Guyana from 100 in 1960 to 252 in 1970. In 1974 the Deputy Prime Minister saw that this problem had increased to such an extent that he felt it necessary to draw national attention to it.

This brain drain from developing to the richer countries may, as Myint reminded us,

> be regarded as a symptom rather than as an important cause of the slow rate of economic growth in the losing countries.... A symptom of a tendency to a serious disequilibrium between the typical pattern of expansion of higher education in these underdeveloped countries and their limited capacity to "absorb" the expanding number of graduates who turn out to be too highly specialized or too highly trained (in the formal academic sense) for their requirements.[42]

He made the further point that the external brain drain has many of the characteristics of the internal brain drain. The unequal distribution of economic resources and the marked income differentials between the two sectors of a dualistic economy result in a strong pull by the richer sector on the human resources of the poorer sector.

A further attempt at coping with this problem was the introduction of near-compulsory national service for the young population. Every young person is now expected to undertake two years' service for the state working on some kind of productive project without receiving an income. While there has been some opposition to making national service compulsory, its "success" in securing "volunteers" lies in the fact that all further educational opportunities and later, according to current popular belief, all jobs in the public sector will only be open to those who have completed their national service. This measure effectively takes the young population out of the labour force for another two years and at the same time postpones the growing discontent among the educated unemployed.

The increase in the supply of educated personnel beyond the demands of the job market has resulted in a rise in the qualification level required for entry into many jobs or into local tertiary level educational institutions. Also, it meant that some applicants are now willing to accept jobs which they would not previously have considered, which is tantamount to an increase in the level of qualification required for these jobs. The personnel director of one of the largest private firms informed the author in June 1974 that many of his most recent applicants for jobs, even as night security guards, had a secondary education, some with three or four passes at the G.C.E. "O" level examination.

One of the indirect effects of this virtual increase in qualifications required for some jobs has been the lowering of the occupational

[42] Myint, "The Brain Drain from the Underdeveloped Countries: A Less Alarmist View," in *Economic Theory and the Underdeveloped Countries*, p. 241.

aspirations of the lesser-qualified, and incidentally, also an increase in the demand for education, keeping more individuals in the schools for a longer period, further reducing the pressure, if temporarily, on the job market.

Suggested Solutions

Some economists using classical economic theory of supply and demand argue that this oversupply of "educated" manpower in the developing countries is not a problem requiring any special policy decision since the market will soon adjust itself and there will eventually be a fall in the demand for education. But this expected downturn in the supply curve of educated manpower has not yet taken place, and judging from the experience in many LDCs, such as Sri Lanka, Philippines, Lebanon, Egypt, etc., this is not likely to happen in the near future. For example, in June 1974 the author learned from the officials of a medium-sized insurance company in Guyana, that, in response to an advertisement for two accounts clerks, the company was inundated with over 120 applicants, nearly all of whom were the holders of G.C.E. "O" level certificates in a number of subjects.

This suggested laissez-faire policy of leaving things alone in the belief that the market will correct itself, ignores the reality of the situation in most LDCs. For many reasons indicated earlier, the private cost of education has been falling in these countries, with a resultant increase in the demand for all levels of education. Simmons notes that when one considers the existing context within which education in the developing countries is provided

> it is not surprising that students continue to pursue higher levels of education despite the rising level of graduate unemployment. Given that costs are highly subsidized and that foregone earnings of education without experience on the job are small in comparison to wages with education and experience, the risk of unemployment in the early years is less significant than the possible maximum return.[43]

To counteract this problem, it has sometimes been suggested that public subsidies to education should either be reduced or eliminated entirely, at least above the primary level. As one economist puts it, "in general, it would be advisable to suppress the demand based on low opportunity cost and high private returns."[44] This will, in fact, mean there will be a closer approximation between private and social costs and private and social rates of return on education, which will undoubtedly result in a considerable drop in the popular demand for education.

But anyone who has any insights into the political situation in many LDCs will immediately realize the difficulties which any political leader in these countries would likely face if he openly supported such

[43] Simmons, p. 29.
[44] *Ibid.*

a view. The author recalls a number of occasions when his Minister of Education, because of the political pressures exerted on him by the masses, had to change his policy on a particular issue to one which he knew was more costly.

In addition, the egalitarian ideal of giving greater educational opportunities to the masses has become a very important part of the credo of most politicians virtually all over the world, including those in the developing countries. This, along with the fact that if education is not subsidized the opportunities for upward mobility among the masses will be extremely limited, strongly influences the willingness of these governments to provide more educational services which both meet the demands of the public and are consistent with their philosophy of egalitarianism.

Some economists have argued that if the economic circumstances of the lower-income groups make it difficult for them to secure post-primary education for their children, then the setting up of a capital market for investment in education, which will make its funds available equally to all socio-economic groups, might be the more appropriate solution. But this approach ignores the whole range of attitudinal variables and the possible lack of collateral among the lower socio-economic groups. The latter factor militates against their borrowing money, especially for enterprises where the outcome might be considered very uncertain.

Another proposal which was at one time advanced to cope with this problem of increasing demand for education and at the same time to overcome the problem of inequality of educational opportunity was put forward by Professor Ron Dore of the Institute of Development Studies in Sussex, England.[45] He suggested that beyond the primary level, all further educational opportunities should be awarded on the basis of a lottery. The planning authorities would probably estimate the manpower needs of the countries and the students who were to receive the necessary training would be selected on some random basis. By restricting the number of places available in the educational institutions, the country would ensure that the social returns to the investment in education would be no less than social costs, and secondly, by allocating available places on a lottery basis it would be assured that the upper soci-economic groups did not receive a more favourable treatment than the lower socio-economic groups. But even though this method of selection would likely achieve its two objectives, it would create its own problems. First of all, it would be very difficult to get people to accept the legitimacy of an educational selection process which would determine the entire future of their

[45] Ronald Dore, "Education and the Developing Countries," Occasional Papers (Brighton, Sussex: University of Sussex, Institute of Development Studies, 1973). (Mimeographed.)

children with the children's own efforts being considered irrelevant to the selection process. In fact, such an approach in which a person's future is not determined by personal efforts but by some deus ex machina—a lottery— is likely only to reinforce the passivistic attitude to life which social scientists have observed is widely shared by the population in these countries and which in itself has been considered an important factor in their underdevelopment.

Secondly, the nature of the education offered in schools, especially education leading to higher levels of technical and professional training, is such that the ability to undertake these programmes is not equally distributed among all students in the population. Some seem to be better able to handle this type of training than others. A selection for post-primary education, if based on the results of a lottery, would ignore this fact and would likely result in a substantial degree of "wastage" of education and training efforts due to the fact that many of those selected on this random basis would not be able to complete their programmes satisfactorily. This approach is likely to overcome the latter hurdle only if there is a drastic reform in both our methods of teaching and in our traditional content of education. This will make it possible for anyone to learn any of the skills needed for the efficient functioning of the society, somewhat along the lines being attempted by the Chinese. But so far, we know very little about how our existing educational and training programmes can be restructured to allow for this possibility or even whether the knowledge base which is now associated with the necessary qualifications for certain jobs can be radically changed and still ensure efficiency in the performance of these jobs.

Another issue is that, unless one denies popular participation or inputs into the political decision-making process, there are always likely to be pressures on the authorities to increase the numbers selected for these higher levels of education if it means that they will eventually be destined for those jobs with very high incomes and prestige.

Dore has since modified his ideas and has come up with what seems to be a more feasible proposal. In his later work[46] he suggested that:

(a) Careers of youngsters in third world countries should start early in life—between the ages of 15 and 17—possibly after they have completed a basic nine years of schooling. Further education and training, for those who require it, must be done on the job or within the industry. Those who need more advanced education and training will be selected for it on the basis of internal tests and work performance;

(b) Since some countries can afford to provide only five to six years of schooling for the entire primary school-age population, a

[46] Dore, *The Diploma Disease.*

selection process will have to take place to screen those primary school graduates who will be allowed to continue their education. Those not selected will directly enter the work force while the others will do so after finishing an additional three to four years of schooling. Selection will be based on the results of aptitude tests and work performance and not on achievement tests since students can usually cram for these.

First of all, while this early entry into jobs seems a sensible idea from an economic point of view, the question which arises is whether the education proposed for the nine-year period—education which will be oriented to the practical needs of the society—will provide enough of an educational base for those who later have to be selected to undertake training for higher technical and professional fields such as engineering, geology, and medicine. This will be of special concern in view of the fact that selection for further education will be based on aptitude and work performance rather than on academic attainment. Secondly, if the present situation of extremely wide income differentials between occupations continues, the process of selection for jobs will become an even more vexing issue. The assessment of work performance and aptitude, especially since the validity of aptitude tests has, so far, left much to be desired, will be a matter in which the subjective impressions of a supervisor will be crucial. This can easily open the way to an increased importance of ascriptive and particularistic considerations in occupational, economic, and social selection.

Those who are against any radical reduction in income differentials in these societies usually argue that such differences are necessary and can be justified on the grounds that (i) they stimulate people to make sacrifices to obtain the levels of education and training required for the different jobs in the society; (ii) they represent differential levels of productivity between workers; and (iii) they will help to speed up needed capital formation since these higher income groups have a greater propensity to save.

There might be some validity in the argument that the maintenance of differential incomes for various occupations is necessary, in the present socio-economic context of these countries, to motivate people to qualify themselves in areas in which there is a short supply of skills. But the point to be noted here is that, when these income differences are inordinate and unrelated to the demand and supply of skills because of the relative inflexibility of wages, their economic function in ensuring an adequate supply of skills needed by the economy is no longer the most important one.

As one World Bank economist noted, "It is important to point out that the classical rationale of the incentive of wage differentials no longer applies when a mechanic earns ten times as much as an agricultural labourer or a doctor one hundred times as much."[47] This writer also went on to illustrate his point by noting that in Uganda the average salary of the secondary school graduate was about twenty times the per capita national income. He further observed that in developing countries generally these wage differences seem to be widening, thus increasing the incentive for individuals to obtain formal educational qualifications, and suggested that the "uneconomic incentives" for more schooling may not be reduced until wages are realigned.

Further it is very doubtful whether these large wage differentials represent compensation for different levels of productivity in these countries. The history of many LDCs indicates that there were important "non-economic" reasons for their emergence. And with the existing wage structures, education has become primarily a means—and an expensive one at that—of sorting out a few potential recruits for the modern sector of the economy (legitimizing the existing marked wage differentials in these societies) and only secondarily one of providing manpower with special types of education and training needed for their economic development.

In many of the economically more developed countries, educational institutions often simultaneously perform the functions both of social selection of individuals for upward mobility and occupational preparation for jobs requiring formal training. This is made easier because of the virtual absence of a dualistic economy with a low wage or traditional sector in which incomes are barely enough to enable workers to keep body and soul together. Added to this is the fact that income differences between manual and white collar workers are usually less marked than they are in the LDCs. It is not being suggested that the role of education in the richer countries is basically different from its role in the poorer countries. But because of the dualistic wage structure and the wide gap in incomes between manual and non-manual workers in the LDCs, considerably more emphasis is understandably being placed by the population on the role of education as an instrument of social and economic mobility as against its role in vocational preparation. The masses have tended to reject the view that the major role of the school is to teach their children those skills and knowledge which will help them to be more productive and to cope more efficiently with life in the traditional sector of those societies. When the relationship between these two functions of education, providing an opportunity for economic and status improvement and offering skill training, is negative or nonexistent, the former function is likely to become more important to the consumer of education, as it has been in most developing countries.

[47] Simmons, p. 27.

These wide income gaps, coupled with the general unresponsiveness of wages to the objective manpower needs of these countries, were probably reducing their levels of labour productivity in another way. They helped give rise to the phenomenon of the shortage of middle-level technical or sub-professional staff to which Adam Curle[48] drew attention some time ago and which continues to plague most LDCs. Students prefer to make every effort to secure training in the professional rather than in the sub-professional fields, largely because of the enormity of the salary differences and the resulting status gap between these two groups. This makes the additional cost of professional, including degree-level studies, a much better investment and creates or reinforces the shortage for middle-level technicians. For example, in Guyana the maximum salary of the chief medical technologist at the largest hospital in the country was lower than the starting salary of, say, an honours graduate teaching at the Government Boys' Secondary School. The result was that it was often easier to find arts graduates than trained laboratory technicians. The same phenomenon in other developing countries was commented on by Myint who noted that "Many underdeveloped countries are acutely short of people to fill jobs at the middle level of skills while suffering from a relative glut of university graduates—a phenomenon which is reinforced by top heavy salary structures in favour of graduates."[49]

The professionals in these countries were inadequately supplied with supporting sub-professional help. This meant that their services were more costly because so much of their time was spent on doing lower-level jobs for which they were receiving the pay of a fully qualified professional.

These marked wage differences not only diverted the supply of trained manpower away from areas which were greatly needed for national economic development but also inflated the demand for more high levels of formal education, making it necessary to the Government to allocate additional resources to this field—resources which might have been more productively used in other development endeavours.

This large supply of academically more qualified individuals, most of whom eventually find jobs in an expanding public sector where wages are based primarily on academic qualifications rather than on "productivity," might well mean that employed, educated personnel are possibly benefitting from a transfer of wealth from the "lesser educated," unorganized masses to themselves, thereby widening the poverty gap in the society. This point has also been made by

[48] Adam Curle, *Educational Strategy for Developing Countries* (London: Tavistock Publications, 1963).

[49] Myint, "Trade, Education and Economic Development," in *Economic Theory and the Underdeveloped Countries*, p. 263.

Singer and Jolly[50] who noted that in situations in which remuneration is determined more by an individual's formal qualifications rather than by the supply and demand for his skills, there is the tendency toward an increase in the supply of persons with these qualifications, resulting in a rise in the average income of such workers without necessarily increasing their productivity. For example, it is a moot point whether an increase in the number of graduate teachers in the primary schools is accompanied by an increase in their level of productivity, at least in sufficient amount to justify the substantially higher wages which are usually paid to graduate teachers in developing countries. But since salaries are based on qualifications, it means that, with the infusion of graduate teachers in the primary schools, the average income of such teachers rises, and unless there has been a corresponding increase in their productivity, which is usually doubtful, some sector of the population will have to pay these additional costs. With the more effective organization of workers in the modern sector, this usually means that it is the unorganized and less-educated farmers and other workers in the traditional sector who are likely to pay for such wage increases. This internal redistribution of income in favour of the "schooled," which it is suggested is taking place in many LDCs, has probably contributed further to the phenomenon of increasing income disparities, both in relative and absolute terms, which has been observed in these countries.

The third reason for suggesting that there should be no radical restructuring of wage differentials in the developing countries is that the existing distribution is necessary to stimulate savings which are badly needed for further investment. But the assumption that the surplus wealth needed for capital formation will come from the higher socio-economic groups if they are allowed to keep their wealth—an assumption based on the known higher propensity to save among the middle classes in the economically more advanced countries—is a doubtful one as far as the LDCs are concerned. In fact, most social scientists who study the third world have observed that the higher income groups tend to use their wealth not so much for local investment nor even for the consumption of locally-produced goods and services, but instead for the purchase of goods and services from the economically more developed countries. Further, the wealthiest groups tend to keep their money in Swiss and North American banks where it does very little good for local economic development.

Another suggested educational solution sometimes put forward is to make compulsory all courses most relevant for the economic development of the country. This means that all children at school will be expected to study tropical agriculture, industrial arts, etc. But

[50] Richard Jolly, *et al., Third World Employment: Problems and Strategy* (Harmondsworth, Middlesex, England: Penguin Books, 1973), p. 71.

this proposal will in itself add a number of problems. First, the situation is not a static one and the skills "most relevant for the economic development of the country" change all the time. Secondly, one cannot, in blanket terms, assess what are the "most relevant" skills. The issue is one of numbers. The economy needs both farmers and clerks and the issue at hand is to ensure that the numbers who are preparing themselves for various types of jobs are more or less in line with the objective needs of the country. Thirdly, skills that are needed by the great majority might not be the most appropriate ones for those who will be working in certain crucial types of jobs. To have every potential administrator do tropical agriculture and gardening might be a waste of resources if it means that such personnel will end up at desk jobs in a Government Ministry. The focus must be the acquisition of skills by those who need them and are most likely to utilize them in their day-to-day activities of earning a living.

And finally, if everyone acquires these "relevant skills" then additional criteria will have to be developed for selecting those who will have to fill the higher income jobs. Assuming that these criteria are to be based on achievement and are to be universally applied, then it is likely that they will manifest themselves in additional school courses, success at which will discriminate between the "more able" and the "less able" candidates. The end result will be that the emphasis in the schools will undoubtedly shift over to these new courses.

The most effective and inescapable solution, therefore, seems to be a radical reduction in the income differentials between the traditional and the modern sectors and between different occupations in the modern sector itself. As long as the present marked income differences remain, students are likely to want the type of training which will lead them out of the low-wage sector of the economy, no matter how important this type of training is for the economic development of the country.

Assuredly, many problems will be encountered in trying to achieve the goal of a substantial reduction in income disparities in these societies. Frank has argued that the dependency status that exists between most LDCs and the major capitalist countries of the world has first to be reduced before the internal economic relationship between the modern and the traditional sectors can be changed. but this in itself presents a difficult problem, especially since resistance to any such change is likely to come from the vested interest groups in the modern sector of the "hinterland" economy, which tend to have a greater congruence of interest with those in the metropolitan "centre" than with those on the "periphery" of the hinterland. As was previously pointed out, the present wage structure in Guyana and other LDCs does not only represent payments for the relative scarcity of skills; there were other reasons for these high incomes which were being enjoyed by those in the modern sector. But with independence, the justification for much of this marked difference in income, especially that part which represented payment for "loyalty" to the colonizing power, should no longer exist. Yet many political leaders in the LDCs continue to maintain and even increase the "loyalty element" in wages, especially among those in the public sector—including the armed forces and the police.

In addition, the more economically privileged groups, through their organized efforts in professional associations and trade unions, have also attempted to ensure that the existing wage differentials remain and that wages will not be regulated simply by forces of supply and demand. We saw this most clearly in Guyana when the Government, under pressure from the Public Service Association and the Guyana Teachers' Association, accepted the principle that every person who graduates from a university and holds a job in teaching or in the civil service will be automatically placed on a graduate salary scale. This measure was introduced to "overcome" a problem faced by degree holders from the University of Guyana (mainly teachers and civil servants), who were finding it difficult to secure positions which specifically required the holder to have a university degree. The move was probably not unrelated to the fact that up to 1972 only 4.7% of the graduates from the University of Guyana held jobs in the private sector, where the productivity of an individual, rather than the mere fact that he had a B.A. or B.Sc. behind his name, was probably somewhat more important in determining his salary.

This question of how income differentials could be drastically reduced will not be discussed here, since the strategies used might have to vary from country to country. Some Governments will see that the answer lies in their taking full control of the "commanding heights" of the economy, in Guyana including the modern sector with the sugar plantations and the bauxite companies, and then attempt to build a national wages policy to reflect the economic priorities of the country. Others will see that the same objective can be achieved with a policy of taxation, of incomes control, of the reduction of the monopolistic powers of the private companies and the organized labour groups in the modern sector, or with a combination of all of these measures, coupled with efforts to pump more funds into the traditional sector to increase its productivity.

The relative merits of these policies are too involved to be delved into here. But in light of the past experiences of these countries, their present dependency on the economically more developed countries, and the vested interest of their own elites in the existing social and economic status quo, it is doubtful if any income redistribution measure that does not involve a radical departure from the existing practices is likely to succeed. The dependence on a free market mechanism to correct the existing differences is, for a number of reasons, not likely to be very effective. Incidentally, Carnoy,[51] using data both from a developed (U.S.A.) and a developing country (Mexico) has strongly argued that increasing inequality of income distribution is a characteristic feature of economic growth under a capitalist system.

Further, in these developing countries, there is usually a small but very powerful elite group with a vested interest in the maintenance of the status quo. Because of the power it wields, any measure aimed at changing the present structure of the societies and which depends for its implementation on the "free flow of the market forces," is likely to be domesticated by this group in its own interest. In short, the assumption of perfect competition which underlies the operation of a free market mechanism is a textbook unreality which ignores the fact that when economic power becomes unequally distributed in a society, those with more of that power tend to use it to influence or manipulate the workings of the market mechanism in their own interest. Even if the objective was to create conditions necessary for that idyllic state of perfect competition, this cannot be done in most LDCs without the Government's active intervention in the economy.

Consequently, one of the major problems of any proposed reform aimed at reducing income disparities in these countries is the likely opposition to such change from the vested interest groups which benefit most from the existing distribution of wealth. Considerable political courage, which can stem only from an overriding concern for the masses as well as the long-term development prospects of the country would be needed to overcome any opposition from the local vested interests.

In addition, reform measures aimed at getting the active support of the masses must be part of a national development policy which closely links the twin concepts of greater equality in the distribution of rewards and greater equality of sacrifice. At the moment, these two concepts seem to be negatively related in many LDCs. The success of any effort at reform will depend on changing the nature of this relationship to a positive one.

Apart from its influence on curbing the educational inflation in the LDCs and making it possible for curriculum reform to be successful, a marked reduction in the existing wage differentials is also likely to have a positive influence on the aspiration levels of the population by making them more appropriate to the economic and occupational realities of a developing country. A characteristic feature of many LDCs, including Guyana, is a growing lack of congruence between their resources and the aspirations of their population. Or as one

[51] Carnoy, "The Political Consequences of Manpower Formation," p. 117.

author puts it, the "want/get ratio" is widening in these countries. This is due to both the internal and external influences. While attempts have been made to control some of these external factors via trade restrictions, such as heavy duties on luxury items, the internal ones which stem from the marked and increasing income disparities locally still remain. And these have continued to influence the occupational and educational aspirations of the population away from many of the types of jobs which need to be done efficiently if these countries are to make any major step towards greater economic development. Further, as educational facilities become more available, the gap between occupational aspirations and the realities of the job market increase, resulting in further demand for yet higher levels of education.

Other Efforts at Educational Reform

While it is being suggested here that wage differentials between various occupations need to be radically reduced as a first step in any meaningful educational reform in the LDCs, it does not mean that there are no common sense educational changes which can be attempted in the meantime. For example, while formal schooling in these countries has been so strongly associated in people's minds with preparation for access to high-income, usually white-collar jobs, it is not always the most sensible approach, when attempting to teach people new occupational skills, to institutionalize such training within a formal school setting. In most cases, it might be much better to take those who are already doing their jobs, to study the nature of the informal training they might have received, diagnose the deficiencies and strengths of such training within the context in which the job is done, and then attempt to provide any necessary additional training, preferably on the job or "in situ" to correct or improve existing practices where necessary.

This approach has two major advantages. First, it will ensure that when the training is done, the economic and social milieu in which the skills have to be practised are fully taken into account. We have seen from this study how attempts at formalizing and institutionalizing craft training in technical institutes has resulted in an increasing rate of unemployment among skilled workers, because they were expensively trained and had priced themselves out of the job market in the traditional sector while the modern sector was not expanding rapidly enough to absorb them. Secondly, such an approach to training has the advantage of starting with the various factors of production used locally on a job and then improving the skills which are being utilized, thus resulting in increasing productivity without creating a demand for too many new or additional factors of production which might be inappropriate within the economic context of these countries.

This does not mean that improvements will need to be made only in the nature of the skill training that has traditionally been provided. It might also be necessary to effect some changes in the other cooperant factors of production in order to achieve an even greater efficiency in the production process. But by focussing the training within the context of the job, as it is performed in these countries, the educator is likely to become more aware of the non-educational variables or constraints in the actual production process which have to be taken into account in devising the most appropriate training programme.

There are many problems which individuals who are educated in formal educational institutions often face, if they are to make an effective contribution to the development of the traditional sector. The skills which they learn in educational institutions such as the technical institutes are often more appropriate in, and suitable to, the needs of a capital intensive economy. A motor mechanic who graduates from the G.T.I. tends to be most effective when he is employed in a "modern" workshop which has the whole range of tools that he has learned to use as a student of the technical institute. Without such tools, and most rural motor vehicle repair shops do not have them, he is at a complete loss as to how to improvise on a job in which, say, tuning a car becomes first a matter of developing a sensitive ear as a diagnostic device rather than relying on some sophisticated technological equipment, such as an oscilloscope. Secondly, he is usually not trained to fabricate substitute parts for a vehicle. Like his North American or European-trained counterpart, he is accustomed mainly to identifying and replacing defective parts with new ones. While the acquisition of such skills makes sense in a North American or European context where car parts are relatively cheap as compared to labour, this is certainly not true in most developing countries like Guyana, where imported car parts are expensive and labour relatively cheap. Thirdly, the mechanic who is trained in a "modern" technical institute learns to specialize in his job. While this is acceptable in the well-equipped, modern workshops in urban centres, such a mechanic is virtually unemployable in a rural car repair workshop which usually needs individuals with almost the complete range of skills required for repairing cars. The nature of the demand for a specialized skill is such that he is not likely to find enough work to keep him fully employed if he sticks to his narrow field of specialization.

Fourthly, as was indicated above, the higher cost of his training, say as a skilled carpenter, often prices him out of this traditional sector since those who earn their living in this sector often cannot afford to pay him enough wages to compensate for the high cost of this training. Similarly, doctors who are qualified abroad or even in up-to-date local medical schools find it difficult to perform their jobs outside the context of modern hospitals with up-to-date diagnostic facilities. In addition, many of them are reluctant to work in the rural areas, largely because of the fact that the residents in these areas— with their low incomes—are usually not able to pay the relatively high fees which these doctors demand, or find it necessary to demand, because of the high cost of their training.

This is not merely a criticism of the education and training offered in most LDCs but, in addition, it represents an attempt to recognize that for reasons mentioned above, such training has been useful mainly to those engaged in economic activities in the modern sector which tend to have the supporting cooperant factors of production to use the type of training provided by formal educational institutions. In addition to the fact that the skills acquired in formal training programmes are not seen to be very useful to those working in the traditional sector, the relatively high cost of producing some of these skilled workers usually prices the trained manpower out of the reach of those in the traditional sector, again denying it some of the benefits from the increasingly heavy national investment in education in these countries.

If trained personnel are to be more effective in the low wage sector of the developing countries, they must be much less expensively trained, and in addition, they must be taught to work with the existing factors of production available in the traditional sector, thereby helping to increase the efficiency with which problems are solved and production carried on in this sector.

Nyerere made a somewhat similar criticism of the educational system of Tanzania when he observed that the effect of education offered in the schools was such "as to divorce its participants from the society it is preparing them for"—a poor and predominantly agricultural society with a very large traditional sector. He noted that "from school, he [the child] acquires knowledge unrelated to agricultural life. Everything we do stresses book learning."[52]

To summarize briefly, the main argument here is that the marked difference in wage levels between occupations in the developing countries, the inflexibility of the wage structure to the demand and supply situation for skills due largely to the pressure exerted by the organized minority of workers, the increasing reduction of private costs of education coupled with the limited alternative opportunities for economic and social mobility among those without a formal education, together contribute to this increasing popular demand for formal educational facilities and an "oversupply" of those with the qualifications needed to enter into the high-wage level sector of the

[52] Julius K. Nyerere, "Education for Self Reliance," in *Self-Reliant Tanzania*, ed. by K. E. Svendsen and M. Jenson (Dar-es-Salaam: Tanzania Publishing House, 1969), pp. 219-39.

economy. Unless the key element in this situation is removed (i.e., the wide income disparities between occupational groups), the educational inflation will continue to be an important feature of the labour markets in these countries since the motivation to get an education to escape into the high-level sector will continue to exist.

It is sometimes suggested[53] that this oversupply of skills, assuming that useful skills are in fact created in the process of schooling, might in itself be a positive factor in economic development. While this may be true in a limited number of instances, this view tends to ignore the fact that unless such levels of education can find other cooperant factors of production, e.g., capital, their use in the production process can be and is usually very limited, And while the radical reduction in the structure of these wages between different jobs would not by itself ensure that greater economic growth will take place in these countries, such a step will remove the major obstacle to reforming their educational institutions in order to make them more effective in providing the population with the type of skills that are most needed for the development of these countries.

[53] M. J. Bowman, "Schools for and against Innovation," *Comparative Education* Vol. 9, No. 3 (October 1965), pp. 270-74.

Bibliography

Books

Adamson, Alan H. *Sugar Without Slaves: The Political Economy of British Guiana 1838-1904*. New Haven and London: Yale University Press, 1972.

Augier, F. R. and S. G. Gordon. *Sources of West Indian History*. London: Longmans, 1962.

Beckford, George L. *Persistent Poverty*. London: Oxford University Press, 1972.

Beeby, C. E. *The Quality of Education in Developing Countries*. Cambridge, Mass.: Harvard University Press, 1966.

Boeke, J. H. *Economics and Economic Policy of Dual Societies*. New York: Institute of Pacific Relations, 1953.

Cameron, Norman. *A History of the Queen's College of British Guiana*. Georgetown: F. A. Persick Ltd., 1951.

Carnoy, M. and H. M. Levin. *Limits of Educational Reform*. New York: David McKay Co. Ltd., 1976.

Clementi, Sir Cecil. *A Constitutional History of British Guiana*. London: Macmillan & Co., Ltd., 1937.

Coleridge, H. N. *Six Months in the West Indies in 1825*. London: John Murray, 1832.

Conant, J. B. *The Education of American Teachers*. New York: McGraw Hill, 1963.

Curle, Adam. *Educational Strategy for Developing Countries*. London: Tavistock Publications, 1963.

Dalton, Henry G. *A History of British Guiana*. London: Longmans, 1855.

Daly, Vere T. *A Short History of the Guyanese People*. Georgetown, Guyana: Daily Chronicle, 1966.

Despres, Leo A. *Cultural Pluralism and Nationalist Politics in British Guiana*. Chicago: Rand McNally & Co., 1967.

Dore, Ronald. *The Diploma Disease*. London: George Allen and Unwin Ltd., 1976.

Fanon, Frantz. *Black Skins, White Masks*. Translated by Charles Lam Markennan. New York: Grove Press, Inc., 1967.

_____. *Towards the African Revolution*. New York: Grove Press, Inc., 1967.

Foster, Philip. *Education and Social Change in Ghana*. London: Routledge and Kegan Paul, 1965.

Francis, O. J. *Report on Survey of Manpower Requirements in the Labour Force, British Guiana 1965*. 4 vols. Georgetown: Government of Guyana, 1966.

Furnivall, John S. *Colonial Policy and Practice: A Comparative Study of Burma and Netherlands India*. Issued in cooperation with the International Secretariat, Institute of Pacific Relations. London: Cambridge University Press, 1948.

Gordon, Shirley. *A Century of West Indian Education—A Source Book*. London: Longmans, 1963.

Holmes, Brian. *Problems of Education*. London: Routledge and Kegan Paul, 1965.

International Bank for Reconstruction and Development. *The Economic Development of British Guiana*. Baltimore: Johns Hopkins University Press, 1953.

Jagan, C. B. *The West on Trial*. London: Michael Joseph, 1966.

Jalée, Pierre. *The Pillage of the Third World*. Translated by Mary Klopper. New York: Monthly Review Press, 1968.

Jayawardena, C. *Conflict and Solidarity in a Guianese Plantation*. London: Athlone Press, 1963.

Johnson, H. *Economic Policies Towards Less Developed Countries*. New York: Brookings Institute, 1967.

Jolly, Richard *et al*. *Third World Employment: Problems and Strategy. Selected Readings*. Harmondsworth, Middlesex: Penguin Books, 1973.

Kirke, H. *Twenty-Five Years in British Guiana*. London: Sampson, Low, Marston and Co., 1898.

Knorr, K. E. *British Colonial Theories 1570-1850*. Toronto: University of Toronto Press, 1944.

Lewis, S. and T. G. Matthews. *Caribbean Integration*. Rio Pedras: University of Puerto Rico, 1967.

Martin, R. M. *The British Colonies, Their History, Extent, Condition and Resources*. 8 vols. London and New York: J. & F. Tallis, n.d.

Maunier, R. *The Sociology of Colonies: An Introduction to the Study of Race Contact*. Edited and translated by E. O. Lorimer. London: Routledge and Kegan Paul, 1949.

Merton, R. K. *Social Theory and Social Structure*. Glencoe, Illinois: The Free Press, 1957.

Mitchell, W. B. *et al*. *Area Handbook for Guyana*. Washington, D.C.: The American University, 1969.

Moore, W. E. *Social Change*. New York: Prentice Hall, 1963.

Myint, H. U. *Economic Theory and the Underdeveloped Countries*. New York: Oxford University Press, 1971.

Nath, Dwarka. *A History of Indians in Guyana*. Revised edition. London: Butler and Tanner Ltd., 1970.

Newman, Peter. *British Guiana, Problems of Cohesion in an Immigrant Society*. London: Oxford University Press, 1964.

Patterson, Orlando. *The Sociology of Slavery: An Analysis of the Origins, Development and Structure of Negro Slave Society in Jamaica*. London: McGibbon and Kee, 1967.

Percival, D. A. and D'Andrade, W. P. *The National Economic Accounts of British Guiana 1938-51*. Georgetown, Guyana: The Daily Chronicle Ltd., 1952.

Pitman, Frank W. *The Development of the British West Indies 1700-1763*. Hamden, Conn.: Archon Books, 1917.

290 / *Education for Development or Underdevelopment?*

Prithipaul, D. *A Comparative Analysis of French and British Colonial Policies of Education in Mauritius 1735-1889*. Port Louis, Mauritius: Imprimerie Ideal, 1976.

Ranis, G. and Fei, J. C. H. *Development of the Labour Surplus Economy: Theory and Policy*. Homewood, Illinois: R. D. Irwin, Inc., 1964.

Riggs, F. W. *Administration in Developing Countries: The Theory of Prismatic Society*. Boston: Houghton Mifflin, 1964.

Rodway, J. *History of British Guiana from 1668*. 3 vols. Georgetown, Guyana: n.p., 1891-1894.

Sherif, M. *Intergroup Relations and Leadership*. New York: John Wiley and Sons, 1962.

Smith, M. G. *The Plural Society in the British West Indies*. Berkeley, Los Angeles and London: University of California Press, 1965.

Smith, Raymond T. *British Guiana*. London: Oxford University Press, 1962.

Spenser, Col. D. A. *The Financial Position of British Guiana 1920-46*. Georgetown, Guyana: Government of British Guyana, n.d.

Sturge, J. and T. Harvey. *The West Indies in 1837*. London: Hamilton, Adams and Company, 1838.

Svendsen, K. E. and M. Jenson. *Self-Reliant Tanzania*. Dar-es-Salaam: Tanzania Publishing House, 1969.

The Red Book of the West Indies 1922, Historical, Descriptive, Commercial and Industrial. London: W. H. & L. Collingridge, 1922.

Theobald, Robert. *The Rich and the Poor: A Study of the Economics of Rising Expectations*. New York: New American Library, 1961.

Thompson, Warren. *Population and Peace in the Pacific*. Chicago: University of Chicago Press, 1946.

Williams, Eric. *Inward Hunger: The Education of a Prime Minister*. London: André Deutsch, 1969.

Young, Allan. *The Approaches to Local Self-Government in British Guiana*. London: Longmans, 1958.

Articles and Monographs

Ahiram, E. "Income Distribution in Jamaica, 1958." *Social and Economic Studies* Vol. 13, No. 3 (September 1964), pp. 333-369.

_____ . "Distribution of Income in Trinidad-Tobago and Comparison with Distribution of Income in Jamaica." *Social and Economic Studies* Vol. 15, No. 2 (June 1966), pp. 103-120.

Bacchus, M. K. "Patterns of Educational Expenditure in an Emergent Nation: A Study of Guyana 1945-65." *Social and Economic Studies* Vol. 18, No. 3 (September 1969).

_____ . "Relationship between Professional and Administrative Officers in a Government Department during a Period of Administrative Change." *Sociological Review* Vol. 15, No. 2 (July 1967).

_____ . "Social Factors in Secondary School Selection in British Guiana." *Social and Economic Studies* Vol. 15, No. 1 (March 1966).

_____ . "Curriculum Development and Social Structure. A Case Study of a Colonial Society." *Perspectives in Curriculum* Vol. 2 (1973).

_____ . *Education and Socio-Cultural Integration in a "Plural" Society*. Occasional Paper Series No. 6. Montreal: McGill University, Centre for Developing-Area Studies, 1970.

_____ . "Manpower Implications of Guyana's Development (1966-72) Plan." *New World* Crop Over Issue Vol. 2 (1966).

Becker, G. S. "Investment in On-the-Job Training." In *Economics of Education*, pp. 183-207. Edited by Mark Blaug. Harmondsworth, Middlesex: Penguin Books, 1968.

Best, Lloyd. "Working Notes Towards the Unification of Guyana." *New World Quarterly* (March 1963).

_____ . "Outlines of a Model of Pure Plantation Economy." *Social and Economic Studies* Vol. 17, No. 3 (September 1968).

Boskoff, Alvin. "Functional Analysis as a Source of a Theoretical Repertory and Research Tasks in the Study of Social Change." In *Explorations in Social Change*, pp. 213-43. Edited by G. Zollschan and Walter Hirsch. Boston: Houghton Mifflin Co., 1964.

Bowman, M. J. "Schools for and Against Innovation." *Comparative Education* Vol. 9, No. 3 (October 1965).

Braithwaite, L. E. "The School Curriculum and the Emergent Needs of Society." *Report on the Conference on Teacher Education in the Eastern Caribbean*. U.W.I.: Institute of Education, 1967.

Carnoy, Martin. "The Political Consequences of Manpower Formation." *Comparative Education Review* Vol. 19, No. 1 (February 1975).

Dewey, John. "Education and Change." In *Readings on the School in Society*, pp. 8-11. Edited by P. C. Sexton. Englewood Cliffs, N.J.: Prentice Hall, 1968.

Dubin, R. "Leadership in Union Management Relations as an Intergroup System." In *Intergroup Relations*, pp. 70-91. Edited by M. Sherif. New York: John Wiley & Sons, 1962.

Evans, P. C. C. "The Ministerial System in Education." *Overseas Education* Vol. 35, No. 2 (July 1962).

Higgins, B. "The Dualistic Theory of Underdeveloped Areas." In *Economic Development and Cultural Change*. Vol. 4, pp. 99-115. Chicago: University of Chicago Press, January 1956.

Hinden, Rita. "The Case of British Guiana." *Encounter* Vol. 2, No. 1 (January 1954).

Kundu, A. "The Economy of British Guiana 1960-75." *Social and Economic Studies* Vol. 12, No. 3 (September 1963).

Lewis, W. A. "Economic Development with Unlimited Supplies of Labour." *Manchester School of Economics and Social Studies* (May 1954), pp. 131-191.

_____ . "Unlimited Labour: Further Notes." *Manchester School of Economics and Social Studies* (January 1958), pp. 1-32.

Michelson, Stephen. "Rational Income Decisions of Blacks and Everybody Else." In *Schooling in a Corporate Society*, pp. 100-119. Edited by Martin Carnoy. New York: McKay, 1972.

Mintz. Sydney W. "The Caribbean as a Socio-Cultural Area." In *Peoples and Cultures of the Caribbean*, pp. 17-46. Edited by M. M. Horowitz. New York: American Museum of Natural History, 1971.

O'Loughlin, C. "The Economy of British Guiana 1952-56. A National Accounts Study." *Social and Economic Studies* Vol. 8, No. 1 (March 1959).

Roberts, George W. "Prospects for Population Growth in the West Indies." *Social and Economic Studies* Vol. 2, No. 4 (December 1962).

Rodney, Walter. "Masses in Action." In *New World: Guyana Independence Issue.* Edited by G. Lamming and M. Carter. Georgetown: New World Group of Associates, West Indies, 1966.

Ruhoman, J. *Timehri* Vol. 7, Third Series (August 1921). Georgetown: Royal Agricultural and Commercial Society, 1921.

Simmons, John. *Education, Poverty and Development.* Bank Staff Working Paper No. 188. Washington: IBRD, February 1974.

Singer, H. W. "Dualism Revisited: A New Approach in the Problems of the Dual Society in Developing Countries." *Journal of Development Studies* Vol. 7, No. 1 (1970).

Singer, P. and E. Araneta, "Hinduization and Creolization in Guyana." *Social and Economic Studies* Vol. 16, No. 3 (September 1967).

Smith, Raymond T. "People and Change." In *New World: Guyana Independence Issue.* Georgetown: New World Group of Associates, West Indies, 1966.

————— . "Social Stratification, Cultural Pluralism and Integration in West Indian Societies." In *Caribbean Integration*, pp. 226-58. Edited by S. Lewis and T. G. Matthews. Rio Piedras, Puerto Rico: University of Puerto Rico, 1967.

Tauber, Irene B. "British Guiana—Some Demographic Aspects of Economic Development." *Population Index* Vol. 18, No. 1 (1952).

Thomas, Clive Y. "The Political Economy of Exploitation in the Caribbean." *Black Lines* Vols. 2 and 3, Nos. 2 and 3, Special Double Issue (Winter 1971 and Spring 1972). Pittsburgh: University of Pittsburgh.

Turner, R. H. "Sponsored and Contest Mobility and the School System." In *The Sociology of Education: A Sourcebook*, pp. 219-35. Edited by Robert R. Bell and Holger R. Stubb. Homewood, Illinois: The Dorsey Press, 1968.

Williams, Eric. "Education in the Dependent Territories in America." *Journal of Negro Education* Vol. 15, No. 3 (Summer 1946).

Wolf, Eric R. "Specific Aspects of Plantation Systems in the New World." In *Plantation Systems of the New World.* Edited by Vera Rubin. Social Science Monographs No. 7. Washington: Pan American Union and Research Institute for the Study of Man, 1959.

Government Reports and Other Publications

Colony of Berbice. "Minutes of the Proceedings of the Colony of Berbice for the Year Ending 30th June 1827. A Proposal to Grant 6000 Guilders out of the Ordinary Funds of the Colony to Establish Free Schools." 10 January 1827. London: Public Records Office.

Development and Welfare in the West Indies, *Report of the Regional Conference on the Training of Teachers in the British Caribbean*, Bulletin No. 39. Bridgetown, Barbados 1957.

Government of British Guiana. *Annual Report[s] of the Director of Education or the Ministry of Education.* Georgetown, 1945-73.

————— . *Census of the Colony of British Guiana 9th April 1946.* Kingston, Jamaica: Government Printer, 1949.

————— . *Census of the Colony of British Guiana, 1960.* Kingston, Jamaica.

_____ . *Census of Guyana 1970.* Georgetown, Guyana.

_____ . *Circular Dispatch 1st October 1845.* Georgetown, 1945.

_____ . *Code of Regulations for Education 1901.* Georgetown, 1901.

_____ . *Education Code 1940.* Georgetown, 1940.

_____ . Reports of Legislative Council Debates 1945-1970. In *Hansard.* Georgetown.

_____ . *Memorandum by the Minister of Education and Social Development on Educational Policy 1963.* Georgetown, 1963.

_____ . *Memorandum on Educational Policy 1968.* Georgetown, 1968.

_____ . *Memorandum on Technical Education,* by Dr. Harlow, Technical Education Adviser to the Secretary of State for the Colonies. Georgetown, 1 December 1952.

_____ . *Memorandum on Secondary Education 1957.* Georgetown: The Daily Chronicle Ltd., 1957.

_____ . *Nine Year Report 1965-73.* Georgetown: Ministry of Education and Social Development, February 1974.

_____ . *Papers Relating to Development Planning 1947.* Georgetown, 1947.

_____ . *Report of the Education Development Committee 1946.* Georgetown, 1946.

_____ . *Report of the Immigration Agent General for the Year 1880.* Georgetown: Immigration Department, 1880.

_____ . *Report of an Investigation into the Public Service* by E. Mills. Georgetown, 1953.

_____ . *Report of the Primary Education Committee 1939.* Georgetown, 1939.

_____ . *Report of the Primary Education Policy Committee 1952.* Georgetown, 1952.

_____ . *Report of the Primary School Teachers' Salaries Structure Committee 1955.* Georgetown, 1955.

_____ . *Report of the Principal of Queen's College 1877, 1880, 1888.* Georgetown: Queen's College.

_____ . *Report on Local Government in British Guiana* by A. H. Marshall. Georgetown, May 1955.

_____ . *Report on Vocational Education for the Government of British Guiana* by William Partin. Georgetown, May 1965.

_____. *Statement by the Minister of Education, C. V. Nunes.* Georgetown: Ministry of Education and Social Development, 8 September 1962.

_____ . *Triennial Report of the Education Department 1954-57.* Georgetown, 1957.

_____ . *Year of Education, 1963.* Georgetown, 1963.

Government of Great Britain. *British Guiana: Report of the Constitutional Commission 1950-51.* Vol. 280. London: H.M.S.O., 1951.

_____ . Board of Education. *Special Reports on Educational Subjects.* Vol. 4: *Education Systems of the Chief Colonies of the British Empire.* London: H.M.S.O., 1901.

_____ . Colonial Development and Welfare. *Memorandum on Education in British Guiana 1942.* Georgetown, 1942.

_____ . Colonial Development and Welfare in the West Indies. *The Future Cost of Education.* Memorandum by the Educational Adviser, Bulletin No. 15, n.d.

_____ . Colonial Office. *Miscellaneous Pamphlets* Vol. 1, No. 1. London: Public Records Office.

_____ . Colonial Office. *Report of a Commission of Enquiry into the Sugar Industry of British Guiana.* J. Venn, chairman. Col. 249. London: H.M.S.O., 1949.

_____ . Colonial Office. *Report of a Commission on Secondary and Primary Education in Trinidad* by F. C. Marriott and A. Mayhew. Col. No. 79. London: H.M.S.O., 1933.

_____ . *Statement by Her Majesty's Government, British Guiana. Suspension of Constitution.* Cmd. 8980. London: H.M.S.O., 1953.

_____ . *West Indian Royal Commission Report 1938-39.* 6607. London: H.M.S.O., 1945.

Government of Guyana. *A Digest of Educational Statistics 1971-72.* Georgetown, Guyana: Ministry of Education Planning, September 1973.

_____ . *Annual Estimates 1945 to 1974.* Georgetown, Guyana.

_____ . *Development Budget 1966-72.* Georgetown, Guyana.

Guyana School of Agriculture. *Reports of the Principal.* Mon Repos: Guyana School of Agriculture, 1966-1975.

International Commission of Jurists. *Report of the British Guiana Commission of Enquiry: Racial Problems in the Public Service.* Geneva, 1965.

University of the West Indies. *Annual Report of the Principal.* Mona, Jamaica, 1950-65.

World Bank, The. *Education: Sector Working Paper, December 1974.* Washington: The World Bank, December 1975.

Unpublished Materials

Bacchus, M. K. "Education and Development in Guyana Since 1945 with Estimates of Educational Needs up to 1975." Unpublished Ph.D. thesis, University of London, 1968.

Baksh, Ahamad. "Education and Economic Development: The Relevance to Guyana." Turkeyen: University of Guyana, Department of Sociology, February 1973. (Mimeographed.)

_____ . "The Pattern of Higher Education at the University of Guyana, 1963/64-1971/72." Turkeyen E.C.D., Guyana, 1973. (Mimeographed.)

Brewster, H. "Some Features of Guyana's Economic Development." Mona, Jamaica: University of the West Indies, I.S.E.R. Library, 1965. (Mimeographed.)

Burnham, L. F. S. "Address to the Regional Conference of the P. N. C." Georgetown, June 1974. (Mimeographed.)

Dore, Ronald. "Education and the Developing Countries." Occasional Papers. Brighton, Sussex: University of Sussex, Institute of Development Studies, 1973. (Mimeographed.)

Government of British Guiana. "British Guiana Development Programme 1966-72." Georgetown, 1966. (Mimeographed.)

_____ . "An Economic Justification for the University of Guyana." Georgetown: Ministry of Education, ca. 1963. (Mimeographed.)

_____ . "Proposals for the Establishment of Senior Schools for British Guiana." Written correspondence by the Principal, Government Training College, 13 January 1953.

_____ . "Report of the Committee on Technical Education 1966." Georgetown: Ministry of Education, 1966. (Mimeographed.)

_____ . "Report on the Development of Technical Education 1966-70." Georgetown: Principal of the Government Technical Institute, n.d. (Mimeographed.)

_____ . "Report of the Educational Commission 1925." Georgetown, 1925. (Mimeographed.)

_____ . "Report on Establishments Enquiry 1969: Manpower Survey Office." Georgetown: Ministry of Labour and Social Security, May 1970. (Mimeographed.)

_____ . "Suggested Curriculum Guide 1962." Georgetown: Ministry of Education, 1962. (Mimeographed.)

Government of Guyana. "Annual Reports of the Principal, Government Technical Institute." Georgetown, Guyana, 1965-69. (Mimeographed.)

Graham, Sarah. "Social Mobility in Guyana." Unpublished Ph.D. thesis, Mona, Jamaica: University of the West Indies, 1973.

Guyana School of Agriculture. "Annual Reports of the Principal." Mon Repos, E.C.D., Guyana, 1965-73. (Mimeographed.)

International Bank for Reconstruction and Development/International Development Agency. "An Appraisal of the Development Program of Guyana." Vol. 4: Education. Washington: IBRD, 27 February 1967. (Mimeographed.)

International Labour Organization. "Report to the Government of British Guiana on Employment, Unemployment and Underemployment in the Colony in 1956." Geneva:I.L.O., 1957. (Mimeographed.)

Phillips, W. J. "The Trade Unions and Guyana's Draft Development Plan 1972-76." Turkeyen: University of Guyana Library, September 1973. (Mimeographed.)

Principal of Queen's College. "Public address by V. J. Sanger-Davies." Georgetown: Queen's College, 15 December 1952. (Mimeographed.)

Sukdeo, Fred. "The Impact of Emigration on Manpower Resources in Guyana." Turkeyen: University of Guyana Library, December 1972. (Mimeographed.)

Thomas, Clive Y. "Inflation, Shortages and the Working Class Interests in Guyana." Turkeyen: University of Guyana Library, November 1973.

UNESCO. "Report of the UNESCO Educational Survey Mission to British Guiana." Paris: UNESCO, 1963. (Mimeographed.)

_____ . "Suggestions for Reform and Improvement of Education." Paris: UNESCO, January 1973. (Mimeographed.)

_____ . "Memorandum to the Minister of Education, Teacher Education Programme." Georgetown: UNESCO Educational Mission, 15 February 1963. (Mimeographed.)

University of Guyana. "Report of the Principal on Research and Research Institutes in the University." Turkeyen: University of Guyana, ca. 1962. (Mimeographed.)

General Index

Abolition of Slavery Act, 11
achievement criteria, 2, 59, 64, 171, 247
adult suffrage, 56
agricultural education, 206-14, 258
agriculture, general, 3, 5, 12, 17, 25, 34, 38, 40, 96, 97, 98, 99, 122, 135; tobacco, 5; cotton, 5, 6, 11; sugar, 5, 6, 7, 8, 12, 14, 34, 38, 50, 249, 252, 263, 264; coffee, 6, 11; rice, 11, 24, 25, 30, 34, 38, 44, 249
A.I.F.L.D. (American Institute of Free LabourDevelopment), 57
Amerindian, 5, 17, 21, 64
Angel Gabriel Riots, 13
Anglican Church, 9, 114
apprenticeship, 60, 253; apprenticeship period, 11, 12, 72
ascribed status, criteria, 1, 2, 31, 59, 64, 76, 171, 247, 248

balkanization, 4
Barbados, 5, 6, 81, 95
bauxite, 1, 17, 34, 37, 38, 45, 50, 252, 263
Berbice, 5, 75, 136
Berbice High School, 135
Bookers, 16, 52, 60, 140, 186, 198, 202, 248, 262
brain drain, 272, 273
Britain, 2, 6, 8, 9, 57, 159. See also England.
British, 6, 8, 19, 20, 21, 28, 55, 57, 61, 72, 75, 127, 167, 186, 193, 214, 261, 262. See also English.
British Guiana Teachers' Association, 117.(See also Guyana Teachers' Association).
Board of Industrial Training, 196

Cambridge, 8
Canada, 2, 192, 217, 262

Canadian International Development Agency (CIDA), 192, 200, 201
Canadian Mission Schools, 68
Caribbean, 4, 16, 22, 139
CARIFTA, 38
Carnegie School of Home Economics, 222
caste, 2, 7, 18
Catholics, 9, 26, 141
Central Board of Health, 228
Central Intelligence Agency (CIA), 36, 57
China, 13
Chinese, 13, 14, 26, 77, 276
churches, 19, 76, 91, 124, 244
Christianity, 12, 124, 244
CIA. See Central Intelligence Agency.
CIDA. See Canadian International Development Agency.
civil service, 14, 23, 24, 40, 60, 179, 184, 188, 189, 194, 248, 249, 256, 272
co-educational, 85
College of Secondary Education, 120
colonial, 3, 6, 19, 21, 56, 61, 63, 66, 74, 96, 109, 115, 126, 127, 128, 179, 259, 260
Colonial Development and Welfare (C.D. & W.), 60, 91, 98, 113, 128, 159, 185, 228, 229
colonist, 10, 72
colour (skin), 1, 2, 6, 7, 8, 9, 13, 14, 18, 22, 24, 30, 31, 71, 76, 188, 247
Combined Court, 20, 24, 55
compulsory education, 1, 15, 19, 20, 28, 29, 66, 74, 75, 78, 79, 80, 82, 245
compulsory school attendance, 1, 82, 84, 257

Index of Persons